Cultural Quarters

Cultural Quarters
Principles and Practice

Edited and written by Simon Roodhouse

SECOND EDITION

intellect Bristol, UK / Chicago, USA

First published in the UK in 2010 by
Intellect, The Mill, Parnall Road, Fishponds, Bristol, BS16 3JG, UK

First published in the USA in 2010 by
Intellect, The University of Chicago Press, 1427 E. 60th Street,
Chicago, IL 60637, USA

A catalogue record for this book is available from the
British Library.

Cover designer: Holly Rose
Copy-editor: Rebecca Vaughan-Williams
Typesetting: Mac Style, Beverley, E. Yorkshire

ISBN 978-1-84150-158-1

Printed and bound in Great Britain by 4edge Limited. www.4edge.co.uk

FSC Mixed Sources
SA-COC-001695
© 1996 FSC A.C.

Contents

Acknowledgements

This second edition owes its success to the original contributors, John Montgomery, John Napier, Rebecca Albrow, John Parkin, Susan Ford and Peter Richards as well as the support of Bolton Borough Council. Similarly thanks are also due to Sarah Campbell, Wolverhampton City Council; Richard Motley, Sheffield Cultural Industries Quarter (CIQ); and Rev. Phillip R. Mason, Victoria Halls Methodist Church, Bolton, for their willingness to provide the initial information and answer questions. Particular thanks go to the Centre for Creative Communities and Jennifer Williams for allowing the reproduction of two case studies. It should also be noted that the case studies have been informed by earlier papers published by Simon Roodhouse in the *International Journal of Heritage Studies* and the *International Journal of Arts Management*.

In this edition thanks go to Ann Galligan, Mattias Legner, Pier Luici Sacco, Tim Vorley, Lisa De Propris and Ping Wei and Louise Johnson for their additional contributions as well as the *Journal of Arts Management, Law and Society* for permission to reproduce an article published in the *Journal of Arts Management, Law and Society*, volume 39, number 3, pp. 187–199.

Contributors

RJ Buswell
Lisa De Propris
Ann Galligan
Alison Holmes
Louise Johnson
Mattias Legner
Monika Mokre
John Montgomery
John Napier
John Parkin
Peter Richards
Pier Luici Sacco
Pring Wei
Tim Vorley

Note on Simon Roodhouse

Professor Roodhouse has substantial experience as an educator, manager and researcher in the fields of management, education, training and cultural policy. He has written extensively and published in national and international journals such as the *Journal of Education through Partnership*, the *International Journal of Arts Management*, the *International Journal of Museum Management and Curatorship* and the *Journal of Arts Management, Law and Society*. In addition he has edited the *Journal of Vocational Education and Training* and sat on editorial boards such as *Arts Documentation Monthly* and the *International Journal of Applied Management*. Currently he edits the *Creative Industries Journal*.

Awards and scholarships have included research fellowships at the University of Bradford, City University, Goethe Institute Cultural Scholarship and a Leverhulme Trust Research grant. Currently he is Professor at the Institute for Work Based Learning, Middlesex University and the University of Technology, Sydney. He was until recently Professor of Creative Industries at the University of the Arts, London, adjunct Professor at the Queensland University of Technology and Visiting Professor at the University of Bolton and Greenwich.

He has direct experience of management in the educational and cultural fields, as the Chief Executive for the University Vocational Awards Council and, latterly, as the founding Director of the Museum Training Institute. His senior management experience in higher education includes Dean of the School of Art and Design, University of Derby, Head of the School of Creative Arts, Northumbria University and Head of Academic Development, Bretton Hall, University of Leeds. In addition he is a Director of his consultancy practice, Safehands (Management) Ltd.

Introduction

This second edition builds on the original volume which provided a practical explanation of the principles and practice employed in considering, developing and establishing Cultural Quarters, using urban examples largely drawn from the north of England, north and southern Ireland and Austria, and focusing on a specific case of a proposed Cultural Quarter in a northern English town.

This book has now been expanded to include additional chapters on the significance of historic buildings, the role of universities and the economics of Cultural Quarters. In addition there are new case studies from Australia and the United States thus providing a book rich in examples of Cultural Quarters practice.

As it remains, however, an essentially practical book largely grounded in the United Kingdom traditions, it is structured to assist local authority planners and economic development staff as well as public agencies responsible for developing the cultural and creative industries. In addition, this book is useful in supporting undergraduate and postgraduate teaching and dissertations in architecture, urban development, or cultural administration and management, particularly the case studies and the detailed first-hand description of how a northern England local authority approached the establishment of a Cultural Quarter.

Cultural Quarters are now a well-established concept internationally, particularly with local government, as a component of urban regeneration schemes. Many of the concepts and arguments involved have been critically analised over the last fifteen years or so and are usefully summarised in the *City of Quarters, Urban Villages in the Contemporary City* (Bell and Jayne 2004). In addition, there has been considerable interest in the creative cities concept, which has been thoroughly examined by Charles Landry in *Creative Cities*, and Justin O'Connor in 'A Special Kind of City Knowledge: Innovation Clusters, Tacit Knowledge and the Creative City'. More recently the branding of cities has been considered, in particular the role of Cultural Quarters, in *Branding Cities: Cosmopolitanism, Parochialism, and Social Change*, edited by Hemelryk, Donald, Kofman, and Kevin. Consequently there is no attempt here to analyze previous papers and publications on the subject but rather to focus on the how and what of Cultural Quarters, largely drawn from a cultural perspective. The later part of the book consists of a detailed analysis of a proposal for a Cultural Quarter in Bolton and the issues surrounding this provide a practical, useful and detailed insight for those wishing to study, develop and establish such concepts.

Chapter 1

An Introduction to the Cultural Quarter Landscape

This chapter sets out to explore some of the arguments for Cultural Quarters and the consequent definitional and policy contortions that have influenced the development of these projects. In addition the principles, criteria for success and characteristics of Cultural Quarters are discussed from an urban planning perspective. As a result it provides a useful context for consideration of the case studies in the following chapters.

1.1 Conceptual Confusion: Arts Industry, Heritage Industry, Creative Industries or Cultural Industries?

Successive United Kingdom national governments and their agencies have defined and redrawn boundaries, resulting in continuous public cultural policy and practice turbulence since 1945, commencing with the establishment of the Arts Council of Great Britain (Pick & Anderton 1999). The pragmatic determination of these boundaries – that is, definitions with no obvious rationale for inclusion or exclusion – lends itself to an interpretation of a public sector domain engaged in restrictive cultural practice, wherein boundaries are constrained enough to match the level of available resources at any given time. It is the government administrative machinery responding to national policy by providing manageable and controllable categories, classifications and frameworks for the allocation of public funds, rather than a rational, inclusive and empirically informed (and hence measurable) system that conforms to the requirements of evidence-based policy (Solesbury 2001). Urban regeneration (Roodhouse and Roodhouse 1997) and the creative industries policy (Roodhouse 2003) by the New Labour administration exemplify this practice.

The impact of this obsession with continuous boundary redefinition through national government machinery and by political parties for the arts, creativity and culture (which commenced with the Department of Education, followed by the Office of Arts and Libraries, then the Department of Heritage and now the Department for Culture, Media and Sport) works against cohesion, interaction and connectivity; although much is said by politicians about joined-up policy and action.

'Joined-up government' is a key theme of modern government. The Labour government, first elected in 1997, decided that intractable problems such as social exclusion, drug addiction and crime could not be resolved by any single department of government. Instead, such

problems had to be made the object of a concerted attack using all the arms of government — central and local government and public agencies, as well as the private and voluntary sectors. (Bogdanor 2005, p. 1)

In particular, it encourages isolationism between national, regional and local government and agencies by relying on departmentalisation and compartmentalisation as the organisational means of delivery. As an illustration, culture resides within the Department for Culture, Media and Sport (DCMS) and is also found in the Foreign and Commonwealth Office, who fund the British Council (British Council 1998, 2004), the Ministry of Defence, which resources a substantial number of museums, galleries and musical bands, the Department of Trade and Industry, which supports creative industries through the Small Business Service, including the export effort of these businesses, the Department for Education and Skills (DfES; Allen & Shaw 2001) and the Higher Education Funding Council for England (HEFCE) which provides entry to work and workforce development in the cultural field (North West Universities Association 2004). This incidentally excludes all the devolved cultural arrangements for Scotland, Northern Ireland and Wales, which are another area of chaos, as the studies referred to are focused on England.

This chaotic organisational pattern is replicated at regional level with DCMS-sponsored Cultural Consortia, the Arts Council, the Museums, Libraries and Archives Council (MLA), the Sports Council, the Tourist Boards, Sector Skills Councils (SSCs) and local authorities, along with the Regional Development Agencies (RDAs) and the Small Business Service, including Business Link, not to mention the plethora of sub-regional intermediaries funded from the public purse, all pursuing differing cultural agendas and definitional frameworks (Hamilton & Scullion 2002). Although attempts are made at overarching regional strategies, there is not as yet a shared understanding of an agreement to a definitional framework to operate and evaluate the effectiveness of these strategies. This leads, for example, to data collection replication, which requires additional resource allocation for coordination. Selwood has recognised this, and suggests,

If the lure of cross domain data remains attractive to DCMS and its agencies, there is a case to be made for a better relationship to be forged between the requirements of cultural policy and the collection of evidence. In short we should replace our reliance on the sometimes random data sets which already exist, and which are collated in a piecemeal fashion, with a coherent data framework. (Selwood, no date, p. 6)

1.2 The Creative Industries Concept

These issues were fore-grounded by the 1997 "New Labour" government engagement in the creative industries concept, which claimed to be a significant contributor to the UK knowledge economy (DCMS 1998, 2001). This concept, generated by Leadbetter and Oakley

(1999), is a contemporary reinvention of the "Old Labour" GLC-oriented cultural model. The Labour-controlled Greater London Council (GLC) provided a significant challenge to the definitional status quo in the early 1980s, at a time of high unemployment, significant industrial decline and diminishing public funds for the arts, by re-introducing the cultural industries model derived from popular culture theorists such as Bourdieu and reinvented by Walpole and Comedia in the 1980s. The introduction of the cultural and creative industries exemplars gave rise to a re-appraisal of the role and function of the "traditional" arts in economic terms (Myerscough 1988), and in relation to new technologies such as instant printing, cassette recording and video making (O'Connor 1999). So, the concept of culture as an industry in a public policy context was introduced. The arts, described by the GLC as the "traditional arts", were subsumed into a broader definitional framework, which included

> the electronic forms of cultural production and distribution – radio, television, records and video – and the diverse range of popular cultures which exist in London. (Greater London Council, Industry and Employment Branch, 1985, p. 11)

The eventual successor body, the London Assembly, and the executive Mayor of London have rekindled the theme (London Development Agency 2003), this time with a focus on intervention in the creative industry networks and linkages. However, creative industries development is derived from a longer history associated with defining and redefining the arts as an industry sector (Roodhouse 1997; Calhoun, Lupuma & Postone 1993) and the relationship of the arts and media as cultural industries, for example, which others have addressed (O'Connor 1999; Throsby 2001; Pratt 1997; Garnham 1987).

The cultural industries' replacement creative industry concept, generated by DEMOS (Leadbetter & Oakley 1999) and constructed as a component of the knowledge economy model, can be found in one (Cunningham 2002) of four key policy themes for the DCMS: that is, economic value. It is argued that the theme of economic value is a maturing of the Thatcherite ethos of efficiency, effectiveness, value for money and market forces. Smith, the first New Labour Secretary of State for Culture, Media and Sport, reinforced this interpretation in his attempts to promote "Cool Britannia";

> ensuring that the full economic and employment impact of the whole range of creative industries is acknowledged and assisted by government. (Smith 1998, p. 2)

It was, after all, a continuation of the cultural economic rationale developed earlier by Ken Walpole (Greater London Council, Industry and Employment Branch, 1985). In a keynote paper for the Australian Institute of Arts Management Annual Conference, Brisbane, Australia, 2002, this was elaborated:

> For the first time, the concept of culture as an industry in a public policy context was introduced. The arts, described by the GLC as the 'traditional arts', were subsumed into a broader definitional

framework which included 'the electronic forms of cultural production and distribution – radio, television, records and video – and the diverse range of popular cultures which exist in London.' (Greater London Council, Industry and Employment Branch 1985, p. 11)

The GLC, a Labour-controlled metropolitan council for London, recognised at an early stage that there was a 'strong and deep-rooted antagonism towards any attempt to analyse culture as part of the economy'. It subsequently required a move away from the traditional approaches to cultural analysis, which has tended to separate culture from 'material production and economic activity'. The London Industrial Strategy, The Cultural Industries, argued strongly that 'What is available for cultural consumption and what opportunities there are for employment in cultural production are, for better or for worse, clearly determined by economics'. Given the high levels of unemployment at the time, March 1985, (over 400,000 people were officially unemployed and there were a further 120,000 people wanting work in London), it is not surprising that the role of 'cultural industries' as an employment vehicle within London's economy was recognised. For example, London's biggest manufacturing sector, printing and publishing, employed 112,000 people, and the University of Warwick's Institute of Employment Research indicated at the time that literary, artistic and sports employment would grow by 30% nationally between 1980 and 1990. (Roodhouse 2000a)

Here attention is drawn to a continuum of development, thus suggesting that the creative industries concept is evolutionary and certainly not radical. The connection with the knowledge economy provides a new dimension. These thoughts have been cited by others such as Caust (2003).

The government, through the Creative Industries Taskforce, chaired by Smith, defined the creative industries' boundaries. The definition employed is largely pragmatic, with little in the way of a rationale (Roodhouse 2003a):

those activities which have their origin in individual creativity, skill and talent, and which have a potential for wealth and job creation through the generation and exploitation of intellectual property. (DCMS 1998b)

The industrial activity sub-sectors within which this activity primarily takes place are:

advertising, architecture, the art and antiques market, crafts, design, designer fashion, film, interactive leisure software, music, the performing arts, publishing, software, television and radio. (DCMS 1998b)

This representation of the UK creative industries generates structural and intellectual location tensions: for example, architecture relates to construction and marginally engages with the arts and antiques trade; similarly, the arts and antiques trade has little or nothing to do with interactive leisure software. It is an emerging policy constraint that the DCMS has yet to embed both intellectually and practically in the consciousness of those working in the field, not least because there has been little consultation with those affected. As a consequence, the concept has more in common with the developing global economic interest in the knowledge economy (Leadbetter & Oakley 1999; Howkins 2001; Caves 2000) than the DCMS-designated constituent activities (the sub-sectors). This is exacerbated by the DCMS's divisional structure, which does not attempt to reconcile the creative industries' sub-sectors.

Of particular note in this definitional discourse is the equitable inclusion of both public and private sector activity in public cultural policy which has led to a re-designation of cultural activity as creative industries and an engagement with convergence arguments generated through advances in technology (Flew 2002; Cunningham, Hearn, Cox, Ninan & Keane 2003). Fundamentally, this growing re-conceptualisation facilitates a reassessment of the traditional forms of policy intervention in support of the arts and culture (Roodhouse 2002). As elaborated by Cunningham (2002), the term "creative industries" offers a workable solution that enables cultural industries and creative arts to become enshrined within a definition that breaks down the rigid sustainability of the long-standing definitions of culture and creative arts to create coherency through democratising culture in the context of commerce, whereby creativity can become coupled alongside enterprise and technology to become sectors of economic growth through the commercialisation of creative activity and intellectual property. Cunningham confirms this:

> 'Creative Industries' is a term that suits the political, cultural and technological landscape of these times. It focuses on the twin truths that (i) the core of 'culture' is still creativity, but (ii) creativity is produced, deployed, consumed and enjoyed quite differently in post-industrialised societies. (Cunningham 2002, p. 2)

This, then, is a move from the traditional arts definition established by the Arts Council of Great Britain and successor bodies, recently re-invented as "the value of the arts" argument (Jowell 2004), to an economic re-conceptualisation of the creative industries that implies a democratisation of the arts (Roodhouse 2002) and opens the door to seriously engaging with the arts as business. This re-conceptualisation was presented as the keynote address to over 650 cultural managers, administrators and practitioners at a major international conference, Culture@com.unity, the arts and cultural domain in New South Wales in Sydney, Australia, organised by the Museums and Galleries Foundation of NSW, Regional Arts NSW, Community Cultural Development NSW and the Local Government and Shires Associations of NSW. Subsequently, these concepts were encompassed in an invited article for the Liberal Democrat policy journal, The Reformer, as a contribution to the arts policy debate.

> Such an alternative perspective allows us to consider a more sustainable future for the arts and heritage as creative businesses, with products, services and markets. Judgement of

excellence is simple, and funding becomes based on a business model. The nature of public sector organisational roles can be re-evaluated in developing this industrial sector just like any other industrial activity. Large businesses and the education sector take over the role of research and development. Government should ensure that risk and innovation is nurtured. No special pleading should be required, though, and a wider range of funding agencies can become involved in supporting and developing the businesses. (Roodhouse 2001a)

1.3 Culture as a Creative Industry

A useful point of departure is the conventional view of culture succinctly encapsulated in the Raymond Williams definition (Williams 1981):

a description of a particular way of life which expresses certain meanings and values not only in art and learning, but also in institutions and ordinary behaviour.

He interprets culture in the widest definitional sense; an inclusive attitude consisting of structured and patterned ways of learning, and explains the artistic component of culture as:

Individuals in groups – characteristically respond to and make meaningful the circumstances in which they are placed by virtue of their positions in society and in history.

This definitional framework leads us into a wider understanding of our society, so for example Williams would recognise Britain's most popular tourist attraction, Blackpool Pleasure Beach, visited by over 7 million people in 1998, and with more hotel beds than in all of Greece and its islands combined, as a cultural centre (North West Development Agency 1999). However this cultural centre would not be welcomed into the approved cultural family of the Arts Council of England, or Re:source (now the Museums, Libraries and Archives Council), although it would be seen as a significant component of the tourism industry.

Similarly, popular programmes on television such as 'EastEnders' and 'Coronation Street' are instantly recognised by social scientists, media academics and others as a significant component of the cultural life of the United Kingdom. Notably the Arts Council and the Film Council do not fund these activities or formally recognise them as a cultural component of equal status to the Royal Opera, not least because they are largely private sector activities and "inartistic". Manchester United Football Club with its fan culture is a United Kingdom and international cultural phenomenon which comfortably falls within the Williams definition. Manchester United is also a business quoted on the stock exchange which does not receive public subsidy, and is able to attract capacity audiences – a successful private sector cultural organisation.

In addition, Williams refers to values as an integral component of culture, and in this particular case he is referring to the values of society such as equality, individuality, and religious freedom. However, little is said, for example, about the role of religion in cultural life, except when policy makers and administrators give consideration to equal opportunities and ethnicity. The arts, religion, and culture have been inextricably linked over centuries, with the Renaissance being an obvious example, and similarly Muslim art and design traditions. The arts and heritage form an important component of this cultural definition.

However it seems that debates over the last decade regarding expenditure of public funds in support of cultural activity and development have lacked coherence and ignored convergence, preferring departmentalisation, with each discipline fighting for its particular corner, often based on a self-defining view of the cultural world. For example the Museums Association in the United Kingdom (Museums Association Bulletin 1996) has defined a museum as:

An institution that collects, documents, preserves exhibits and interprets material evidence and associated information for the public benefit.

This definition includes galleries; however it excludes environmental heritage activity, botanical gardens and aquaria.

What is interesting about these debates is the focused attention on particular arts and heritage constituencies at the expense of others, with little demonstrable interest in responding to, and encouraging emerging and different traditions. Furthermore, increasingly over this period these arguments have not been concerned with the intrinsic nature of the arts and whom they benefit, so much as how they relate to the contemporary government policy of the time. So we find for example that in the United Kingdom during the 1940s and 1950s arts development (Roodhouse and Roodhouse 1997) was entirely devoted to the creation of arts centres in new towns, with the assumption that every town should have one. It was also associated with the representation of Britain after the war and a celebration of the future.

Since the 1970s there has been little or no debate by administrators and policy makers about the purpose, value and nature of the arts, but rather a focus of attention on how the arts and heritage can meet national and local government policy in the areas of the economy, urban regeneration, regionalism, social cohesion, and community development, to name a few.

Whilst this is laudable, we should be considering the importance of culture as a defining mechanism for communities such as Wolverhampton, Sheffield, and Bolton. In other words, arguing for coherence and convergence; the arts and heritage in culture; and culture as a manifestation of society: the richness in diversity concept. By taking this stance it is possible to incorporate the wider issues that concern society, such as the environment, employment, urban regeneration, social cohesion, safety, and community development, all of which directly influence a Cultural Quarter concept.

The other issue that complicates these debates, and again is rarely discussed in public, is how society decides what art is, including a shared view of aesthetics. In other words many of the public agencies such as the Arts Councils are charged with promoting the arts as excellence, making excellent art accessible and educating society in the excellence of the arts. Whilst this may be admirable it poses problems such as what is excellence in the arts and heritage fields, determined by whom and using whose criteria? In other words we have established a number of national and regional agencies that have implicitly been given by their remit the task of determining our corporate sense of aesthetic.

If consideration is then given to activities including the arts and heritage as businesses, (the cultural as opposed to the creative industries) with products, services, and markets, then, for example access questions are immediately answered. The judgement of excellence is simple (fitness for purpose), and funding becomes conventionally based on business planning models. So the issue for public sector policy and funding agencies responsible for implementation is more to do with how to support the establishment and growth of cultural businesses as opposed to making aesthetic peer group decisions about the quality of the individual's creative output, which is a subjective procedure.

Such an alternative perspective allows us to consider a more sustainable future for the arts and heritage as cultural businesses. Funding becomes based on a business model, and as a consequence the cultural public sector agency role changes to provide business support in developing this sector just like any other industrial economic activity. It leads to the suggestion that large businesses and the education sector take over the responsibility for research and development. In this way government ensures that cultural risk and innovation is nurtured. No special pleading is required, and the art for art's sake argument (Jowell 2004) is avoided. A wider range of funding agencies with interests in social and economic development can become involved in supporting and developing the businesses.

We can then place our understanding of the creative industries in a wider definition of culture to encourage cohesion, access, participation, and ownership. Culture as an all embracing framework gives us a mechanism for making sense of our activities at a community, regional, and national level. A good example of this is the development of a cultural strategy in Rotherham, an old steel community in South Yorkshire (Rotherham Metropolitan Borough Council 2000), which defined culture as having:

A material dimension:

- The performing arts – music, drama, dance;
- The visual arts – craft, sculpture, fashion;
- Media, film, television, video, language;
- Museums, artefacts, archives, design;
- Libraries, literature, publishing, writing;
- Combined Arts and festivals;
- The Built Heritage – architecture, landscape, urban parks;

And a value dimension:

- Relationships and shared identity;
- Shared memories and experiences;
- Standards;
- What we consider valuable to pass on to future generations.

It is obvious that a cultural definitional framework encompassing far more than the traditional arts and heritage facilitates engagement and interaction with many other components such as the built environment, beliefs, play, and shared memories. A museum, as a focal point for reflection and interpretation of past cultural activities, becomes a sustainable project where public funding is clearly justified. However, this should not prevent us from seeing that the combination of the arts and heritage as an integral component of the culture of a community, region, or nation, with the notion of culture as an industry, providing the most effective and powerful future strategy for all those engaged in such activities.

Culture then as an industry challenges the traditional large institutions, which absorb the largest share of public funds. Whilst they have an important role to play, such funding issues can be resolved by establishing these institutions as businesses, with public sector money targeted at what is needed to "grow" the business. This approach, becoming more popular with the introduction of Trusts and Public Private Partnerships (PPPs), can encourage the private sector, such as Blackpool Leisure Beach, to become involved in public sector activity. In Sheffield, for example, the Council was having difficulty meeting the required expenditure on its museums, galleries, and libraries, leading to redundancies and reduced opening hours. The city placed the department in Trust, retaining ownership of the estate, collections, and other assets, but with an independent management contracted to run the services for six years in return for a guaranteed grant income. Acting commercially to a business plan, the Trust allowed the private sector flexibility to operate the institutions as a business with the assurance of public sector support.

Institutions such as these can be seen as creative businesses engaging with customers, developing markets, and providing services and products which contribute to the development of local, national, and regional culture. This may require a re-examination of the role of local government or Arts Councils towards acting as contract and risk managers with a wider understanding of business development. However, such developments will not only limit public expenditure but also provide more flexibility for the managers. Many local authorities see a long-term future for the cultural services and arts in contributing to regeneration, quality of life, social cohesion, and economic development, using vehicles such as Trusts.

If administrators and policy makers continue the static debate on public subsidies dedicated to the arts, the condition of our institutions will never improve. We now need to ensure that activities encompassed in a cultural framework such as Quarters, are derived from the needs of communities and what they are prepared to pay for. This approach relies fundamentally on ensuring that the relationship between organisations and individuals in communities is strong, and that the organisations reflect the needs, aspirations, and creative potential of the people of the town or region. The most effective way of delivering this organisational and individual interaction is to consider cultural activity as creative businesses, occurring in Cultural Quarters, which are a market place for making, buying, and selling goods and services.

1.4 Defining Cultural and Cultural Industry Quarters

A useful definitional parameter for the case studies and practical application of the Bolton experience is informed by Montgomery (2003), O'Connor (2004), Bell and Jayne (2004), as follows:

A Cultural Quarter is a geographical area of a large town or city which acts as a focus for cultural and artistic activities through the presence of a group of buildings devoted to housing a range of such activities, and purpose designed or adapted spaces to create a sense of identity, providing an environment to facilitate and encourage the provision of cultural and artistic services and activities.

A distinction can be made between a Cultural Quarter and a cultural industries quarter. The latter is dedicated to cultural business development e.g. the Sheffield Cultural Industries Quarter, and the other is an identification of a geographical area in which cultural activity is encouraged to locate, a physically defined focal point for cultural activity e.g. Wolverhampton Cultural Quarter.

A Cultural Quarter represents the coherence and convergence of the arts and heritage in culture, and culture as a manifestation of society. Cultural Quarters provide a context for the use of planning and development powers to preserve and encourage cultural production and consumption.

Up to the present time, Cultural Quarters have invariably developed from an existing embryonic cultural presence, as a result of a public sector initiative. Cultural Quarters are often part of a larger strategy integrating cultural and economic development, usually linked to the regeneration of a selected urban area. A Cultural Quarter is a complex cluster of activities – networks embedded in a particular place.

By selecting this description of a cultural or creative industry quarter there is a deliberate exclusion of the cluster concept which is regularly applied to the cultural and creative business activity. However there is a correlation between quarters, precincts used in Australia, and districts in the United States. For example, Brooks and Kushner share a similar definitional framework when quantifying the North American version of Cultural Quarters, cultural districts (Brooks & Kushner 2001) illustrated in the Pawtucket, Rhode Island case study later in the book.

They adopt a classificatory approach to cultural district strategies to facilitate analysis, which is:

Cultural District Strategy Classifications

- **Administration (*delivery structure*):** How does the institutional landscape change as a result of creating a cultural district?
- **Degree of Public Involvement (*funding and regulatory structures*):** How is the government involved in the district?
- **Degree of Change in the Cultural District (*spatial relationships, refurbishment, and new build*):** How much physical change is evident in the district as a result of cultural designation?
- **Programming (*cultural activity*):** What is the content, centralised or decentralised programming of cultural activity?

From this it is apparent that the ingredients for a Quarter are similar to those in North America, that is: spatial and build issues, cultural activity, and delivery structures. However, little reference is made in this model to the meaning of a Quarter; that is a sense of place, the people's history, and culture.

A distinction needs to be made at this stage between Cultural Quarters, creative industry quarters, and cultural iconographic regeneration, which includes examples such as the new Royal Armouries in Leeds, the Tate Modern Cornwall, or the Baltic Contemporary Visual Arts Centre, Newcastle upon Tyne. Although these singular projects often provide a focus for regenerative activity the distinction lies in designation; a spatial area for a particular form of development.

1.5 The Ingredients for a Successful Cultural Quarter

As Graeme Evans says,

> *The phenomenon of collective production in 'Marshallian districts' has been evident from pre-industrial artist and crafts-based communities to contemporary cultural industry quarters in 'post industrial cities'. It is not new, and even with the threat of the 'placelessness of communications technology and new media practice' has continued to grow in importance as a physical manifestation of production and consumption of cultural goods and services, a market place.* (Evans, 2009 cited in LEGNÉR, M. & PONZINI, D. (2009))

John Montgomery (2003) also draws our attention to the history of Cultural Quarters, with examples of the Left Bank in Paris, the Lower East Side in New York, and Soho in London.

Similarly, Brown, O'Connor and Cohen (Brown, O'Connor and Cohen 2000) suggest that the models we consider are derived from the North American experience of the urban village and the British industrial district model based on pre-Fordist economies of small and medium-sized enterprises clustering around complementary skills and services, both competing and collaborating at the same time. Science and business parks are a typical example of this approach, and proved popular in the 1980s. It is suggested that:

> Quarters are complex clusters of activities – they are networks embedded in a particular place. The complex networks of activity and exchange are given the context – they take place. This place acquired is a series of associations which can be iconic, but are also spatially embedded social networks.

Montgomery describes Cultural Quarters from an urban planning perspective as:

> The use of planning and development powers to both preserve and encourage both cultural production and consumption. Moreover, Cultural Quarters are often seen as part of a larger strategy integrating cultural and economic development. This is usually linked to the redevelopment or regeneration of a selected urban area, in which mixed use urban development is to be encouraged, and the public realm is to be reconfigured. In other words Cultural Quarters tend to combine strategies for greater consumption of the arts and culture with cultural production and urban place making.

He cites Canter, *The Metaphor for Place* (Cantor 1997) as providing a useful description of the necessary characteristics of all successful urban places as follows:

Activity: economic, cultural, and social;
Form: the relationship between buildings and spaces;
Meaning: sense of place, historical and cultural.

He goes on to suggest that it is possible within this framework to establish indicators that can be used to assess the relative success of Cultural Quarters. The Montgomery model is elaborated by Parkin with reference to DETR (1999) and DETR/CABE (2000) as follows:

Cultural Quarter Principles

Placemaking
- Form to follow function;
- Balance harmony with contrast, history with context, familiar with new and stimulating;
- Straightforward yet with rich local meaning;

- Building backs to backs and fronts to fronts;
- Create microclimates, e.g. to trap the sun and protect from the prevailing wind;
- Ability to respond to change;
- For meeting and easy contact;
- Density need not be high;
- Visually simple, free of clutter;

Space
- No indeterminate spaces that are neither private nor public;
- Identifiable meeting places need to be created, but informal (e.g. sitting space "created" by the users)
- Movement (walk), transactions (gather), and assembly (linger) to be facilitated;
- Objects need to be carefully placed in spaces;
- High culture to have pride of place;
- Safe, well maintained, and active (surveillance and protection);
- Elegant and generous (open spaces/crescents/parks/squares).

Activity
- Active edges and frontages leading to "transactions" because of a movement or visual relationship;
- Pedestrians come in and activities spill out;
- A "hot spot" for activity, created by an overlap and congestion of activity;
- A mix of uses necessary, but these are difficult to prescribe;
- Perhaps "constellations of use" that can be combined in close proximity;
- Temporal activities, i.e. morning, afternoon, and evening;
- Mixture of uses with public–private interaction.

Fabric
- Spaces must be attractive, stimulating, and delightful to the senses by use of colour, texture and surfaces, ornament, materials, and decoration.

Movement
- Strong paths, landmarks (tower, corner, statue), edges, and nodes (meeting of paths);
- Network of public spaces, web of connections, hierarchy of routes;
- Enclaves to mesh;
- Wider network of green corridors;
- Location of entrances important.

The case studies incorporating the Cultural Quarter principles found in Chapter 5 and 6 provide examples of differing approaches to Cultural Quarter development from the highly structured or the organically developed, to the creative entrepreneur or state-led development. However, all the selected examples concern themselves with the re-use of old buildings, new build, the bringing back into life an area of a town or city, sustaining and creation of jobs and businesses, as well as University engagement, but above all else they fundamentally rely on a cultural anchor of one kind or another.

1.6 Criticisms of Cultural Quarters

Critics of the Cultural Quarter approach to regeneration focus on the artificial planning and building development-led approach, suggesting that this has little to do with communities, their needs, or creative activity. This debate is often typified as a top-down versus bottom-up, or directed as opposed to collaborative, with the engagement of communities, their needs and creative activity being the collaborative bottom-up means of developing Cultural Quarters rather than the building-centred directed profit-oriented mechanism.

The Sheffield Creative Industries Quarter regeneration example commenced with creative individuals taking over a redundant building associated with the old cutlery industry in a derelict city centre area near the railway station and University, to provide a venue for popular music. As this became more successful, recording studios were established and more people moved into the area, including artists. The primary motivating factor for those involved in the early stages was to meet their needs for a live and cheap venue for their kind of music. As happens in many cases, including the Manchester Cultural Quarter development, local authorities and other public agencies progressively take control, with the result that gentrification creeps in and the creative individuals move out to another "poor" area because they cannot afford the rents or purchase price of accommodation.

Sometimes it is also concerned with a generation or cohort of creatives who enjoy being associated with each other, who want to locate and interact with each other, who eventually begin to fragment and follow their own personal and professional interests. This driving away of the creative core is cited as a weakness of the structured approach to Cultural Quarter development.

The Custard Factory in Birmingham is a regeneration project that relied less on individual artists and more on a creative entrepreneur with vision and determination to succeed despite the odds to provide high quality facilities at competitive prices for creative businesses. The individual entrepreneur model does not fit comfortably into a planned public sector-led system with the associated regulatory requirements, procedures, and collective decision-making processes.

Finding cheap places to live and work provided the driver for the artist-led Newcastle studio development, and triggered in the 1970s and 80s artist-owned studio cooperatives such as SPACE and ACME. ACME, a London-based charity established in 1972, is the largest artist support agency in the United Kingdom with over 380 studios, 25 units of living accommodation, and working with 4,000 artists. Yorkshire Arts Space Society, part of the Sheffield creative industries quarter, performs a similar function. Often this type of activity profiles a physical location, attracting investment and over time gentrification, referred to earlier.

Chapter 2

The Cultural Economics of Quarters

Pier Luici Sacco

This chapter provides an introduction to the economics of Cultural Quarters by suggesting that the conventional approaches to measuring this activity are redundant as cultural activity and in particular the cultural and creative industries have become increasingly important to the knowledge economy. A new paradigm is required which places more emphasis on the social contribution these activities make to local development through horizontal value chains and the virtual as well as physical clustering that is a Cultural Quarter. This has implications for urban policy planners in terms of city branding and identification as well as the recognition of the social fabric of individual urban environments. Culture is used as a general description in this chapter to include the creative and culture al industries and reflects the position taken in chapter 1.

2.1 Introduction: Culture and Economic Development

Over recent years considerable attention has been given by both economic analysts and public organisations to the issue of the economic impact of cultural and creative activities. An important watershed in this respect has been the publication, in 2006, of the "Figel" report, which was the first systematic attempt at measuring the economic size of the cultural and creative value chains in the European Union, in terms of turnover, number of jobs, and growth dynamics. The reported data was a surprise to many, as the report maintained that, in its entirety, the sector was worth approximately twice the automobile manufacturing sector (in terms of turnover), and, by the same token, was at least the equivalent of most of the EU's recognised leading economic sectors. There is the inevitable controversy about the reliability of these data, but nevertheless, even when due adjustments would have been made, the actual orders of magnitude are still significant in comparison with other industrial sectors. Thus, consequently, there is evidence to support the assumption that culture and creativity are driving forces in the EU economy.

This recognition does not imply, however, that there is wide agreement on why and how cultural activity boosts the economy. Despite the fact that the cultural and creative industry turnover is high, it is also to be noted that culture receives substantial subsidies from public and private institutions, and therefore only part of the overall value of the macro-sector comes from genuine market transactions. Moreover, for cultural and creative professionals the labour market is often high qualification and low pay where a substantial number of players on the demand side try to live on these salaries and often do not manage to. Advocates of the economic developmental role of the cultural and creative industries therefore have to counter the argument that cultural value chains are not stable and solid enough to credibly compare with the "old" production economy in terms of established and proven long-term growth potential.

At the centre of the controversy there is a basic misconception that needs to be clarified. If the developmental role of the cultural and creative industries is mainly measured in terms of its ability to generate economic value added, whether directly or indirectly, all that matters is how, and to what extent, the sector contributes to increasing the overall level of economic activity. Therefore, it matters insofar as it causes the occurrence of market transactions. If, alternatively, the developmental role includes both the creation of value added *and* the creation of suitable pre-conditions for the generation of further economic value, an alternative form of evaluation is required which incorporates economic and social impact. In the first case, evaluation is framed in terms of sales of goods and services with a cultural content. In the second case, effects such as the generation of individual and social capabilities and functioning, of social cohesion, of individual and collective identity are included. These components often defy economic measurement, but may nevertheless have a remarkable developmental impact. Consequently to understand the economic contribution of these industries to local strategic development it is necessary to refer to the "extensive" view.

The contraposition between the two developmental views of culture may be traced back to their implicit functional role: culture as a (macro-)sector of the economy amongst others or culture as a basic developmental *asset*, its economic dimension being a part of the whole picture. The key issue becomes how deeply interconnected it is with most or all of the other economic sectors, and to what extent such interconnection contributes to enhancing the local economy's overall vitality, competitiveness, and so on.

Typically, cultural activities tend to be organised into clusters, and interestingly the two alternative views just introduced act as the main clustering factors. In the traditional, value-added, macro-sector-centred view, the driving force behind cultural clusters is vertical integration, i.e. the spatial aggregation of players operating at various stages of the same value chain. In this case, cultural clusters cannot but be clusters of activities all directly pertaining to the cultural and creative fields, characterised by more or less rich and articulated input-output relationships and by various levels of economies of scale, scope, and agglomeration. Alternatively, the system-wide (developmental) view focuses upon horizontal integration, i.e. the strategic complimentarity amongst players operating in different value chains, so that the driving force between spatial aggregation becomes the common need to take advantage of the indirect social and economic effects of cultural activity on a variety of different levels such as the access to innovative thinking, social animation, urban atmosphere, and so on.

Not surprisingly, from a historical point of view vertically integrated (homogeneous) quarters have come first, as a direct consequence of the translation of the "cultural" urban industrial revolution. In the early twentieth century, the transposition of technological innovation to the cultural sectors paved the way to cultural mass markets for media such as music, cinema, and performing arts, which led to a natural impulse to concentrate such activities in specialised quadrants of the city, and to characterise these activities as entertainment. Attendance of cultural/entertainment shows was then a way to employ one's leisure time, and therefore concentrating all the facilities in a few physical places was, on the demand side, a way to facilitate the choice of potential customers giving them an easily explorable and comparable menu of alternatives in one location. On the supply side, this approach enabled suppliers to take collective advantage from the physical concentration of a critical mass of potential audience.

As the *productive* dimension of culture has gone beyond pure entertainment to find new and sometimes unexpected complementarities with scientific and technological research, social animation, and education, a new logic of spatial aggregation has emerged. The main concern was no longer establishing physical hubs of entertainment facilities, but to create spatial connections between potentially related activities belonging to different fields, in order to exploit the economic and social value of diversity to the same extent as the previous aggregation logic strived to exploit the economic and social value of homogeneity. As the transition took place, the nature and structure of Cultural Quarters has changed accordingly, and continues to develop to explore different models and solutions that reflect more effectively the current needs and meet the upcoming challenges.

The purpose of this chapter is to review the basic economics of Cultural Quarters and to explore change as a consequence of the transition from an entertainment-based to a wide cultural economics system. The structure of the chapter will include a brief review of the main issues about the impact of culture on urban development. In the subsequent section the basic economics of traditional Cultural Quarters compared with "new wave" Cultural Quarters is explored. Finally, key conclusions are drawn and likely future developments are discussed.

2.2 The Developmental Role of Culture in Urban Settings

There are many different ways in which culture may have an impact on the local economy. The most significant are discussed in the following sections.

Attraction of Resources

Culture sometimes is an inward investment or relocation factor for firms and human capital, insofar as there is an understanding of how a thriving cultural milieu can create economic opportunities. From the point of view of firms, different local conditions such as individual and social attitudes toward the production, circulation, and use of knowledge may make a big difference on their locational choices, irrespective of the firm's size. A culturally active milieu, if adequately supported by a large enough level of social capital, certainly favours the emergence of open-minded, change-friendly organisational environments, and makes room for incentive schemes based on non-monetary forms of compensation that involve training, workshops, and other forms of knowledge-intensive activities, thereby making room for the individual and collective accumulation of cultural capital. This may lead in turn to a positive feedback growth cycle, as more skilled workers become interested in further investment in their intangible capitals, but also more financial investors and venture capitalists are attracted to the same milieu.

It is important to stress that this particular attraction-driven growth dynamics is not necessarily linked to "creative class" factors. Different urban environments may be attractive for a variety of different reasons in a knowledge-intensive economic and social scenario: there are a large number of factors concurrently at work, and they may interact in very complex ways. For example, issues of knowledge base, quality of life, and diversity may be weighed against those of accessibility, social equity, industry structure, or scale: a far more intricate conundrum than the simple "3T" formula (Technology – Talent – Tolerance), the Richard Florida (2002) model that has won popularity. Perhaps the most compelling (and convincing) critical appraisal of the limitations of the "creative class" way of thinking of urban attraction dynamics is that of Peck (2005). He takes up former criticisms by Glaeser (2004) and Malanga (2004) questioning the association between cities faring well in Florida's "3T league tables" and actual growth and occupation performance, but goes on to stress that the major shortcoming of "creative class" explanations of local development – and this is an irony if one thinks of the sociological origin of the term "class" – is their basic neglect of issues of social inequality, marginality, and poverty, which is easily conducive to new forms of dualistic societies based on the contraposition between the "creative haves" and the "creative have-nots". And thus, in terms of social sustainability, there is an argument that the long-term attractiveness potential of a city basically depends on its ability *not* to encourage such kind of dualistic dynamics, but rather to develop a socially inclusive milieu.

The primary tension between "creative class" and local community value lies in the issue of instrumentality. From the creative class point of view, the emphasis on creativity and creatives stems from the fact that the latter are the people that (according to Florida) "bring the money" in the current scenario, and thus realise a social goal (to make cities thrive), whereas from the local community point of view, the emphasis is on the social practices of creativity and their *meaning*: having the opportunity to live a creative life is an end in itself, and all of its further implications are secondary. But the paradox is that only when one reasons in non-instrumental terms economic and social value can be generated in a sustainable way.

The latter is a point where implications go far beyond anecdotal wisdom: It has to do with the basic properties of intangible assets that are crucial to define, and develop, to arrive at suitable norms of substantial and procedural rationality in the post-industrial context. From the point of view of both substantial and procedural rationality, the optimal accumulation of intangible assets (such as human, social, or cultural capital) requires an intrinsic motivational drive – in the absence of which, people will not do what is meaningful to acquire knowledge and skills, relationships, or cultural experience, but only what is instrumentally functional to their stated goals – and, as a consequence, their conduct will be too narrowly focused and lacking that 'serendipity dimension' that easily distinguishes between the truly committed and the opportunist.

The literature on the relationships between culture and local development processes provides little of relevance, both at the theoretical and policy levels. Issues related to the effect of culture on human capital are hardly mentioned although they are fundamental to understanding the developmental role of culture in the current scenario. This is at least partly due to the fact that a conceptualisation of the role of culture in shaping the codes of rationality for the production and accumulation of intangible assets is lacking. In fact, the crucial condition for viable culture-led local development is the existence of social governance mechanisms that encourage individuals and groups to give importance to intrinsic motivation and to link social approval and recognition to commitment toward knowledge-intensive activities and experiences. This is a basic pillar of the emerging knowledge society and urban policy makers may have to learn to take this dimension into account when designing social mechanisms and regulations.

Innovation

Innovation is the name of the game in today's globally competitive world. Innovation, however, is a subtle and complex idea that escapes understanding when analised through a narrow disciplinary lens. To make sense of this concept, multiple perspectives have to be employed: economical, sociological, anthropological, socio-psychological, geographical, technological, to mention a few. And yet, despite this complexity, that calls into question a number of heterogeneous factors and encourages an "anything goes" approach; there has been interest in the specific role of culture in fostering innovation. Recently, the European Community (KEA 2009) presented a document that illustrates systematically the many different connections between innovation and culture, arguing that they occur at several levels, and putting forward some preliminary indications for the future mainstreaming of policies aimed at developing those connections.

It seems therefore that innovation-related policies may be an important part of any culture-led local development model. Clearly, the effect of culture on innovation is hardly rationalised in terms of the same, almost tautological links that connect science and technology. The impact of culture is more subtle, but no less interesting, nor important: culture acts as a sort of global platform that creates the social conditions for the onset of innovative waves, by providing people with opportunities to revise and even re-shape their cognitive background through contact with unexpected, including challenging, situations and contexts. Seen from this perspective, culture may become the engine of a new model of endogenous growth where the acquisition of cognitive capabilities through cultural attendance and their socialisation through culturally mediated interaction may cause an innovation-based productivity shift that can be dynamically reinforced. It is interesting to note that this particular type of innovation-based growth dynamic does not overlap with the attraction-based model, but is complementary. Therefore, a culture-led local development dynamic may be the effect of the confluence of several distinct factors, that are open to strategic complimentarity and spillover.

The implications of this new field of theoretical research and policy design are neither trivial nor negligible. In particular, it is important to stress how the dynamic mechanism briefly described earlier crucially hinges upon the *actual* acquisition and development of cognitive skills and upon their effective socialisation: in other words, it depends on the success of intrinsic motivational factors in driving individual and collective behaviours. In the case of innovation, the contradictions described earlier in the instrumental rationality dimension become clear: so on the one hand there is the need to move across unknown territories to develop new ideas that can have a successful business translation, but on the other there is a fundamental suspicion and lack of interest in anything that does not fit comfortably into existing schemes and can therefore be safely evaluated in terms of cost-benefit trade-offs. When faced with this dilemma, the instrumental rationality model inevitably relates to circumscribed territory where things "make sense" and are amenable to evaluation, thus ignoring the key factors which are more likely to be conducive to real innovation. This is why, in his still seminal work about the nature and economic effects of innovation, Schumpeter (1911/1934) argues that the entrepreneur is following a peculiar norm of rationality that is escaping the narrow calculations of the ordinary *homo oeconomicus*.

The links between cultural experience, creativity and innovation are therefore much more substantial than one could expect at first sight, and are rooted in the very foundations of the rationality norms that govern non-instrumental behaviours. And this deep link does not lend itself to mechanistic recipes that sound like "do this, and that will happen", which are the daily bread of instrumental rationality and are reflected in approaches like the "creative class". The formation of an innovative wave cannot but be the effect of self-organisation; a product of that "spontaneous order" which is the hallmark of the Austrian school, that is to say, the core of Schumpeter's background as an economist. One can operate upon the contextual conditions for the emergence of innovation, in terms of resources, social attitudes, infrastructure, education, and so on – but it is a matter of fact that similar contexts will typically generate different outcomes, and not only in terms of performance. The socio-psychological micro-structure that prevails in the different contexts will have a significant bearing on the outcome, and in ways that cannot easily be anticipated. Therefore, it is hard to justify and implement a culture-based innovation policy if there is no interest for the intrinsic effects that it produces, that is to say, if one does not give value to the very fact that people and groups may acquire culturally transmitted cognitive competences. Judged from the standpoint of instrumental rationality, there may be safer, less vague ways of pursuing the goal of excellence in innovation, and certainly amongst them there are ways that are more easily evaluated and can thus command more political and social consensus.

Consequently the route of culture-based innovation policy development and implementation is more likely to be taken by these local communities where the socialisation of knowledge as a goal with an intrinsic value has been successfully accomplished, at least to a degree and it is there that one can expect *to see* new, powerful innovation waves.

Cultural Production: Cultural and Creative Industries

A third fundamental pillar of a culture-based local development model including creative industries is production itself not least because of its increasing importance to any economic system. There is also a history. Cultural production per se is one of the most ancient human activities, with roots going back to a pre-industrial past. So what makes cultural production so relevant in the late industrial and post-industrial phases of socio-economic development is the volume and economic value of cultural production. To appreciate this, it is necessary to explain the main stages of the process.

In the pre-industrial era, cultural demand was basically traceable back to cultural commissioning, and in particular to mecenatism: a situation in which the commissioner makes use of his political and economic power to offer to cultural producers a "free zone" to work and operate, shielded against the necessities of daily life. It is important to stress that, in the pre-industrial context, the channels of creation of economic value and political power are basically disconnected from cultural commissioning, which as a result appears as a way to make use of otherwise accumulated resources to self-celebrate one's own power and prestige, in ways and forms not accessible to the majority of others. But cultural production also occurs at the bottom line of economic production, and incorporates all of the social relationships that underlie the latter.

With the industrial revolution, we witness the beginning of a process, to develop cultural industries, where ever-expanding markets centred on the creation and circulation of cultural products rely on the new possibilities unleashed by technological change devising more and more sophisticated interfaces to attract new audiences. This process generated printed books, magazines, and newspapers, vinyl records and latterly CDs, cinema with film and then digital, radio-television broadcasting, video games and recreational software. It is an astounding broadening of modes of cultural experience delivery largely associated with the growth in leisure and entertainment, and one that could never have been imagined in the nineteenth century, when the industrial revolution was, in other fields of production, already well on its way. In this new era, cultural production is no longer a pre-economic type of activity, based more on the economics of gift than market exchange, as it was customary in pre-industrialism. On the contrary, it becomes one of many ways to create economic value. Culture, therefore, does not lie at the bottom of the value chain as a peripheral activity, but becomes one component of the chain itself amongst many. The real issue becomes that of its relative dimension (in terms of turnover) with respect to that of more traditional productive sectors. An issue that, in Europe at least, has been taken seriously until recently, whereas in North America it has long been credited with making a recognisable contribution to the economic and political discourse. The reasons for this European neglect are manifold. The fact that in Europe culture is heavily subsidised from the "public purse" leads quite naturally to consider it as a meta-sector that absorbs economic resources rather than creates them. In addition the European tradition of industrially organised cultural production has been seen, especially through the legacy of the Frankfurt and French schools, as mass manipulation, overlaid with conflicting socio-political implications. This has provided an important background for the continued, explicit public support of cultural production as a way to defend pluralism and to prevent at least partially the commodification of culture.

As a result the "rediscovery" of cultural industry in Europe as a primary engine of economic and social development is relatively recent. The urge to find workable ways to re-activate de-industrialised, stagnating local economies cited in other chapters left behind by the post-industrial transition has allowed the bypassing of doubt and controversy, once it became clear that cultural activity was likely to be one of the sectors of the future post-industrial economy for which demand was rising, in large part due to technological progress and people with more leisure time. It is understandable that when, at the end of 2006, the European Community published its report on the levels of economic turnover of European cultural industries (KEA 2009), the results were surprising. Some of the most widely reported highlights included the turnover of the whole cultural and creative sector in Europe was roughly twice as big as that of the automobile industry, and that the relative weight of the sector was similar to giants such as ICT, real estate, and food-beverages-tobacco. However, in the United Kingdom the cultural and creative industries as contributors to the knowledge economy had been taken seriously since the 1980s.

The articulation of the cultural and creative sectors is complex and the Throsby (2001) concentric circles model provides a helpful explanation. It assumes the cultural value of cultural good is the ultimate source of value for these sectors. The core of the concentric circles consists of "unconstrained" creative ideas and contents, with a progressive decrease of cultural content in favour of commercialisation. Overall, there are four distinct circles; the first two pertain to the cultural industries, whilst the others to the creative industries. It consists of, respectively, the "non-industrial" cultural core (visual arts, performing arts, and heritage), the cultural industries (film and video, television and radio, video games, music, and books and press, design, architecture and advertising) and the related industries (those that produce technological interfaces for cultural and creative products: PC, MP3 players, mobile phones etc.).

Another recent contribution to the understanding of this complex and rapidly evolving field is the report on creative economy for the United Nations (UNCTAD 2008), that attempts to bridge different possible approaches including "creativity", "creative products", "cultural industries", "creative industries" and "creative economy": creativity as a measurable social process is, from the economic point of view, considered not only in terms of economic outcomes (transactions with a market value), but also for the whole cycle of creative activity, through the interplay of four forms of capital – social cultural, human, and structural or institutional – that determines in turn the expansion of the "stock" of creativity – the creative capital, namely, the ultimate outcome of the cycle (one could in fact adopt a "circular flow" view of the creative process, where market transactions occurring on cultural and creative markets are not the end of the game, but are functional to the "reproduction" of the stock of creative capital). UNCTAD defines creativity as "the process by which ideas are generated, connected and transformed into things that are valued" (UNCTAD 2008, p. 10). The UNCTAD report attempts to provide a synthesis of the literature on cultural and creative industries and as a result defines them as:

- working through cycles of creation, production and distribution of goods and services that use creativity and intellectual capital as primary inputs;
- relying upon a set of knowledge-based activities, focused on – but not limited to – the arts, potentially generating revenues from trade and intellectual property rights;
- dealing with both tangible products and intangible intellectual or artistic services with creative content and economic value;
- being at the cross-road amongst the artisan, services, and industrial sectors; and
- constituting a new, dynamic sector in world trade (UNCTAD 2008, p. 13).

The UNCTAD report makes an important contribution to the global acceptance and recognition of cultural and creative industries as a key choice for local socio-economic development, and therefore paves the way to more generalised interest by the policy makers and advisers. However, the rather particular mix of instrumental and non-instrumental motivations that are found across the spectrum of this rather heterogeneous and diverse meta-sector is likely to continue to generate further discussion, both at the theoretical and policy levels. Moreover, with the further unfolding of the post-industrial transition that is progressively unveiling a process of "culturalisation" of the whole economy; it becomes increasingly difficult to distinguish between which industries are creative and which are not. One can argue for example that "all industries are cultural because they all produce products that besides having functional applications are also socio-symbolically significant" (Mato 2009, p. 73, and, for a critical rebuttal, Miller 2009). Certainly, there is ample room for believing that not only the local developmental impact of cultural and creative industries will increase over time, but also their active role in driving the already cited, and ongoing "culturalisation" of the economy will be increasingly recognised and strategically accounted for by other economic players. In fact the next phase of the process may be, in terms of the positioning of culture and creativity along value chains, the further migration of the latter to the top of value chains, by producing contents and meaning that will be deliberately appropriated (and, when necessary, paid for) by apparently non-cultural producers, to shape the perceptions of value of their customers by finding more and more sophisticated ways to associate such contents and meanings to their products.

2.3 Cultural Quarters: Recreational Spaces or Creative Hubs?

Cultural Quarters as clusters of spatially concentrated cultural facilities into a specific urban neighbourhood, described in chapter I, are a typical presence in many urban contexts, and in some cases are long-standing components of the urban landscape. As already stated, the spatial agglomeration of cultural facilities responds to intuitive but economically compelling arguments. As cultural audiences have multiple and diverse interests, it is perceived to be beneficial to concentrate all the facilities in physically related locations, so that all Quarter organisations have the opportunity to draw from the whole basket of potential customers. This concentration effect is most likely to outweigh competition deriving from the presence of so many other similar facilities. In the alternative scenario in which businesses are scattered throughout the city, there is less competition but also significantly fewer potential customers, and especially if a given facility is relatively small, isolated from obvious transport routes and less well known compared to better publicised organisations. Moreover, customers that choose one facility one night, once having learnt of possibilities, are tempted to come back again and choose another activity. In larger cities where these services and products are rich and diversified with big audiences, there are different, thematically characterised Quarters (the gallery district, the cinema district, the theatre district, and so on).

This is the first and most obvious (demand side) agglomeration economy leading to the emergence of Cultural Quarters. But there are other agglomeration economies which are clearly equally relevant, amongst them scale, transportation, scope (and the relative, connected economies of information and visibility). Being part of a Cultural Quarter, individual companies and organisations can exploit the scale factor in terms of easier availability of services, skilled workers, raw materials, and relevant production supplies, which tend to locate nearby to take advantage of the high concentration of potential customers, the more so the bigger the cluster. Moreover, further economies of scale may result from public administration choosing to locate different types of public services such as tourist information and business support in the vicinities of the Quarter to further enhance its attractiveness and functionality. They can likewise exploit economies of transportation not only by staying close to other potential partners and service providers, but also by securing better contractual conditions from shippers and transporters when bundling shipments with those of other players in the Quarter. Again, a further element of transportation economy may emerge when the critical mass of the quarter encourages the city administration to plan better connections to the area in terms of public transportation and motorways. The economy of scope is perhaps the most evident and intuitive in the case of a Cultural Quarter. The main rationale behind the emergence of a Cultural Quarter is the bundling of its services and goods with branding and joint marketing under a common label, and often these campaigns may be partly or even entirely covered by public funds as a part of city marketing strategies, as a distinctive element of city identity. Similar effects occur with reference to the production and dissemination of information about the activities and events taking place in the Quarter, as well as production, funding, and promotion opportunities for the players operating in the Quarter.

As to the economic impact of a Cultural Quarter, there is a direct component related to the actual operation of the companies and organisations that make up the quarter, and an indirect element. The direct component is the production of the value added by all the Quarter players. They produce goods and services, whose selling generates different sources of income in the form of rents, wages, and profits, whereas there may be a part of the supplied goods and services which are not sold on the market and are supported by public or private subsidies. The indirect component is the demand for goods and services which are not produced within the Cultural Quarter but can be traced back to the presence of the Quarter itself such as housing and restoration services, retail shops, and wholesale supplies. But there are also indirect "environmental" effects, the most important and well understood of which is the effect on the real estate. Generally, the presence of the Cultural Quarter adds value to the real estate, and especially so if the Quarter occupies facilities that were previously abandoned or needing restoration. But the positive real estate effect may only occur as the Cultural Quarter attracts knowledge workers and professionals to the area, and consequently paves the way to high-end shops and service providers. As it is well known, this effect introduces the conditions for the progressive "gentrification" of the Quarter surroundings. It favours the gradual takeover by high income professionals and residents leading in turn to the transformation of the area into a cosy or even "posh" shopping district, and the subversion of the cultural identity. But the indirect "environmental" effects may have a more complex nature, in that the aura of the Cultural Quarter may reverberate to a significant extent to the identity, visibility and attractiveness of the city as a whole, its social patterns of use of time and space, and level of social cohesion.

These indirect, "environmental" effects are strongly linked to the actual nature of the activities and the function played by the Quarter in an urban context. Whereas vertical integration is typical of Cultural Quarters with a recreational specialisation, the complex architecture of relationships of a productive Cultural Quarter calls for forms of horizontal integration. In the case of a traditional Quarter with a prominent recreational character, cultural facilities are places whose aim is to attract final customers willing to pay, to spend some time and enjoy. In a more mature developmental model of culture, however, there are many different functions that culture can and must perform, and this is reflected in the spatial organisation of cities; the level and quality of social commitment and control that is achieved through cultural production; and the type of place and city identification generated. In this wider framework, the attraction of a potential audience is no longer the sole criterion. When cultural production and not only dissemination combine with the link between culture and innovation and the attraction of talent and resources, new location criteria are necessary. Amongst these, closeness to production facilities (recording, rehearsal, and digital processing studios), to science and technology parks and specific industrial clusters, amenities, colleges and universities, to downtown areas with particular symbolic value become important.

Similarly if the emphasis moves from entertainment and leisure to entertainment *plus* production *plus* complimentarity with other productive sectors there are then a number of different factors that act in parallel to determine location choices and thus how cultural activities fit into the spatial logic of the city. The spatial concentration of producers, that traditionally was a driving location factor only for certain fields of cultural production, most notably visual arts, is now taking over the full spectrum of cultural and creative production. Unlike entertainment-based quarters, forms of spatial concentration are not determining functional specialisation but rather encouraging further, complex locational choices whose dynamics still need further study and clarification. More fundamentally, though, a new extended economic framework is needed to conceptualise, measure and evaluate all the indirect effects that culturally and creatively focused activities produce on the various aspects of urban life, bearing in mind that economic and social components are closely intertwined and therefore call for an interdisciplinary paradigm.

Important differences exist in this respect between North American, European, and the new, emerging phenomenon of creative production in Asian countries. In Europe, where most cities are characterised by historical city cores rich with heritage, social life, and fascinating ambience, industrial development has progressively pushed productive activities away to sub-central and peripheral areas, as such activities are generally noisy, polluting, and cause congestion to the local traffic flows. But with the post-industrial transition where most "new economy" productive activities have a low environmental impact if any, there has been a massive "flow-back" phenomenon that has led many new businesses, and in particular cultural and creative producers, to occupy centrally located positions in order to exploit this centrality thereby infusing new vitality to Quarters that were colonised by the offices of banking, insurance, and financial services firms, as well as by other forms of "tertiary" nine-to-five occupations. They were inevitably subject to late-afternoon desertification that made them grim, lifeless, and even unsafe. The infusion of cultural and creative production to the city centre not only breaks down the nine-to-five "curse" as the time schedules of creative people are notoriously different than those of office staff, which results in a dramatic change in nightlife vivacity.

In North America, most cities lack city cores characterised by a strong urban identity and in addition most residential neighbourhoods are localised in semi-central and suburban areas. This of course further intensifies the nine-to-five effect. Notable exceptions are these cities, mostly on the East Coast (but also across the West Coast 'Cascadian' region with San Francisco, Portland, Seattle, and Vancouver) where a city core can be found, incorporating "European" characteristics. There is an additional reason for cultural and creative activities' spatial compactness located in the city core to preserve their identity and urban centrality, but also to encourage a richer mix of functions and often different central locations. There are also a few cases (Kansas City, for instance) where the relatively low prices of the urban downtown have caused an inflow of cultural and creative producers, thereby creating a new urban identity that is not linked to the idea of a (non-existent) city core, but rather to the spatial concentration of cultural facilities in the first place.

In Asia a major distinction from Europe and North America is that there is no particular interest or concern in preserving and articulating the symbolic meaning of the older parts of the city or those that host particularly ancient buildings, unless the latter carry a special functional or symbolic importance per se (temples, gardens, imperial residencies). The localisation of cultural and creative activities follows pragmatic criteria of availability and adequacy of spaces and, at least momentarily, does not have a big impact on the overall urban identity, despite the fact that public interest in and private and public investments in this field are rapidly increasing.

It is worth noting that converting redundant urban space for cultural use is becoming a trend with worldwide implications. In the recovered spaces, production and entertainment facilities are co-located in innovative (and sometimes surprising) ways, often blowing new life on former (abandoned) industrial spaces requiring new functional destinations. In spite of the heterogeneity of the various experiences taking place in different economic, social and geographical contexts, there are common factors that comprise this global tendency known as "creative dismissions". A creative dismission is the conversion of a facility previously used for non-cultural purposes into a cultural and creative functional centre. In many cases, these facilities are, as already identifiable, factories or warehouses, but other examples include hospitals, prisons, schools, and military installations. In some cases, these projects can be large geographical spaces thus generating a major impact such the case of Zollverein in Essen, or the *Baumwollspinnerei* area in Leipzig, both in Germany. The latter is a project (which is a work in progress) entirely carried out with private capital, and consists of the re-conversion of a large former cotton mill factory (one of the largest in continental Europe), that now hosts artist studios, art galleries, fashion design, and crafts workshops, but also commercial outlets. The project has been made possible through the coincidence of several factors: the low real estate prices prevailing in Leipzig after the burst of the post-reunification price bubble; the presence in Leipzig of one of the most renowned (and sought after by collectors) painting "schools" of the contemporary art scene; the availability of large and apt spaces in a sub-central position in the city; the establishment of a mixed-use quarter where the revenues from rents to classical commercial activities could be partly used to keep rental prices for creatives and galleries low enough to make them affordable. This has enabled the organisers to discriminate between potential tenants on the basis of quality. This latter aspect is particularly important, and interesting: Once the place had became well known for the presence of prominent artists and galleries there has been, unsurprisingly, a rush by artists and galleries to locate to exploit the notoriety and reputation effect. From an economic perspective, the landlords could have capitalised this rent by giving out spaces to best bidders, regardless of quality. But the effect of this would have been the destruction of reputation with the eventual flight of good quality artists and galleries and the eventual takeover of talentless affluence as the "identity marker" of the place. In spite of its semi-peripheral position, *Baumwollspinnerei* has become a key player in Leipzig's cultural life (which, by the way, is quite lively and selective, because of its world-class orchestras and long historic tradition in publishing), and is now attracting not only local visitors and creatives, but international visitors (the complex hosts galleries whose main headquarters are in North America, Mexico, or India, as well as several international artists choosing to live and work in the premises), thereby affecting, although in slow and subtle ways, the "central place geometry" of the city.

The *Baumwollspinnerei* example is a clear illustration of how successful the creative dismissions process can be. It relies on site-specific alchemies which call for subtle exercises of non-conventional, intrinsically motivated forms of rationality, in this case avoiding maximising rental income at the expense of quality. Interestingly, the global geography of creative dismissions is remarkably rich and constantly expanding with most of the currently active projects organised into international, constantly expanding thematic networks – such as Trans Europe Halles (TEH) or the European Network of Cultural Centres (ENCC). They carefully monitor members' compliance with some fundamentals, such as absence of speculative motives, social inclusiveness, and financial transparency. In other words, the vitality (and viability) of creative dismissions basically rests on an adherence to ethical codes which place a high value on the integrity of the cultural mission, irrespective of their narrowly economic impact.

The creative dismissions theme provides a helpful illustration of the key issues that arise when conceptualising the creative quarter (or, more extensively, of the city) as a creative hub. It is not merely a matter of dealing with talented people, or of providing the right facilities, and not even of investing enough resources to fuel the place's "creative push". It is basically a matter of finding a way to involve the whole social fabric of the city in the pursuit of cultural excellence and integrity, and in the construction of a collective identity in which culture becomes a cornerstone of the local approach to quality of life, social relationships, and entrepreneurship. Localisation choices are more a consequence than a cause of this. It is well known that, in many cases, location choices of cultural and creative producers have been strategically exploited by real estate developers to "hip up" previously disregarded areas of the city. Certainly, real estate developments transforming previously underrated areas into eagerly sought ones are spectacular examples of renewal. But this is only the appearance. The substance is that cultural and creative activity is manipulated and instrumentalised, which undermines, rather than builds up, the social cohesiveness of the city, and that in the long run turns it into a cultural and creative *showroom* rather than in a cradle of new ideas and experimentations. This is what the creative dismission movement has understood so well by enshrining social orientation and functions to preserve the spirit and practical implications of the cultural transformation of urban space. But clearly, the major issue is concerned with the level of governance of the urban space and the sensitivity of urban policy makers and their understanding of the subtleties of post-industrial rationality. If fundamental strategic choices are influenced by classical and familiar standards of instrumental rationality, all a city can hope for is a brief season of cultural and creative vitality, overtaken by massive gentrification with the very thing that attracted cultural production and consumption threatened and ultimately moving elsewhere. In other words, the instrumental exploitation of culture paves the way to the immunisation of the city against further attempts at cultural stimulation: once the real name of the game becomes apparent, people become much less willing to play, and the city loses relevant opportunities in a global scenario where the economics of knowledge rules. After all, culture is a process with a very high dependence on initial and "boundary" conditions. It cannot be engineered. It asks for new, and specific, methods of policy and social governance. Without this awareness, speaking of cities as creative hubs results in misunderstanding and disappointment.

2.4 From the Economics of Cultural Quarters to the Cultural Economics of Quarters?

In the vertically integrated, entertainment-driven model of a Cultural Quarter, the latter is a specialised functional area the city, that contributes to the local economy, but whose relevance basically depends on its economic dimension, that is how much value added it generates compared with the overall level of the city's economic activity. In a horizontally integrated, production-driven model of a Cultural Quarter, however, the quarter is no longer a *component* of the city fabric, but becomes one of its basic *constituents*, insofar as it provides a social and economic use of space (and time) model that can impact on most or all of the other parts of the city. This may happen as culture changes its role from being one of the many possible ways to spend one's leisure time to one essential aspect of daily life (and an essential constituent of *quality* of life). In this respect, Cultural Quarters are no longer specialised functional units, but hubs that irradiate and condition the whole organisational model of the city, which becomes increasingly penetrated by a system-wide cultural logic.

Vertically integrated clusters (and Cultural Quarters are no exception) typically produce forms of "mental lock-in": due to the spatial concentration of similar or affinity activities, there is the tendency to proceed by small, incremental forms of change and innovation, rather than by radical, decisive innovations, and therefore with time the Quarter loses its spirit and energy and tends to decay. Over-specialised Quarters do not manage to meet the increased demand for novelty and variety, and as soon as the competitive pressure forces the relocation of some of the players, the whole social fabric of the Quarter tends to collapse. Horizontal integration and the increasing confluence of different culture-related functionalities therefore represents an important condition to preserve the vitality and the dynamism of the Quarter in the long run – let alone its social sustainability. This new, emerging organisational model, however, presents many more degrees of freedom with respect to the traditional, entertainment-driven Quarters, and it is easy to conjecture that many different models will emerge in different social, economic and geographic contexts. Likewise, the logic of "new wave" Cultural Quarters will progressively spread to other sections of the city as the transition toward a fully fledged model of a knowledge and creative economy takes over as a driving force of mature, post-industrial economies.

In this context Cultural Quarters can be considered as "research and development labs" for experimentation and development of new forms of urban sociality, the most successful of which could become characteristic of advanced urban environments. This is especially true for the historical cores of European cities, whose dimensions and characteristics make it likely for them to evolve into specialised cultural hubs in the years to come.

Chapter 3

The Role and Function of Historic Buildings in Cultural Quarters

Mattias Legner

3.1 Introduction

Historic buildings such as old warehouses or shops often play an important part in making a Cultural Quarter come alive and give a sense of the place's past. Consequently, the past, as symbolised by these buildings and environments, should always be seen as a vital cultural asset when establishing a Cultural Quarter. History epitomised in the built environment is often the most visible and concrete aspect of a place's uniqueness.

Without this visual experience of the past, an important part of the "culture" of a place is lost. This is why the built heritage of any Quarter has to be developed sensitively. There are however a number of issues we have to address in order to successfully adapt these historic environments for creative uses:

- Why are historic buildings appreciated today?
- How are the most important characteristics of the built environment identified?
- How can redundant industrial buildings be adapted and re-used for the purposes of creative industries without destroying a sense of the past?
- How are complete environments (and not just individual buildings) recreated that can convey a historic sense of place?

These issues all connect with the re-use and rehabilitation of redundant urban environments as opposed to the restoration of unique individual architecture. In urban environment adaptive re-use, the possibilities of making insertions and changing both the exteriors and interiors are much greater than restoration projects, in which the purpose is to restore the building to an earlier state. Consequently, creative industries are much more likely to be located to recently deindustrialised areas than a block of seventeenth-century buildings in the centre of a town. Such buildings are most likely already to be attractive and as a result occupied with rental levels being much higher than small creative businesses are willing to pay. Another type of facility increasingly available for redevelopment throughout Europe today are military bases, of which many have important historic buildings, and monuments which are of increasing interest to cultural organisations and creative businesses.

An example of this is the re-use of one wing of a deserted fort (built in 1816–1830) in the former industrial centre of Daugavpils, Latvia. Following a private donation by Rothko's

Arsenal of the Daugavpils fortress planned for re-use as a gallery of world-renowned artist Mark Rothko.
Photograph: M. Legnér.

family, the beautiful classicist wing known as the Arsenal is destined to become a gallery displaying the works of abstract expressionist painter Mark Rothko, born in Daugavpils in 1903. There is an annual culture festival held inside the Arsenal to commemorate the heritage of Rothko and his art. Today the fortress is mostly abandoned, partly used as social housing for the poor in a city mostly populated by ethnic Russian and suffering from mass unemployment following the closing of many mills.

3.2 The Re-appraisal of Historic Environments

There is evidence to suggest that many people working within creative industries are concerned about their working environment and seem to like working in historic environments: exposed brick walls, high ceilings, and tall iron frame windows have all become the everyday attributes of many businesses that wish to be associated with arts, creativity, and culture (Zukin 1995). One reason for this appreciation is that the city built heritage has undergone a major re-appraisal in the Western world in the last three decades. So today it is more difficult not to appreciate historic buildings, whereas 30 or 40 years ago almost all office workers seem to have preferred working in highly modern, newly constructed buildings. In 1960s Sweden, the thought of refurbishing a previously industrial building to provide new offices was peripheral and unpopular. There were, however, a handful of professionals working with adaptive re-use for cultural or creative functions before the mid 1970s (Legnér 2009a).

Things were however changing and American architectural historian Barbaralee Diamonstein (1978, p. 15) commented on the growing movement of historic preservation:

More and more, people seem to prefer what the past has to offer in the way of handicrafts, custom design of hardware and moldings, attention to details (newness still prevails, though, when it comes to choosing appliances).

There are important reasons why this re-appraisal has occurred. One is that deindustrial-isation, i.e. the decline of the manufacturing industry and the decrease of the labour force used for manufacturing, today has progressed much farther and faster than expected in European countries in particular. Not that industrialisation has left the world, but it is migrating from the European Union and the United States where manufacturing jobs are increasingly seen as dull, dirty and low paid. Manufacturing jobs, then, are moving to other parts of the world which makes it possible to begin seeing the "industrial epoch" as an historic age, rather than an age we are currently living in (Storm 2008). There are simply no more large brick buildings with tall windows and chimneys being built. Another, and perhaps more obvious reason, is that deindustrialisation leaves an abundance of abandoned built environments often in key city locations, consequently raising the question of what should be done with them. Should they be demolished and replaced with new developments such as shopping centres or housing estates? Is there any value in or motivation to preserve the best elements of the industrial past and generate re-use as a contribution to new economic development?

These questions are, of course, rhetorical but they need to be asked in order to understand why we are re-using some built environments which are not architecturally unique whereas many other areas are razed and constructed anew. In the United States, the Environmental Protection Agency estimates the number of existing brownfield sites (old industrial sites) to be about 450,000, and increasing (EPA 2009). Needless to say, there is a growing demand from national governments to regenerate these vacant areas not least to replace lost businesses and jobs. A third reason is concerned with the growth of the environmental movement and the resulting "greening" policies. Energy and physical resources can be saved by re-using buildings instead of demolishing and constructing new ones. Re-use is much more energy efficient than any other type of intervention in the built environment, and conserving the built environment is therefore an important contribution to sustainable development (Rodwell 2007).

Finally, the benefits of re-using historic structures in urban space are summed up in a clear way by Worthing and Bond (2008, pp. 49–52):

- There are significant benefits to the wellbeing of individuals as well as groups;
- There are educational benefits: we can understand aspects of past societies better;
- Existing buildings should be re-used for environmental and financial reasons;
- Historic environments contribute to a sense of place through their character and visual aesthetics;
- Historic areas attract tourist revenue and make significant contributions to local and regional economies.

In other words, there are significant benefits from social, environmental, as well as economic perspectives in re-using older built structures.

3.3 Identification and Rehabilitation

The most important aspect of rehabilitation is the functional continuity of a building (Stratton 1997). A voluminous power plant, for example, could easily be re-used for a gallery such as Tate Modern in London or for other large gatherings such as concerts or theatre, whereas re-using it as an office might be less appropriate because of the cost of converting the large open spaces compared with a new construction already designed for such a purpose. In Swedish Västerås which used to be the centre of the manufacturer ASEA (today called ABB), there are plans to re-use a huge 1940s power plant both as an exhibition centre of Swedish industrial heritage (Ståhl 1999) as well as an indoor water adventure centre.

Furthermore, an old foundry which was used to forge steel goods can easily be rehabilitated into metal artisans' studios. This was the case with the John Gutierrez studio in Baltimore, Maryland (United States). Gutierrez also re-used objects found in the nearby vacant buildings – such as cog-wheels and other metal scraps – to decorate the site (Legnér 2007).

Other spacious industrial buildings have been used as rock climbing gyms or cinemas. Another example of matching large industrial spaces with relevant function includes parts

A rail shaped as cog-wheels found at the site of Clipper Mill, designed by local artisan John Gutierrez. Photograph: M. Legnér.

Could *Pannhus 11*, a deserted power plant in Västerås, be re-used for indoor water adventures demanding high ceilings and large spaces? Photograph: M. Legnér.

of a former copper mill in Västerås, the building *Culturen,* re-opened in 2000 for teaching, displaying, and experiencing arts such as theatre, film, radio broadcasting, dance, music, workshops, and painting.

Before planning the re-use of a building it is important to identify what are its most striking and interesting features. If these features are ignored, much of the building's integrity will be lost, and also its attractiveness to potential investors. What are the distinctive features and spaces that characterise these historic buildings? All features and spaces do not carry equal weight in determining the character of a historic property. The more important a feature or space is to the historic character of a property, the less it can be changed resulting in less flexibility in re-use. In addition there are "periods of significance", implying that there is a defined historic period in which the building was given its most valuable features. The US authority National Park Services (NPS) has developed a policy solely concerned with historic rehabilitation (and not restoration) of buildings:

> ... *features and spaces that have been so substantially changed outside the period of significance or are so severely deteriorated as no longer to convey historic character can be more readily altered than those aspects of a property that retain a high degree of integrity.* (NPS 2009a)

In short, this generally means that if a building has been modified considerably after it was first built, it becomes easier to modify the building once again. Much of the historic authenticity has already been lost and cannot be recovered.

Regarding the interiors, the NPS identifies primary and secondary spaces (NPS 2009b). Primary spaces are the most important ones to preserve. Primary spaces are those that are essential in conveying the historic and architectural character of a building. They are often entrance halls, corridors, and other public or in other ways representative areas. Secondary spaces are ones that have not been as critical to the function of the building. As a consequence, significant parts of the interior may be altered without damaging the integrity of the interior.

Windows and doors are often deemed the most striking exterior features of a building, since they are highly visible. Changing the appearance of the windows, for example by removing old frames or by using other materials, can decrease the integrity of the building considerably. A developer who recently wished to rehabilitate an early nineteenth-century workshop at Clipper Mill, Baltimore, had to find a workshop that was able to re-produce similar steel window frames which needed to be replaced since the building had been severely damaged by fire. The building was to be used for living quarters and creative industries. The developer wished to place balconies on the front facade, but this was denied by the NPS since it would have diminished the features of the building. Putting balconies on the exterior of an industrial building is a clear breach of respect for the structure's historic use. In the end, the developer was allowed to put a few balconies on

Window frames at Clipper Mill replaced with similar ones manufactured solely for this purpose.
Photograph: M. Legnér.

The former communist headquarters and later orphanage in Disna, Belarus, now destined to be re-used as a cultural centre. Photograph: M. Legnér.

the back of the building by re-using steel girders from the old building (Legnér 2007). In Providence, Rhode Island (United States) the same developer also re-used the interiors of old brick buildings when setting up combined living spaces and studios for artists. Art displaying the historic uses of the buildings was set up in public areas, as well as pictures displaying the rehabilitation work in progress.

Doors and windows also prove to be the most striking and valuable features of a deserted brick building in the small town of Disna in northern Belarus. The Town Council wished to re-use this building, one of few surviving both world wars (Disna was occupied by German forces in both wars) and the following Stalinist vandalism of the 1950s, in order to begin developing cultural tourism attractions in the town. The building in mind was first built to provide the local financial centre. After the revolution it became the communist party headquarters, and on the dissolution of the Soviet Union an orphanage for fifteen years. Contemporary knowledge and skills about the re-use and rehabilitation of historic buildings is largely lacking in Belarus today as it is in many countries emerging from the soviet era. This has encouraged partnerships enabling historic building re-use expertise to be made available. In the case of the Disna project in Belarus the town cooperated with Swedish authorities funded through SIDA (Swedish Development Agency). As a result the building will become a combined Town Council and cultural centre; out of

Part of the tobacco plant in Durham, North Carolina, was turned into a creative industries hub in 2007. This building is now used by a company developing mobile phone solutions. Photograph: M. Legnér.

which as confidence grows further new attractions will emerge in this beautifully situated area in the junction of the Disna and Dvina rivers (Legnér 2009c).

In the creative industries re-use of the old tobacco plant in Durham, North Carolina (United States), which is today renowned for its medical University rather than the tobacco industry, the developer used the heritage of different brands, such as Lucky Strike, to connect with the industrial past of the site. A tall water tower with the brand name on the side was kept as a "beam" or "icon" pointing out the place to everyone in the vicinity. The area was rebuilt as a park housing small biotech industry and software programming businesses (Legnér 2009a).

Similar principles of rehabilitation are practised in other countries, even if they are far from always articulated in policies as clear as that of the NPS.

In Norrköping, which used to be the industrial centre of Sweden, many industrial brick buildings from the beginning of the twentieth century are now re-used by creative industries, retaining their key external characteristics but having been completely changed on the inside, a historic shell with a contemporary interior. Currently, a former water power plant is being rehabilitated to be used as a multimedia centre with a dome theatre, located next to the University main building (Legnér 2009b). Another water power plant has been re-used as a science park housing small knowledge business, but without compromising the striking external building features, among them a glass wall facing the river. In some buildings, such as *Strykbrädan* (Ironing Board), wooden floors and beams and steel columns have been left in place.

The most high-profile re-use in the so-called Industrial Landscape of central Norrköping was the turning of a large paper mill building from the 1920s into a symphony and event hall. Thanks to a joint venture between the five largest developers in town, most of the building – located along the riverside – could be preserved, making the necessary alterations highly visible, thereby not confusing their appearance with the original features (Legnér 2008).

Finally, it is difficult to provide universal recommendations on how to successfully re-use a building; each case brings together a unique combination of elements. Both historic and future functions of a building need to be considered in order to safeguard the continuity in the use of a building and in particular to avoid destroying the "sense of place" referred to above. Alternatively, some buildings have been extensively modified losing their historical significance or have been vacant for such a long time that they may more easily be re-used for entirely new purposes.

3.4 Creating Environments

A key factor when rehabilitating complete collections of buildings is time. It is difficult to create sustainable and attractive environments if the redevelopment has short timelines. Often when this is the case, government incentives are involved with substantial investments made in a short period of time. Norrköping's Cultural Quarter, the Industrial Landscape, has developed rather slowly over a period of more than 30 years, and is beginning to reach a mature phase. For many years developers have complained that regeneration is too slow and that the antiquarian officers of local and regional authorities have too much influence on redevelopment. However, they are beginning to realise that this slow-paced development has had its advantages. Slowing down redevelopment has meant more thought through and careful restoration and re-use of the building stock, and more public access to previously sealed off areas. Time has proven that this area is developing and surviving with a high degree of public engagement (such as intimate negotiations between property owners, developers, and the municipality), and independently of large government subsidies.

The urban landscape with its tall buildings and narrow streets and the integrity of the historic buildings has been preserved. This is as a consequence of investments made by the developers, legal protection of the area by county and national government antiquarians, the city's planning of public spaces and moving of public institutions such as offices and schools into the district. The Industrial Landscape has changed from having been a closed and prohibited to the public industrial site to becoming a public space with a range of cultural attractions – museums, exclusive shops, a gym, a symphony hall – and a University campus complete with a science park and technology hub, and soon to establish a multimedia centre of international ranking.

Part of the Industrial Landscape in Norrköping showing the old entrance to the area, now entrance to Museum of Work. Photograph: M. Legnér.

The public spaces are crucial to a Cultural Quarter since the concept is to mix functions based on "live, work, play" encouraging people to be present, stay, and move around in the Quarter. The area not only needs to be perceived as safe but also as aesthetically attractive. The design of plazas, streets, pavement, lighting, and signage becomes important. There also needs to be reason for activity after normal working hours. This seems to be a problem for many Cultural Quarters which focus on creative industries: streets appear more or less deserted after 6:00 pm. A place such as the Richmond Riverfront in Virginia (United States) is desolate most of the day and all night despite beautiful walkways and engaging public art relating to the history of the former confederate capital. The reason behind these empty streets is not the absence of residents, but because cultural amenities, offices, and commercial venues are completely missing. This is evidently the opposite problem for the Vienna MuseumsQuartier where activities are too much focused on museums, exhibits, and day time coffee shops to allow for night time activities.

In Tampere, Finland, the industrial district redeveloped for culture, entertainment, and creative businesses in the 1990s has addressed this problem by integrating workplaces with a night time economy involving cinemas, restaurants, and bars. It is clear that If there are no possibilities of social interaction in the Quarter, people will not go there (especially not at night) even if there are exquisite historic buildings and well-designed public spaces.

Public art at the Richmond Riverfront. In 1849, the slave Henry Brown escaped to freedom in a box similar to this one. Photograph: M. Legnér.

Chapter 4

Universities and Cultural Quarters

Simon Roodhouse and Tim Vorley

4.1 A brief History of Universities

Waterhouse (2002, p. 6) focuses our attention on technical education as the point of contact between universities and business. He suggests that

> A fundamental part of education, wherever it occurs, is technical. Technical education is not simply practical, it is about particular types of action to make and manipulate physical things. Technical learning begins at birth. Technical education as a specific social institution began when techniques had reached a certain level of complication and sophistication.

This gave birth in Europe to the apprenticeship system, with its overlay of secret knowledge and mystique. In spite of the printing press, the computer, and communications technology, the restrictive practices of these medieval guilds are still with us – known today as professional bodies or associations such as the General Medical Council, the Law Society or the Institute of Civil Engineering. This concept of technical education as a social institution has often been distinguished from vocationalism:

> a vocation is a calling, and the highest vocation, certainly in Europe, is to the priesthood and the European universities were invented to deliver vocational education in the strictest of senses. They were set up by the Church to train clerks, i.e. clerics. Indeed, all the great civilisations of the old world had similar institutions with an identical purpose. (Waterhouse 2002, p. 6)

These origins are still evident today in the oldest universities. They were essentially the training colleges of their day.

The classic model of the late medieval University was the Sorbonne in Paris. Like other European universities the Sorbonne had four faculties. The lower faculty, the Faculty of Arts, generally trained young men in the skills of the clerk (church employee) and the three higher faculties were those of theology, medicine, and laws. The whole purpose was vocational, with the degree as a licence to practice and the doctorate as a licence to teach. However, much of this seems to have been forgotten. Medicine, law, and theology as subjects worthy of study were the equivalent of the creative industries today.

As Waterhouse (2002, p. 7) points out,

universities in the early modern period were in no sense technical. They were about language, social interaction, beliefs and ideologies. They were not about making things or manipulating the physical world by action. (This even applied to faculties of medicine. If a surgeon was needed, people visited a barber not a doctor). By the eighteenth century the universities were largely moribund, their social function having become the perpetuation of the aristocratic elite.

In 1792 the Legislative Assembly of the French revolution abolished the Sorbonne and three years later the Hautes Ecoles were established. They were dedicated to practical and technical learning – astronomy, geometry, mechanics, applied arts, natural history, medicine, veterinary science, and rural economy, the new industries of their day – comparable to media studies or business and management. These actions were indicative of an explosion in technical knowledge during the seventeenth and eighteenth centuries, which had occurred almost entirely outside the universities. Investigation, experimentation, and learning had largely taken place without formal structures or teaching institutions; the Hautes Ecoles were designed to help put this technical knowledge into practice and fuel the industrial revolution.

However, the French model of the Hautes Ecoles did not sweep across Europe. With the notable exception of the University of Berlin, under Von Humboldt, existing universities were slow to change. Industrialists, princes, or enlightened regimes found it easier to establish new institutions of higher technical learning than to change the power structures of the universities. So, for example, England in the mid nineteenth century saw the foundation of the University of London and the first of the civic universities, often driven (for reasons of public health) by the medical school. Elsewhere in Europe colleges of mines, engineering, and commerce were being established. Later we had the development of technical schools and colleges; these were specialised professional schools for teachers, nurses, artists, and designers, all of which eventually went to provide the heritage of the English polytechnic system.

None of these types of institution had degree-awarding powers, though various professional diplomas were created. Throughout the course of this development the word "vocational", like the word "professional", was used to give dignity and status to practical, socially useful, and in some cases technical, activities. The next stage of evolution, as suggested by Waterhouse (2002), requires universities to re-conceptualise themselves as a service industry, not a priesthood of occult technology, or a restrictive academic guild. In place of the student and teacher come the customer and facilitator of learning. Replacing the campus is the distributed system which technology enables institutions to extend into the workplace.

Consequently, the ultimate value proposition for universities, Waterhouse (2002, p. 10) argues,

is not that they can teach, nor even that they can sell research, but that they can assess: they accredit learning and are awarding bodies. It is this social certification of successful learning that individuals, employers and ultimately society pay for.

The next reinvention for the sector is contemporary vocationalisation and responsiveness to economic imperatives rather than learning. So what is being said here is that universities have engaged in a form of vocationalisation and that technical needs of business have generally been met outside the system, although the universities have engaged in the practice of the new industries. This leads us naturally to the consideration of the knowledge transfer functions of universities as a means of contributing to the economy.

4.2 The Changing Role of Universities and the Rise of the Knowledge Economy

Blunkett (2000), speaking on modernising higher education as Secretary of State for Education and Skills, argued that change was necessary:

> higher education policymaking is now subject to new constraints caused by the rapidity of change, a situation unthinkable in the 1960s Robbins era. And this change is related to the fundamental socio-economic development of the last quarter of the twentieth century: globalisation.

These views are echoed by the Institute of Directors:

> Education and skills are crucial ingredients for business success. Businesses need to have an educated and skilled workforce in order to enhance their productivity, quality of service and overall competitiveness. Business success is important because it can result in employment and wealth creation and so contribute towards financing the public services through taxation. (Wilson 2006)

The interest in globalisation has created a new environment for the knowledge economy. For the purposes of clarity, in this case, globalisation is understood to mean

> the growing interdependence of countries world-wide through the increasing volume and variety of cross-border transactions in goods and services, and also through the more rapid and widespread diffusion of technology. Not just an economic phenomenon, but frequently described as such. (New Zealand Ministry of Foreign Affairs and Trade 2006)

In higher education policy terms it has been interpreted as a need for virtual universities, international alliances, expansion with diversity and excellence, wider participation and expanded student numbers, and a role in securing economic competitiveness and social cohesion. Vocational relevance to improve competitiveness and social inclusion, and generate wealth may then be summarised as the British New Labour higher education strategy.

As Brennan (2005) suggests, in this setting, learning is seen as an integral and ongoing feature of working. This is reflected in the UK Department of Education and Employment (DfEE) Green Paper (1999) which highlights the rise of the knowledge economy, or the learning society. Brennan argues, in this version of human capital theory, that intellectual capital has become critical to economic success. This approach focuses on the importance of knowledge creation, and the application and manipulation of "new" knowledge in the workplace.

The authors of a 'Review of Training Packages in Australia' (Australian National Training Authority 2003) suggests that this new knowledge is different such that:

• The production of new knowledge within organisations and enterprises is different from the knowledge outlined in traditional subjects or disciplines, and common in educational and training programmes;
• New knowledge is high in use-value for the enterprise or organisation. Its deployment has immediate value but, as it is context specific, its value within the enterprise or organisation may be short-lived;
• New knowledge is not foundational and cannot be codified into written texts such as competency standard descriptions, procedural manuals, or textbooks; rather it is constructed within the context and environment of the immediate workplace;
• New knowledge is therefore rarely the product of individuals but is constructed through collaborations and networks that exist within specific sites and particular contexts.

Brennan (2005) reasons that this new knowledge is conceptualised as practical, interdisciplinary, informal, applied, and contextual rather than theoretical, disciplinary, formal, foundational, and generalisable. She posits that relevance no longer equates with the 'application' of knowledge to the workplace, but instead, the workplace itself is seen as a site of learning, knowledge, and knowledge production. When this view of the nature of knowledge in the workplace is linked with an analysis of the skill requirements generated by changes to the way work is organised, it would appear that a higher proportion of workers are now expected to use their technical and generic knowledge and skills to contribute to the production of new knowledge within the workplace. The application of skills previously learned outside the work context may no longer be sufficient.

A view proffered by Brennan is that current demands for work based learning differ from those involved in formal University award courses in that they:

• Do not rely on the intervention of institutionally based teachers or organisationally based workplace trainers;
• Are not structured around pre-determined vocational outcomes;
• Are not determined by qualification frameworks and endorsed training packages;
• Are not guided by specific content;
• Are not organised around the "enabling" disciplines.

Instead, the main characteristics of work based learning, as identified by Brennan (2005), are that it:

• Is context bound, driven by specific and immediate work requirements;
• Emphasises learning over teaching or training as a defining characteristic;

- Depends on the responsibility for learning being spread between a number of people within the workplace;
- Is consistent with new learning concepts such as learning networks, learning organisation, and communities of practice.

The changing nature of work is relevant to the integration of work based learning into higher education in that it points to significant changes in the "content" or curriculum of higher education programmes, as well as where and how it should be delivered or achieved. It also suggests that the historic dominance of universities in knowledge production is being eroded, and that knowledge production increasingly becomes a collaborative activity based in and around the workplace. As the University Vocational Awards Council (UVAC) report indicates, if higher education is to continue to make a contribution to the knowledge economy, it becomes necessary for higher education to expand work based learning and recognise the workplace as a legitimate site of knowledge production and commercialisation. In order to realise this universities need to build formal and informal relationships with the creative industries, employers, operatives, students, and their own staff.

In this context *partnership* and *collaboration* between employers, employers' organisations, workers, further and higher education providers assumes a particular significance. The concepts of *lifelong learning* and learning *for, at* and *through* work, also highlight the importance of *continued training*, individual *personal and professional* and *workforce development*. In turn, the notion of continuous learning and its recognition emphasise the need for vocational *progression routes* in and through higher education. These elements have become cornerstones of recent policy affecting higher and further education (Brennan 2005) along with the need to commercialise University activity.

However, it should be noted that there is scepticism about the extent and nature of changes in the work context and its implications for the development of knowledge and skills, regarding them as primarily aspirational, rather than descriptive of the current contexts of work. Nevertheless, as so many elements of these analyses have become incorporated into the policy agenda for education and training in the United Kingdom, they effectively become a reality for both learners and providers. The Higher Education Funding Council for England (HEFCE) inevitably reflects this:

> *A key role for universities … is … activity to meet the needs of business and the community, contributing to economic and social development both regionally and nationally. We are committed to encouraging and rewarding partnerships between HEIs and business, the transfer of knowledge and expertise, and the development of employment skills.* (HEFCE 2004)

So, what does this mean for the University as a corporation? As Mould, Roodhouse and Vorley (2009) state, the role of the University has changed in the last twenty-five years with the (re)emergence of a "third mission" (teaching and research being the first two) which is concerned with the commercialisation and transfer of academic activities to the economy, a process known as knowledge transfer. Charles (2003) describes how the former blue-sky priorities of ivory tower institutions are increasingly challenged by demands for vocational training and employable skills, which is arguably unsurprising in light of the transition from elitist to mass higher education. Further to this, Claes (2002) notes that while the core function of the contemporary University is currently blue-sky research-based teaching, this is subject to increasing negotiation. Gray (2001) aptly identifies this amidst the transition from tradition to science as the source of intellectual authority. Indeed, Kerr (1963) observes the "multiversity" to be a more appropriate interpretation of the contemporary University on account of their increasingly diverse remit and function. The shift from a historical and societal institution to an innovation-led and commercially orientated institution can be seen as a result of the third mission outlined by the 1993 UK government White Paper 'Realising Our Potential' (Cabinet Office 1993).

Mould, Roodhouse and Vorley also point out that as a result of this transition, Gumport (2000) finds the universities attempting to (re)legitimise their role as a societal institution, and shed the perception of higher education as an industry. As societal institutions, universities assume a broad range of social functions which Gumport (2000) finds to include "cultivation of citizenship, the preservation of cultural heritage(s), and the formation of individual character and habits of mind". In contrast, Gumport (2000) also identifies the corporate model of the University as to "produce and sell services, train some of the workforce, advance economic development and perform research". Kerr (1987) describes this tension between higher education as a societal institution and higher education as an industry, as the "accumulated heritage versus modern imperatives". He continues to note these conflicting ideologies as critical to the future form of the University and to higher education in industrialised nations. Undoubtedly this ongoing transformation of higher education in the United Kingdom has become dominated by the dawn of third stream activities as universities endeavour to resolve, reassert, and (re)legitimate themselves as quasi-public institutions. Indeed, Godin and Gingras (2000) observe universities to be highly significant to the knowledge-based economy, finding them to be at the "heart of [knowledge production] systems and that all other actors rely heavily on their expertise".

However, while the ideology of the entrepreneurial University is largely accepted, it is important to note the more moderate interpretations of "academic capitalism" (Slaughter and Leslie 1997) and the "enterprise University" (Marginson and Considine 2000), which contest the extent of the entrepreneurial University's role and capabilities, and how organisational contradictions are resolved. Further to this, working with business and commercialism, in the context of an entrepreneurial University, was reinforced through alternative sources of public finance including the University Challenge Fund, and the Strategic Development Fund, to realise their value to the knowledge-based economy. These alternative sources of "third stream" funding do not, and are not intended to, replace diminishing teaching and research income, but create the opportunity for greater future financial autonomy through generating alternative income. Geuna and Nesta (2003) identify the paradigm shift associated with the rise of the entrepreneurial University as having resulted in the dominant norm becoming the management of industrial research agreements, assessment and protection of intellectual property, and the commercial translation of science rather than blue-sky research.

4.3 Universities, the Creative Industries and Cultural Quarters

In many cities throughout the United Kingdom, particularly in the northern deindustrialised cities, there has been an increasing focus in public policy on the generation of CQs and associated economic and social benefits to the city/region, as well as individuals, firms, and institutions that are affiliated (Bell and Jayne 2003; O'Connor and Wynne 1996; Roodhouse 2006).

The accepted definition, as stated in chapter 1, of a Cultural Quarter is a geographical area of a large town or city which acts as a focus for cultural and artistic activities through the presence of a group of buildings devoted to housing a range of such activities, and purpose-designed or adapted spaces to create a sense of identity, providing an environment to facilitate and encourage the provision of cultural and artistic services and activities.

A distinction is made between a Cultural Quarter and a cultural industries quarter. The latter is dedicated to cultural business development e.g. the Sheffield Cultural Industries Quarter, and the former is an identification of a geographical area in which cultural activity is encouraged to locate, a physically defined focal point for cultural activity e.g. Wolverhampton Cultural Quarter case study.

A Cultural Quarter then represents the coherence and convergence of the arts and heritage in culture, and culture as a manifestation of society. Cultural Quarters provide a context for the use of planning and development powers to preserve and encourage cultural production and consumption (the creative industries).

Up to the present time, Cultural Quarters have invariably developed from an existing embryonic cultural presence, as a result of a public sector initiative. Cultural Quarters are often part of a larger strategy integrating cultural and economic development, usually linked to the regeneration of a selected urban area.

A further distinction needs to be made between Cultural Quarters, and Tate Modern cultural iconographic regeneration, which includes examples such as the Royal Armouries in Leeds, or the Baltic, Contemporary Visual Arts Centre, Newcastle upon Tyne. Although these singular projects often provide a focus for regenerative activity the distinction lies in designation; a spatial area for a particular form of development.

Mould, Roodhouse and Vorley have suggested HEIs are often involved in the designation of these areas, become key institutions in their establishment and benefit from the development. In the case study of Sheffield's Cultural Quarter (CQ), Sheffield Hallam University (SHU) is a key stakeholder. One such benefit is that the universities can forge stronger links with the creative industries located in the surrounding, newly established infrastructure of buildings, office space, and studio space. In Sheffield for example, there are also strong links between the CQ and the adjacent science park, which focus particularly on the development of technologies related to film, photography, and music recording. This has led to the proposal from the City Council to develop a "Cultural Campus" in the CQ which would house SHUs fine art, media studies, and design departments (Roodhouse 2006, p. 28). The links between the HEI and the city manifested themselves in the shape of the Cultural Industry Quarters Agency (CIQ Agency) which composed of a non-executive board with members from local businesses, the science part, the City Council, and SHU. The CIQ Agency set out a number of tasks to improve the development of the CQ including improving transport links, green development as well as retail and catering outlets that housed the shops, bars, cafés, and restaurants that are needed to sustain a successful CQ (Roodhouse 2006, p. 30). The formalisation of links between HEIs and the creative industries is furthered by the physical existence of these CQs. To continue with the example of SHU, it established links very early on with the CQ (through the CIQ Agency) and subsequently, SHU was instrumental in establishing the Northern School of Film and Television, which made use of the studio and office space in the newly developed CQ. This illustrates the University's capacity to engage with industry, support the local economy, and work between the public and private sector to enhance the local creative economy not least for the benefit of its graduates and first destination statistics, a measure used to judge University performance.

City Councils recognise their University as a major cultural employer and want to retain the talent which emerges from that University. This creates a stronger connection between the students and staff of universities with the local creative industries, all with a greater affinity to commercialise. This has been demonstrated in the Wolverhampton CQ case study where the strategic approach recognises the industrial past associated with craft-oriented small businesses. Local authorities and the University are investing in the creative industries, to create new craft-based small businesses for the future. These complement other activities and relates to digital technology companies located in the science park. This overarching coherent approach toward policy (exemplified in the case of Sheffield by the CIQ Agency), combines existing Council cultural assets with private sector organisations and other major institutions such as the university. Many of the students are training to enter the creative industries, as Wolverhampton University has a substantial faculty of Art and Design, and so the CQ stimulates the growth of nascent creative enterprises and acts as a hub for production, presentation, and sale of cultural goods and services.

Those HEIs which have engaged with CQs in the early stages of their development can be seen to benefit from the increased connectivity and communication with industry. As more creative graduates move out of the University (due to the increased student numbers in higher education) into the surrounding office and studio space of the CQ with their newly formed creative industry business, the spaces gradually fill up and inevitably push up rental prices, which can potentially cause a homogenisation and corporatisation of the creative industries. Indeed the rising expenses means that subsequent years of entrepreneurs are forced out of the CQ to non-subsidised, less connected areas, as was the case with the Manchester CQ development referred to in the Bolton example, where local authorities and other public agencies gradually gained "control" of the spaces (through compulsory purchase orders) from the inhabited "creatives", forcing up the prices to gain more rental income. This is potentially detrimental to the CQs as they can stagnate, losing the innovative dynamism associated with "creatives", which is implicit to the success of the CQs themselves, that is the creative milieu. The continued success of the CQ, and its links with HEIs, is dependent on developments such as providing incubator space for both nascent and more established enterprises.[1] However, this process is further complicated as private sector investment in CQs demand a competitive return on that investment through rental income etc, and is largely unconcerned with facilitating the grassroots development of the creative industries.

Mould, Roodhouse and Vorley point out with creativity largely concerned with "activities which have their origin in individual creativity, skill and talent" (DCMS 1998), intellectual property (IP) and protection becomes critical to the success of the industry. Within the creative industries, creativity can be tangibly officiated (and thereby commercialised) though IP (Cunningham 2004; Howkins 2001). HEIs have been slow to recognise the importance of IP (Lambert 2003) and as a result slow to realise its commercial potential particularly in terms of non-scientific creative knowledge. The importance of IP cannot be understated as "creativity by itself will not make anybody rich; intellectual property laws do that" (Healy 2002, p. 97).

IP therefore is a valuable commodity, and if the complex processes surrounding the legality and ownership of IP can be clarified, then the commercialisation and transfer of creative knowledge from HEIs will be better facilitated. The role of IP protection in promoting economic growth has been well documented in industry (Gould & Gruben 1996; Maskus 2000) and so to have a more developed perspective on the IP protection by HEIs will not only aid commercialisation and knowledge/technology transfer, but also increase profitability. Indeed as Gould & Gruben (1996, p. 346) suggest "under a regime of open markets, we might expect competitive forces to stimulate innovation and intellectual property protection to induce even more of it". However, the ownership of this "creative IP" is an issue which can lead to the intense "profitisation" of IP. Healy (2002, p. 98) suggests that "the axial principle of the new economy is not creativity", and "the goal is not so much the fostering of creativity as the ever more fine-grained control of existing goods". However, this intense profitisation of IP and associated commodification of creativity (i.e. the "concentrated ownership and control of ideas" (ibid.)) potentially marginalises the wider societal role of HEIs (Gumport 2000; Lawton Smith 2006).[2]

Education and training for those wanting to enter the workplace and those in work within the HEI is also an important factor in encouraging relationships. Many universities have established departments, courses, and modules focused on the creative industries, of which business and management has come to constitute an important focus. The Research Centre in Creative Industries at Queens University Belfast for example combines staff from management, economics, the humanities, and engineering to understand the dynamics of the creative industries. Similarly the Centre for Creative Empowerment at the University of Portsmouth develops and evaluates creative pedagogy and its policy implications for the creative industries. The need for research to understand the dynamics of the creative industries supports business development and enables University staff to keep in touch with the industry, often developing joint projects or operating as a sole trader. Collectively these factors contribute to realising the creative potential of HEIs, and more specifically the commercialisation and transfer of non-scientific creative knowledge and technology.

4.4. Conclusion

This chapter suggests that there has been a long history of University involvement with vocationalism, employers, and training. There has also been a tradition of engaging with the creative industries over time. However, it needs to be recognised that the University sector is not homogenous consequently the business development and commercialisation agendas do not necessarily relate to every institution. Part of this complexity is the individual nature of creative businesses which is also mirrored in the University sector with individuality reflected in their missions. Meeting national or regional economic needs might only be one component of corporate University activity and of limited interest to academic departments whatever the national government policy might be. It has been observed that universities are effective at absorbing prevailing public policy without threatening core interests.

Those institutions with an established interest in the creative industries which may have one or more faculties of art, design, performing arts, music, architecture, media, animation are most likely to be involved not only training individuals to enter the workforce, but also developing the workforce, and supporting business growth with their engagement in Cultural Quarters. It is in the interests of these universities to support creative businesses in the locality through mechanisms such as Cultural Quarters as a means of generating employment for graduates, having access to expertise to support teaching and as a living research laboratory. What is missing in this scenario is the formalisation of relationships between Cultural Quarters and the appropriate University. There are University science and technology parks, but more importantly perhaps, Cultural Quarters in partnership with universities can be the new creativity parks.

Notes

1. However, there have been some examples of how this "gentrification" process can be halted. The Birmingham Custard Factory is a regeneration project that relied on one creative entrepreneur who was able maintain the quality of the space without the increase in rental prices (Roodhouse 2006, p. 23).

2. Community engagement of HEIs and their "wider societal role" includes (but is not restricted to) the setting up of incubator spaces which provides subsidised rental areas for nascent creative ventures (Roodhouse 2006), as well as providing entrepreneurial and business advice (Cunningham 2004).

Chapter 5

Cultural Quarter Practice in England

R.J. Buswell
Lisa De Propris
Alison Holmes
John Montgomery
Simon Roodhouse
Pring Wei

This chapter provides selected case studies of Cultural Quarters, largely drawn from the north of England. Each case study includes a description of the scope, characteristics, structure, and management arrangements, as well as the outputs derived from adopting such an approach to urban redevelopment and sustaining creative cultures. The selection includes the Sheffield City Council-led Cultural Industries Quarter, which is one of the earliest and most frequently quoted examples of this activity in the United Kingdom, and is often referred to as the model for establishing a Cultural Quarter. In addition to this, the Sheffield City Council's approach to the Museum and Art Gallery service is also included, to illustrate the cultural and creative industry inconsistencies found in a single geographical area. Next, the Cultural Quarter development in Wolverhampton has been selected as an example of a typical town with a long and important industrial history falling in the shadow of a large city. Birmingham Jewellery Quarter is also featured as a long standing historically important part of the city that has and continues to undergo change. This section concludes with a brief analysis of activities in Manchester, including Salford Quays.

5.1 Sheffield Cultural Industries Quarter

Sheffield CIQ is an example of a cultural industries quarter – the organisations located in the quarter are cultural and creative businesses.

The area of the Sheffield Cultural Industries Quarter is defined in Sheffield City Council's CIQ 'Area Action Plan' as extending to some 30 hectares and located just to the south east of the city's administrative, retail, and commercial core. The area is roughly triangular in shape, and is bounded by Arundel Gate and Eyre Street to the north, St Mary's Road to the west, Suffolk Road to the south and Sheaf Square and Howard Street to the east. Sheffield Hallam University occupies much of the area to the immediate north, with parts of its estate within the CIQ itself, including a new Business School, the Northern Media College, and the proposed School of Cultural Studies.

The CIQ is within a ten-minute walk of Sheffield City Centre, the main-line Midland Station is a few hundred yards away, and access to the trunk and motorway networks is good. For a period of some fifteen years the CIQ has been undergoing a transformation. By the mid 1980s the CIQ had become a classic *zone of transition*: a marginal area of the city centre, which was once a thriving industrial and workshop centre, but had become

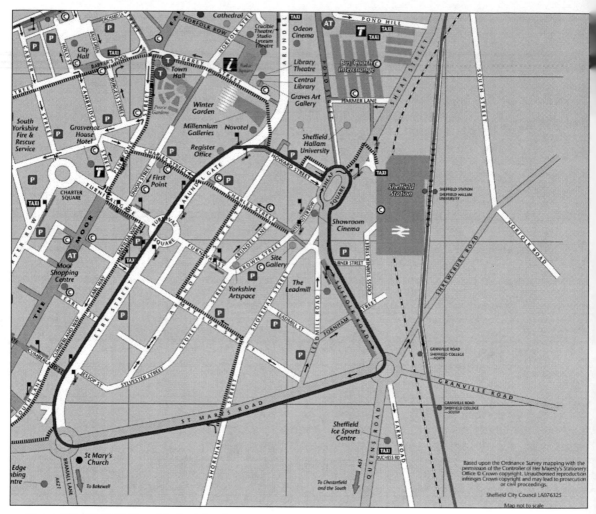

Map of Sheffield Cultural Industries Quarter.
Key: Black lines indicate the Cultural Industries Quarter, Sheffield.

characterised by vacant and derelict buildings and gap sites. Slowly at first, but with a marked quickening in the pace of development from the mid 1990s, the CIQ is now recognised as a centre for a wide range of cultural production. This includes fine arts, photography, film-making, music recording, graphic, and product design. Important initiatives within this spectrum include the Yorkshire Arts Space Studios, the Audio Visual Enterprise Centre, the Leadmill nightclub, Red Tape Studios, the Sheffield Science Park, the Site Photography Gallery, the Workstation managed workspace, and the Showroom Cinema complex. The Quarter is also home to Yorkshire Art Space Society, the Untitled Photographic (now the Site) Gallery, and a cluster of some 300 small businesses related to film, music and TV, design and computers. Important links have been established between the Cultural Industries Quarter and the adjacent Science Park, particularly with regard to the development of new technology in film, photography, and recording, while there are now proposals to develop a Culture Campus in the area which would house Sheffield Hallam University's fine art, media studies, and design departments.

It should be recognised that Sheffield is a city with a long tradition of cultural production, particularly in fine arts, music, film, and video. In the early 1980s the City Council started to develop a cultural industry policy, aimed at supporting these activities and assisting economic regeneration of a former car showroom. Two resultant building-based projects – the Workstation and the Showroom – were seen as central to the development of the CIQ. The buildings were owned by Sheffield City Council and were developed by a specially formed registered charity, Sheffield Media & Exhibition Centre Limited (SMEC). The charity set up a development subsidiary, Paternoster Limited, who took a 125-year lease on the building. Paternoster Limited run the Workstation purely as a commercial enterprise, charged with operating the building for the benefit of its tenants, and covenants profits to the parent charity (SMEC) for the benefit of the Showroom Cinema operation. The Showroom also receives revenue grant support from Sheffield Arts Department, the British Film Institute, and Yorkshire and Humberside Arts.

The area designations, and many of the projects within it, have been championed by the former Sheffield City Council, the Department of Employment and Economic Development, and latterly by the Cultural Industries Quarter Team within the Chief Executive's Department. Over 70 organisations now occupy units in the building, ranging from the Northern Media School, graphic designers – the Designers Republic, the Community Media Association, the Yorkshire Screen Commission – and various film production companies such as Picture Palace North and Dream Factory. Typical of the sector, tenant companies are small to medium size, employing from two to six staff members, although certain companies employ 25 and upwards.

By 1997, despite the impressive growth of new organisations, facilities, and venues, the CIQ lacked a strong sense of place. There were very few shops in the area, and few bars other than some traditional pubs catering for students of Sheffield Hallam University. An important strand of both the 1998 CIQ Vision and Development Strategy and the Action Plan for the CIQ was to encourage secondary mixed-use, particularly along ground floor

The National Centre for Popular Music, now the Sheffield Hallam University Students' Union.

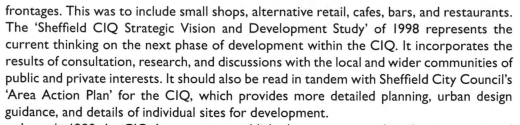

frontages. This was to include small shops, alternative retail, cafes, bars, and restaurants. The 'Sheffield CIQ Strategic Vision and Development Study' of 1998 represents the current thinking on the next phase of development within the CIQ. It incorporates the results of consultation, research, and discussions with the local and wider communities of public and private interests. It should also be read in tandem with Sheffield City Council's 'Area Action Plan' for the CIQ, which provides more detailed planning, urban design guidance, and details of individual sites for development.

In early 1999 the CIQ Agency was established to promote and implement an agreed Development Strategy for the CIQ over a five-year period. The agency's mission is to further develop the CIQ, building on the successes and, importantly, the broad character and nature of the CIQ as a cultural production centre and as an urban place. The aim is to create a thriving cultural production zone with large numbers of small and medium enterprises, a centre for excellence in knowledge creation and creativity, a visitor destination, and a largely mixed-use area, with various complementary activities generating pedestrian flow throughout the day and into the evening, including residences. The agency is comprised of a non-executive board with members being drawn from local businesses, Sheffield Hallam University, the Science Park, and Sheffield City Council. The board is supported by a small, full-time management team. The agency's five-year strategy (to 2004) had the following targets:

- 50 active exporting firms in the cultural industries, and an overall doubling of the businesses base within the area;
- an additional 350,000ft^2 of workspace for cultural industries;

- 4,200 jobs (3,000 direct, 1,200 indirect), of which 2,500 will be net additional jobs;
- 50 new retail, catering, and entertainment outlets provided by private investment;
- 500 additional permanent residents;
- completion of a new urban culture campus for Sheffield Hallam University;
- the completion of a number of cultural projects, including a Photography Gallery, Fine Art Gallery, and Centre for Performing Arts;
- continuation of a two-pronged training and education strategy aimed both at enterprise development and community access to new technologies and the cultural industries;
- considerable upgrading of the urban public realm to provide a more pedestrian-friendly environment, including established access points and routeways and two new urban squares.

In the past four years substantial private sector investment has been attracted into the area in the form of bars, nightclubs, restaurants, and student apartments. A major visitor attraction, the National Centre for Popular Music opened in 1999, although this closed after failing to attract sufficient visitor numbers. Despite those particular difficulties the SCIQ as a whole continues to grow. A new 1,000 capacity bar and live music venue opened in the summer of 2000, Red Tape Studios is launching a new Internet School, Modal's National Music Convention has been attracted to the Quarter, as has the International Documentary Film Festival. Yorkshire Artspace has developed a new building, Radio Sheffield are opening a new headquarters in the SCIQ, the old Roberts and Belk cutlery factory is being developed as a managed workspace with ground floor cafe bar, and the former Leadmill Bus Garage is being redeveloped for six cafe bars, offices, and apartments. Most of these are private sector initiatives and committed schemes currently amount to some £80m. These will provide for some 100 new creative businesses, a further 800 new jobs and 300 new local residents (the data was provided by Sheffield CIQ for the trading year 2003).

The majority of the strategic cultural developments have been delivered by a series of bespoke development companies, which also have charitable status, including Sheffield Media and Exhibition Centre Ltd, Music Heritage Ltd, Sheffield Independent Film Ltd, and Yorkshire Arts Space, and often combine public monies with bank finance. More recently, private sector investment has increased significantly in the area, with schemes including Truro Works (student accommodation), the Leadmill Garage (proposed leisure and entertainment complex), and Butcher Works/Fletcher Works (proposed managed workspace and silverware gallery). These building-based projects have been fundamental to the overall development of the CIQ. This area of the city centre was previously almost totally derelict. Success can be judged by the many new start-up cultural businesses, the establishment of the Quarter as a vibrant business environment, the upgrading of the physical environment, and more recent business relocations. In 2002 the CIQ Agency revealed that the Quarter was home to some 270 businesses and organisations, including film, TV, radio, science, and technolology, new media, training and education, live performance, music, arts, crafts, metalworking, and a range of support producer and consumer services. Additionally, new build, private development is now providing millions of pounds worth of residential, student, and business accommodation.

However, what is significant is how the Cultural Industries Quarter has limited connections with other cultural services in the city. So the Art Gallery and Museums do not form any part of the Cultural Industries Quarter, although this service has been an integral part of the Sheffield city cultural infrastructure for years. Similarly libraries are excluded. This demonstrates a narrow interpretation of culture, with what seems to be a particular interest in music, media, film, photography, and aspects of design, that is creative industries. Consequently an explanation of the establishment of the Sheffield Art Gallery Museums Trust is included here to illustrate the lack of cultural coherence, and perhaps a tendency to engage in "new solutions" at the expense of existing infrastructure that has served the community well.

Sheffield CIQ Features and Benefits

A building-based project approach has been fundamental to the overall development of the CIQ.

Success can be judged by the many new start-up cultural businesses: a 2002 estimate reveals that the CIQ is home to some 270 businesses and organisations, including film, TV, radio, science and technolology, new media, training and education, live performance, music, arts, crafts, metalworking, and a range of support producer and consumer services (data provided by Sheffield CIQ for the trading year 2003).

The establishment of the Quarter as a vibrant business environment, the upgrading of the physical environment, and more recent business relocations have generated new build, with private development providing millions of pounds worth of residential, student, and business accommodation.

The CIQ is unconnected to other cultural policies and activities in the city, for example the Museum and Art Gallery Trust.

Establishing one physical location and focal point for activity has an adverse effect on other wards in the city.

Although connections with higher education seem to be good, relations with further education are unclear.

Establishing and developing the Quarter has been a long-term Council-led strategy.

The Quarter does not include all the sub-sectors of the creative industries as defined by the Department for Culture Media and Sport.

The Quarter was not designed to incorporate amateur arts; it is focused on providing a physical infrastructure and support for professional production.

5.2 The Other Sheffield Cultural Industries Quarter: Sheffield Art Gallery and Museum Trust

The Trust model reflects a Cultural Quarter that represents the coherence and convergence of the arts and heritage in culture, and culture as a manifestation of society.

Sheffield City Council had over many years reduced expenditure on its Museum, Gallery and Library services in order to service debts accrued as a result of building substantial facilities for the World Student Games. As a result the decline in funding for the Art Gallery and Museums Department became increasingly critical, to the point that staff were being made redundant, museums placed on reduced opening times and no resources for temporary exhibitions. However the city had acquired Trust experience both in the past and relatively recently when its leisure facilities were transferred to a Trust vehicle. Consequently it was no great surprise that the Council considered applying a similar solution to the Art Gallery and Museum Department. The approach that was adopted involved the Council retaining ownership of the buildings, collections, and other related assets, with the management of the service being given over to an independent Trust, including the transfer of staff. The Trust, which is an independent constitutional body, then entered into a contract with the Council to provide the management for the Art Gallery and Museums owned by the Council for at least a minimum of six years, and in return receives a guaranteed grant income. However no attempt was made to relate this to the Cultural Industries Quarter model, which does not employ the Trust vehicle.

North American cities are familiar with the Trust structure as a means of public sector engagement in cultural services, representing one feature of the landscape; however in Europe the experience is very different. National and local government are the landscape, playing the dominant role in cultural provision, with local government at regional level being the single most important source of funding (Roodhouse & Taylor 2000). This is a long tradition found not only in the United Kingdom but also in Germany, France, the Benelux countries, and Mediterranean states. It comes then as something of a surprise to find a large and well-established City Council, Sheffield, breaking the conventions of local authority practice in the cultural field by divesting the direct provision of galleries and museums to an independent Trust. This is even more unusual when the city has been politically dominated by a succession of Labour administrations since 1945, with only a recent change to Liberal Democrat control in May 1999.

Sheffield is a proud northern city of 530,000 people with a long history of steel and cutlery making which has suffered from a serious decline over the years in these activities, with the consequent job loss and resultant shrinking of the local economy. Pressure on spending limits continued for those areas outside education and social services, where much of the funding additions have been targeted by national government.

There was an inevitability, given these circumstances, that the City Council would give careful consideration to the cost effectiveness and efficiency of all its services, including

Sheffield Art Gallery and Museum Trust New Galleries.

cultural services. This exercise resulted in a decade of cost-cutting, with an obvious negative impact on the services and managers operating these services.

Revitalisation of the city economy was the priority, with the establishment of a Cultural Quarter; hosting the World Student Games, which required building a substantial sports and entertainment infrastructure, and working in partnership with national government to support existing businesses to modernise and to attract inward investment through the Sheffield Development Corporation to replace the redundant manufacturing companies. As part of this policy drive cultural tourism regeneration of the city included negotiations with the Victoria and Albert Museum, London (due to the failure of the Bradford City Council bid) to establish a northern outlet in Sheffield City Centre as part of the "Heart of the City" regeneration project. City Council resources have as a consequence been drawn away from the provision of traditional non-statutory services such as museums and galleries. This lack of investment and actual reduction in revenue budgets was diagnosed by the Sheffield cultural managers as a long and lingering illness with a very uncertain prognosis.

The preferred alternative to a "slow and uncertain death" of a once proud and nationally well-respected City Council service was the establishment of a Trust. It was almost an inevitable outcome given the pressures described earlier, and historical familiarity with the Trust "vehicle", not least the giving of individual donations and collections to the City Council in Trust. It was the wheel of history turning full circle, because the Mappin Gallery collection, which is a core component of the Sheffield Galleries and Museums Trust, was given in Trust to the City Council due to the financial stability, certainty, skills, and stewardship offered at the time. This historical perspective was reinforced with the recent experience, referred to earlier in establishing Trusts to operate sports and leisure facilities, generating a receptive political climate for the idea of a Trust for galleries and museums.

Sheffield Council Gallery and Museums Service

The City Council Arts and Museums Service, prior to the establishment of the Trust, comprised the Bishop's House, the City Museum, Graves Art Gallery (the Graves Gallery and Collection was not given in Trust, and was never a separate charitable Trust), Mappin Art Gallery, Ruskin Gallery, Kelham Island Industrial Museum, and Abbeydale Industrial Hamlet. In addition the service was responsible for off-site storage of the collections that could not be housed and displayed in the galleries and museums. The staff employed totalled 55, and the annual City Council support for 1997/8 was £1.28m, supplemented by £341,000 from Arts Council stabilisation funding.

The city Museum houses the decorative arts, archaeology, and natural history collections. The Museum started life in 1875 in Weston House, a private residence situated in extensive parkland purchased by the city to become the first public museum, known as the Weston Park Museum. The surrounding gardens became a public park, and in 1937 the Museum was rebuilt and greatly enhanced by physically attaching it to the adjoining Mappin Art Gallery.

The Mappin Art Gallery was the first public gallery to be opened in Sheffield (in 1887), and originally housed the collection of the local brewer and benefactor, John Newton Mappin. The Mappin Art Gallery Trust dates back to when the Mappin Collection was bequeathed to the City in 1883 on the death of John Newton Mappin. A condition of the bequest was that the Council erected a suitable building to house his treasure. In 1940 the gallery was bomb damaged, and in 1964 the original Victorian galleries were restored and new galleries built, which now house contemporary art exhibitions.

The Graves Art Gallery, situated above the central library in the centre of the city, is a purpose-built gallery comprising eight galleries of differing sizes. Alderman J.G. Graves was the benefactor and presented his collection to the city and the twentieth-century collection is housed here.

The Ruskin Gallery was established in 1985 to house the John Ruskin collection, which was originally founded in 1875 in the St George's Museum in a small cottage in Walkley, a suburb of Sheffield. This collection, of international importance, is now housed in the Millennium Gallery.

Bishops' House is a grade two listed seventeenth-century town house situated in Meersbrook Park and was acquired by the City Council in 1976. Although none of the original furniture survives, the house has collections which interpret both the building and the Tudor and Stuart periods.

The arts (incorporating galleries and museums) were one of three divisions, including libraries, which formed the Leisure Services Directorate in 1993 under the leadership of Keith Crawshaw, who reported to the Leisure Services Committee of the Council. Prior to the establishment of the Leisure Services Directorate there had been four cultural services: libraries, arts, galleries, and museums, all with three separate chief officers reporting to the libraries and arts committee, chaired for many years by Councillor Enid Hattersley, a politically powerful and well-established figure in the city.

Councillor Hattersley retired in 1983/4, and so did the Chief Officer for Galleries, paving the way for further change. This resulted in the creation of the post of Director of Arts, which ultimately led to the merging of the museums, galleries and arts services in 1995. Since 1983, with no clear political champion, there has been a general decline in these services with a resulting reduction in the number of visitors enjoying the museums, galleries, and libraries. In addition, internal reorganisation of the services led to staff not being replaced, and significant annual cash reductions in the expenditure budgets. There were also the inevitable constraints for Council managers on borrowing and trading activities as well as restrictive legal frameworks. The general decline was accelerated in the early 1990s with the closing and/or transfer of sports centres to Trusts, or contracting out of services to private sector management teams.

In the case of the museums and galleries the progressive reduction in resources and staff reorganisation resulted in the collapse of the quality of the temporary exhibition programme, and the inability to acquire works of art and objects for the collections. Good will was stretched to the limit, and the curatorial staff used all their networks to borrow works of art and objects to be able to mount temporary exhibitions as an important means of articulating the permanent collections and attracting visitors. There was no investment in information technology; opening times were drastically reduced, and at one stage serious consideration was given to closing down the Graves and Mappin Galleries, with compulsory redundancies. This was blocked by a combination of the force of public opinion and the trade unions directly involved.

In wider Council terms the servicing of the capital debt used to build the sports facilities for the World Student Games (as a contribution to regenerating the city) was becoming increasingly burdensome, particularly as the Conservative national government placed more and more constraints on Councils. This restricted borrowing was accompanied by progressive annual reductions in the grant aid from central government as well as control over local taxation. National government encouraged the contracting out of services.

Setting up the Sheffield Galleries and Museums Trust

It became clear that the use of the Trust vehicle was a real political option due to the positive experience gained through the transfer of the sports and leisure facilities. Not least rate relief could be gained, as well as providing a means of protecting the service from further Council cuts. It also had the potential to enable the services to grow.

The Council's view of Trusts was explained by Keith Crawshaw, the Director of Leisure Services, as:

• the Trust can produce a more focused approach to service delivery, and business development opportunities may be more available, utilising other experiences and resources;

- opportunities may arise to involve a wider group of stakeholders, for example local community interests, in managing the business by involvement on the management board;
- the Trust may have access to external resources, both revenue and capital, which are not available to the local authority;
- it has potential to develop new ways of working in an external environment;
- cash savings can be made where the Trust can benefit from charitable NNDR relief provisions and VAT relief.

However the negative aspects of a Trust approach to the galleries and museums were also recognised:

- the need to sustain ongoing management input, and capacity to sustain relationships;
- the problems of making Trusts properly accountable for the spending of public monies or the use of public resources, because, under Trust arrangements direct control by the City Council cannot be exercised;
- cost savings are not always evident, and additional costs are often incurred in the short term as a result of legal and accountancy requirements;
- legislation may preclude the City Council from having direct control; relationships will need to be built using influence rather than control;
- charitable NNDR relief depends upon fairly strict statutory tests and it is not achievable for every aspect of leisure provision. It will depend upon whether the charity is in rateable occupation, and the use to which the premises are put. To qualify may require that the whole model of occupation of a particular facility may need alteration, thereby affecting income potential.

Quite apart from assessing these advantages and disadvantages, the Council had to decide on the appropriate Trust model if it wished to proceed. It was generally felt that a charitable Trust was the preferred option, although consideration was given to management buyouts, and worker controlled industrial provident societies. It was also recognised that external funding agencies such the regional arts and museum bodies would need to be consulted to ensure that their current funding partnership with the city could be accommodated in any future arrangements.

Running parallel with these internal discussions, an approach was made to include the Council's arts activities (including galleries and museums) in the Stabilisation Programme, a national lottery fund administered by the Arts Council. The application for £1.15m over four years was successful, and work commenced in 1997. The grant came with conditions, and the stabilisation programme specified:

- the award is made to the Sheffield City Council on condition that once the Trust (Sheffield Galleries and Museums Trust) is legally constituted as a limited company with charitable status and takes control, the benefits and conditions will be transferred to the Trust;

- Sheffield City Council has committed to continue its core funding of £1,050,848 per annum for the next three years to the end of March 2001, and will additionally guarantee a realistic minimum grant for the following seven years to allow the Trust to plan effectively;
- Sheffield City Council also commits to providing the ongoing transfer of funds for support costs from the building budget, Arts Directorate budget, and the "Heart of the City" fund as outlined in the stabilisation strategy submitted in June 1997.

The stabilisation fund required the establishment of the Trust by the City Council, as a limited company with charitable status, and this provided the spur for the Council to take the final decision to proceed with divesting itself of the galleries and museums service. In so doing the City Council agreed to provide funding of £1.21m for 1998/9, £1.51m for the next two years, followed by an amount of £1.51m for the following three years of the Trust's operation.

Similarly a City Council application to the Millennium Commission to build a new £13m gallery, the Millennium Galleries, in partnership with the Victoria and Albert Museum, London as part of the city centre regeneration ("Heart of the City"), was also in the process of being approved. The purpose of this gallery was to display major exhibitions from the collections of the Victoria and Albert Museum, London. The Council also had to determine the most effective means of managing this project, and decided to include the Millennium Gallery in the Trust arrangements under consideration.

Approval was given by the Council to commence the setting up of the Trust in May 1997, with a view to completing the transfer in January 1998, and the Sheffield Galleries and Museums Trust established as a legal entity by 1st April 1998.

It is worth noting here that the industrial museums were excluded from the Sheffield Galleries and Museums Trust. The facilities transferred to the Trust were City Museum, Mappin Art Gallery, Graves Art Gallery, Ruskin Gallery and Bishops House, and the Millennium Galleries project. In the case of the Kelham Island Industrial Museum this was set up as an independent Trust in partnership with Sheffield Hallam University, and also included the Abbeydale Industrial Hamlet. The Industrial Museum Trust became the Sheffield Industrial Museums Trust in April 1998.

An equally important decision was taken by the Council when setting up the Trust that there would be no transfer of the collection assets; significantly the collections remain in Council ownership for the benefit of the people of the city. Amongst other considerations it was recognised that this was an important control that could be sustained through a collection agreement. The buildings also had controls exercised through the lease arrangements, although all non-building and non-collection related assets passed from City Council control to the Trust. This led to determining levels of accountability, and it was thought that this could be achieved by:

- the City Council influencing the objects of the Trust and/or articles of association for any trading arms which may be established;
- the provisions of any leasing arrangements that will be put in place regarding the use of City Council property and assets;
- the terms of any funding agreements.

An example of this is that the Council insisted the existing galleries and museums remain free at entry to the public, although the Trust could charge entry to temporary exhibitions.

There was a further suggestion that the equivalent of national government's Public Accounts or Select Committees should be established to undertake the monitoring of the Trusts and carry out detailed appraisals of their activities.

in effect the City Council were agreeing to the transfer of the management of its galleries and museums to a Trust, providing a guaranteed income over an agreed period of a minimum of six and maximum of ten years, with assets remaining in Council ownership and the buildings leased back to the Trust. The leases offered to the Trust were not commercial, but financially nominal, that is at no significant cost to the Trust. The Trust could negotiate for a further four years funding beyond the six years thus providing a ten-year period to deliver the mission and objectives of the Trust on behalf of the Council. Building repair and maintenance remained the responsibility of the Council.

The management of the collections was the subject of a separate but related agreement between the Council and the Trust. This covered conservation care, research, display, interpretation, loans, and curatorial responsibilities (including acquisitions and disposals).

The Council put in motion the legal actions needed to set up the Trust, and also approached individuals who would be willing to become trustees. Sir Hugh Sykes, a well-respected local businessman with extensive public service experience, was chosen and accepted the position of Chair of the Trust. The Council also began the process of appointing a Director. Dr Gordon Rintoul, whose knowledge and experience of independent Trusts was recognised (having established Catalyst: The Museum of the Chemical Industry), was appointed as the first Chief Executive in January 1998.

The Sheffield Galleries and Museums Trust

The Trust formally came into being in April 1998 as a registered charity and limited company, with the purpose of managing the non-industrial museums and galleries in Sheffield on behalf of the City Council. These were the Graves Art Gallery, Ruskin Gallery, the City Museum, Mappin Art Gallery, and the Bishop's House. The Trust was expected to take over the management of the Millennium Galleries when it opened in the spring of 2001. The board of trustees number between eleven and fourteen members and the day to day responsibility for the operation of the Trust is delegated to the Chief Executive and the management team.

The vision for the Trust is:

> *"To be one of the leading gallery and museum organisations in the United Kingdom."*
>
> ('Enriching the Future', Sheffield Art Gallery and Museum
> Trust corporate plan 1999–2002, February 1999)

The mission flowed from this:

To enrich the lives of our audiences by:

- *providing imaginative exhibitions and displays of regional, national, and international importance of interest to local people and visitors to the city;*
- *the development of innovative approaches to interpretation, education, and enhancing public access;*
- *the provision of exceptional customer service;*
- *the care, preservation and development of collections.*

('Enriching the Future', Sheffield Art Gallery and Museum
Trust corporate plan 1999–2002, February 1999)

Strategic aims and objectives were developed which were intended to articulate the mission, and these included:

- Creating a programme of high quality exhibitions and displays which meet the needs of local people and visitors to the city;
- Generating the widest possible understanding and enjoyment of the collections and exhibitions through the development of effective educational and public programmes;
- Improving the operation of the sites in the care of the Trust and their facilities to enhance the service offered to users;
- Increasing public awareness and the use of the Trust's resources, services, and facilities through effective marketing;
- Documenting, storing, preserving, and researching our collections to the recognised professional standards;
- Managing and developing human and administrative resources in the pursuit of the mission and the aims of the Trust.

At transfer the Trust took responsibility for 55 staff, and by 2000 had an establishment of 70, with 32 male and 38 female, which included nineteen part-time employees. It has risen to 80 with the opening of the Millennium Galleries, and its 800m^2 temporary exhibition space.

In financial terms the Trust commenced life with an annual grant of £1.21m, followed by £1.40m for a further two years, and £1.51m for the next three years, guaranteed for three years with an agreement to provide a further £0.5m to manage the Millennium Galleries. In addition the Trust received £1.15m from the Arts Council Stabilisation Fund up to 2002. It is, then, in the remarkable position of knowing that it has a guaranteed income of £2.6m over a three-year period, and a predictable income for up to six years. This has advantages for the managers of the Trust, particularly in terms of stability and in planning with confidence, which is important for temporary exhibitions and trading activities.

The range of the collections in the care of the Trust fall into five key areas:

• Social History;
• Archaeology;
• Decorative Arts;
• Visual Arts;
• Natural History.

The Trust also has in care the collection of the Guild of St George, which was originally assembled by the great Victorian thinker John Ruskin.

The total accessioned collection amounts to 674,446 items, with the largest numbers in Natural and Social History, which is not unusual in a large municipal museum and gallery service in the United Kingdom.

The Management and Financing of the Trust

At the time of writing, the organisation and management structure of the Trust is a conventionally hierarchical model, and one expected to be found for Trusts with similar aims and objectives. The management team comprises the Chief Executive, the Exhibitions and Collections Manager, the Finance and Administration Manager, the Education and Public Programmes Manager, and the Operations Manager. All other staff are designated to these managers. This is explained in figure 1.

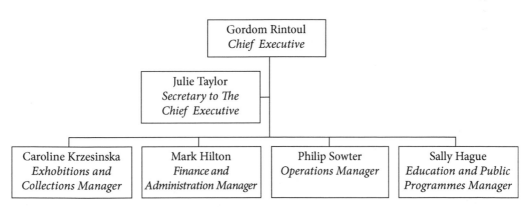

Figure 1: Management Team.

The management team reflects the organisational structure found in figure 2, which again follows similar lines to that of other independent museums and galleries.

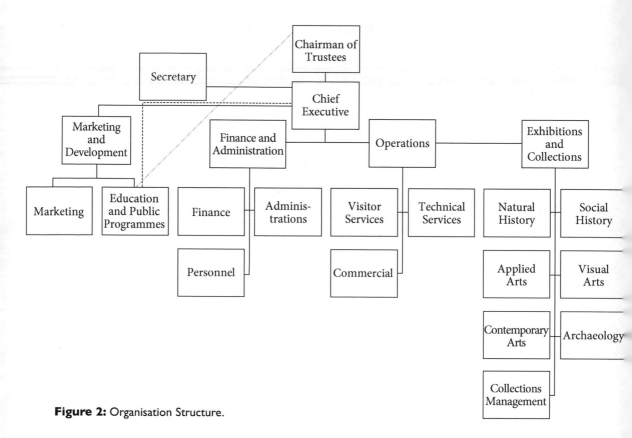

Figure 2: Organisation Structure.

It is the lines of reporting and the freedom to act to realise the Trust's approved business plan, which differentiate the management of the Trust from that of the City Council. The Chief Executive has far greater flexibility to deliver the objectives of the business plan, and is only accountable to the Chairman and board of trustees. The post holder does not have to act as a local Council officer, with limited executive powers and extensive reporting lines to sub-committees, committees and the Council, as well as the Chief Executive of the Council. In other words a chief officer of the City Council is expected to serve two bosses, the councillors (politicians) and the Executive of the Council. The primary function of the Council is to deliver public services to the highest standards for the benefit of the city. Inevitably, because it is a public service using public money, levels of access and accountability are high.

On the other hand the Trust's Chief Executive is employed to deliver "day to day responsibility for the operation of the Trust" and is accountable to the board of trustees, as mentioned earlier. The Chairman of the trustees is accountable to fellow trustees, the charity commissioners, and the various stakeholders, including the City Council, who financially support its work. There is no direct public accountability as found in City

Council services. It is a far simpler system but the freedom to act comes with strings attached.

Conditions that form part of the agreements with the funding agencies have to be met, timescales matter, and there is no one to bail out the Trust if it gets into financial difficulties through its activities, including trading. In a public service environment risk is minimised, and it is unheard of for a City Council to become bankrupt.

The total income for the first three years relied on grant aid from the stabilisation fund, the City Council, and the "Heart of the City" regeneration programme. The planned projections beyond this period recognise that the stabilisation fund will cease, and the shortfall replaced by an increase in private sponsorship, other public sector grants, and trading activities. It has also been the case that the management of the Millennium Galleries, and additional revenue grant given to the Trust for this purpose has assisted in ameliorating the shortfall. However, there are plans for modest steady growth of trading activities from the shops and specific exhibition admission fees, as well as sponsorship. These trading activities were at minimum levels when operated within the City Council. Retailing, selling of reproduction rights, catering, room hire, corporate membership, and picture loans activities has grown from a low initial baseline. This is the growth area for the Trust, and consequently detailed consideration has been given to visitors to the galleries and the museums. There is a planned progressive growth in visitor numbers, which is to be expected with the introduction of the Millennium Galleries and the re-introduction of marketing literature and temporary exhibitions, as well as the extension of opening times.

Apart from the dependence of visitors and trading turnover, private sponsorship has also been identified for expansion. This is due to a perception that the private sponsor is generally unwilling to give financial support to the City Council, as the contribution is often thought to be used to reduce fiscal deficits and rarely seems to reach the specific activity or organisation the sponsor intended it for. Consequently it is easier for a potential sponsor to target their financial contribution to a discrete organisation with clearly defined aims, and lines of accountability. As a consequence the Trust is confident that there is an untapped sponsorship market to exploit. Targets and operational plans have been drawn up to achieve the income projections. However the visitor performance from 1998 to 2000 fell short of the original targets, and this it seems reflects the inadequacies of the inherited methods used to collect this data, as well as gallery closures for refurbishment programmes. With the opening of the Millennium Galleries performance has significantly improved.

It is worth noting that as part of the progressive cost-cutting to the Museum and Gallery service when in City Council control referred to earlier, expenditure on marketing and publicity was reduced to an absolute minimum, hence the need to re-introduce a marketing and publicity campaign at an early stage in the Trust's life.

From a Trust management perspective, however, these are the challenges associated with this freedom to act.

Advantages and Challenges of the Trust

The Trust has been operational for several years and there is no doubt that a new lease of life has been given to the work of the galleries and museums. It is also the case that there is less political interference in the operation of the Trust, and it is recognised that the galleries and museums are progressively being revitalised with the Millennium Galleries and the refurbishment of the Mappin Art Galleries and Western Park Museum. Investment has resulted in the following:

• New information technology systems;
• Improved opening times;
• Higher quality temporary exhibitions;
• More staff;
• Refurbishment of the galleries;
• Better marketing and publicity;
• Establishment of an acquisitions fund;
• New educational and public programmes;
• Partnership with Tate Gallery and Victoria and Albert Museum, London.

The partnership with the City Council is progressing satisfactorily, and close working relationships between the two managements have been established, particularly with regard to the Millennium Galleries.

It is significant that the downward spiral of year-on-year financial cuts, non-replacement of staff, and lack of capital investment has been stopped and reversed. From the City Council's point of view there is a planned and predictable financial commitment, one less service to directly manage, and the opportunity to change the operation of the Leisure Services Directorate into a more strategic role with strengthened monitoring and appraisal functions, as well as contract managing capability. It seems to be a "win-win" situation for the Council and the Trust.

However the challenges continue with:

• Maintaining and increasing visitor numbers;
• Increasing the earned income from shops, specific exhibition admission charges, catering, and private sponsorship;
• Council appraisal and accountability;
• Linkages with other cultural infrastructure in the city such as the cultural industries quarter.

Nevertheless, as long as the Trust improves the performance of the galleries and museums, and those living in the city can tangibly benefit from this, then the relationship will strengthen and grow. However, if the Trust does not make a material difference to the lives of those living and visiting the city it cannot be expected to continue being paid to manage the Council's galleries and museums. As a result, the quality of the management team is critical to success. Similarly increasing pressures are being placed on the City Council to ensure that the services it provides are good value for money, deliver the agreed outputs, and meet the needs of the community. It is within this context that future difficulties may arise.

This approach has several advantages, such as enabling the independent management to attract resources from a number of different sources, to be unfettered by committee structures and the general bureaucracy associated with Councils, and to act commercially, working to a business plan with clearly defined targets and outputs. The Trust accepts the risks involved in managing art galleries and museums, whilst the Council for the first time can predict its commitment to ensuring a service is maintained for the benefit of the community. It is in effect enabling the private sector, through the Trust vehicle, to operate as a business, with the assurance of public sector core funding support. In a recent survey on behalf of Re:source (English Regional Museums Report 2001) of the strategic ambitions of 26 local authorities, with regard to their Museum services, the local authorities interviewed confirmed that they saw a long-term role for the services (whether in direct or indirect control) in contributing to regeneration, widening participation, lifelong learning, quality of life, social cohesion, and economic development. In particular the Chief Executive of Sheffield City Council said:

> - *The cultural sector, including museums and galleries, are a crucial part of the renaissance of city centres, particularly for core cities and influence beyond their boundaries, that is the city region;*
> - *They add to the quality of life and make the city a good place to live and work;*
> - *They play a key role in the knowledge economy;*
> - *They contribute to making the city successful, and as a result the city region, by generating the new economy through knowledge;*
> - *They assist in enabling the city to tackle the economic imbalance between London and the regions;*
> - *They are an educational resource beyond that of schools, playing a part in lifelong learning, through informal learning and contributing to the interpretation and dissemination of knowledge;*
> - *Epitomises civic pride, a sense of place, and belonging to a community as well as articulating community coherence, and feeling comfortable with the past.*
>
> (Re:source 2001)

In other words contributing to the culture of their particular communities in a direct and measurable way was recognised as a strategic goal. It was also seen by many Council members that their museums, galleries, and arts organisations were the "family silver", needing to be retained, nurtured, and developed for the benefit of their town. However it raises the fragmented nature of cultural policy and planning in the city.

Sheffield Art Gallery and Museum Trust Features and Benefits

An effective solution to retaining and developing the family silver and revitalising Council building assets.

A dynamic and beneficial partnership with the Victoria and Albert Museum, London, which raises the profile of the local Museum and Art Gallery service as well as the city.

Epitomises civic pride, a sense of place, and belonging to a community as well as articulating community coherence, and feeling comfortable with the past.

Plays a key role in the knowledge economy.

A networked learning centre, with schools, colleges, and universities.

The attraction of non-Council funds.

New exhibition spaces, including high quality space for local artists.

A popular local attraction, and an integral part of the tourist effort of the city.

A close physical proximity to the cultural industries quarter.

The revitalisation of a failing and under-invested public service.

5.3 A Reinvention of the Craft Industries, Wolverhampton Cultural Quarter

Wolverhampton CQ is an example of a Cultural Quarter rather than a cultural industries quarter – the organisations located in the Quarter provide cultural and creative venues for the public.

Wolverhampton has developed a rich industrial heritage over time. It has grown from a mediaeval regional centre for the wool trade into becoming a major centre for the making of locks, buckles, metal toys, and general hardware, followed in the early nineteenth century by such products as tinplate and enamel.

With the introduction of the industrial revolution Wolverhampton became an important centre for the working of iron and steel, and manufacture of machine tools and engines. It has since built on this tradition to become a focal point for engineering, innovation, the construction of automobiles and motorcycles, as well as the production of paints and varnishes. However, like many other cities and towns the 1970s and 1980s saw recession and the closure of companies.

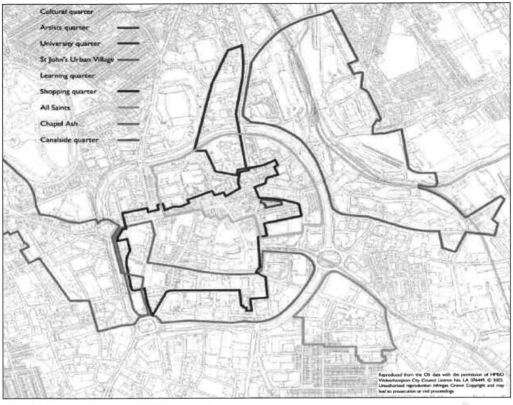

Legend:
- Cultural quarter
- Artists quarter
- University quarter
- St John's Urban Village
- Learning quarter
- Shopping quarter
- All Saints
- Chapel Ash
- Canalside quarter

Reproduced from the OS data with the permission of HMSO Wolverhampton City Council Licence No. LA 076449. © 2003. Unauthorised reproduction infringes Crown Copyright and may lead to prosecution or civil proceedings.

Map of the Cultural Quarter and Other Zones in Wolverhampton.

Over the last two decades however, Wolverhampton, has been reinventing itself by supporting and encouraging the University, which now has 20,000 students. Wolverhampton has also become a regional centre for leisure and entertainment which has a successful nightlife, attracting over 30,000 people each weekend, has improved all the major city centre cultural and sporting facilities, and has refurbished the main shopping centres. It also has substantial pedestrianisation and urban fabric improvement, and has established a science park for technology-based businesses.

However, Wolverhampton is still heavily dependent upon traditional manufacturing industries, with 23 per cent of all jobs in this field. A high proportion of these people work in high technology and high productivity sectors. Nevertheless, the manufacturing sector will continue to decline, leading to potential and rising unemployment levels over the next ten years. Service sector jobs have grown, but not enough to replace the projected losses from manufacturing. The challenge is to create 4,000 new jobs in the next decade to maintain total levels of employment and to find ways in which local people can gain the skills required to access these jobs. One of the growth areas for these jobs has been identified as the cultural industries.

Wolverhampton has started to work towards the development of this sector, using regeneration funding to provide clusters of workshops and support mechanisms – as in the Artists' Quarter, the theatre buildings and a second phase of the Art Gallery project. It is also working with others to regenerate areas of the city that may prove attractive to the service of the leisure sector – St John's urban village, the old Hall Street developments and the Canal Quarter.

The Council is an important provider of leisure and cultural opportunities, spending more than £20m a year on access to leisure and culture. This includes support towards:

- three galleries and museums;
- 21 libraries and archives service;
- concert halls, rehearsal spaces, a theatre, and the media centre.

The development of creative industries in Wolverhampton is being encouraged by the zoning of the town centre conservation area as a Cultural Quarter, which includes the Museum and Art Gallery, as well as part of the University. This is a key component of the Wolverhampton Town Centre Action Plan, which the Council considers a top priority;

> To encourage a wide range of quality leisure, cultural and educational activities at different times of the day and evening, which appeal to all members of the community and complement existing shopping facilities.

The fundamental drivers for redeveloping the town centre are physical regeneration, and substantial improvements to the nightlife of the town. The Cultural Quarter with its Council, cultural assets, including the civic hall, the Town Centre Theatre, the University Arena Theatre and the Art Gallery – which attracts over 170,000 visitors a year and is housed in a very popular grade two listed building close to the University – provides the nucleus for the day and night time activity by attracting people to performances, exhibitions, and related events, which in turn, supports cafes, restaurants, and bars. The media centre, the Lighthouse, is also located in the Quarter. It was established in the early 1990s, and has attracted £2m capital grants.

The existing leisure and cultural facilities, the range of buildings suitable for use, the historical and architectural importance of this part of the centre, and convenient access to bus and rail stations has determined the area as suitable, not only for housing this type of activity, but for positively increasing it.

Within the Cultural Quarter, an Artists' Quarter has been established. This Quarter is to be developed over time in partnership with the private sector, which will be supported and encouraged to convert existing vacant and under-used premises in the area for craft workshops, dance and drama studios, artist workspace, galleries including exhibition space, and some residential accommodation. This development is intended to complement other facilities being developed, for example the Wolverhampton Art Gallery, which will provide some workspace and a gallery area, and the newly refurbished Grand Theatre. In particular, the Artists' Quarter will provide:

- Studios and workshops;
- Speciality shopping, cultural and leisure facilities;
- Improved street furniture, including lighting and upgrading of street finishes, as well as the introduction of public art features, to mark the Quarter;
- Street activities such as a street craft stalls;
- Diverse educational facility, which provides access to the arts for all members of the community;
- New living accommodation, particularly suitable for the needs of tenants, and which is intended to complement the provision within the nearby town centre, urban village;
- Affordable living and working space for artists to make, sell, and display their products;
- A visitor attraction.

As has been mentioned, the Art Gallery has also established studio space, as well as refurbished the interior of the gallery itself. This development is to reassert the importance of the gallery as a landmark building and popular leisure venue.

Wolverhampton Art Gallery and retail outlets.

The initial development of £1.925m concentrated on the refurbishment of the Art Gallery building fabric, both internally and externally, to produce a controlled environment for the artefacts, and a comfortable venue for visitors, as well as increasing the physical accessibility through the provision of an atrium and passenger lift. It also includes a new digital art suite which enables visitors to develop their skills in this discipline. The next phase, amounting to £691,000, included the refurbishment of the Georgian shops in Lichfield Passage to form three commercial retail units on the ground floor and thirteen craftsmakers' studios on the two upper floors. These studios have now been named the "Makers Dozen". The claim for the "Makers Dozen" is that it provides workspace for both the new graduates to start up enterprises to undertake their first commissions and pieces for trade fairs and gift markets, as well as offering space to more established makers, who already run small businesses that need efficient and unproblematic space to produce medium volume orders and exhibition pieces. They will also bring their expertise, selling skills, and resources to the studios, and provide mentors. Spaces range from 64ft^2–285ft^2, and are let on flexible terms. The two developments described attracted a Heritage Lottery Fund grant, the European Regional Development Fund, Single Regeneration Budget, Advantage West Midlands, and Wolverhampton City Council funds.

The third phase of development, totalling £6.6m, is intended to generate additional exhibition space to show the gallery's nationally recognised twentieth-century collection. In total over 25 per cent more of the permanent collection will be on display to the public, along with a major expansion and improvement of the educational services.

The innovative aspect of this approach is combining the exhibition of past and contemporary work with production and sales. The redevelopment of the Art Gallery and associated craftsmakers' studios has attracted over £13m from the Heritage lottery fund, the ERDF, and SRB, the Arts Council, and Capital Challenge, with initial work commencing in 1992. It should be noted that Wolverhampton City Council has a policy of supporting the revenue consequences of approved capital investment.

Retail outlets, part of the Cultural Quarter.

However, the Learning Quarter is zoned some distance from the Cultural Quarter, and consequently there is little physical interaction. In the Learning Quarter the central library (which has attracted over £5m capital investment from the Wolfson Foundation, the new opportunities fund, and the City Council) attracts 2,000 users a day, is positioned alongside the further education college, adult education centre, and housing schemes for the young disadvantaged, on an island site. A management committee of the key stakeholders has been established to oversee the development of the Learning Quarter. As learning is an integral component of culture, and in this case the University is an influential partner in the Cultural Quarter development, the lack of connectivity to create new synergies is disappointing, and may be related to a planning-led zoned approach which takes less account of the nature and purpose of the Quarter.

However, when this case was written there was no management structure for the Cultural Quarter, and individual officers within the Council responsible for cultural services in the Quarter undertake capital developments with the approval of the Council,

---

Wolverhampton Cultural Quarter Features and Benefits

An economic model, focused on job generation for a town with an honourable industrial heritage.

A town centre regeneration tool, which is property and nightlife-led.

The combination of existing and well-established cultural facilities with creative industry businesses and the university.

The linking of exhibition, sales, and production by connecting the gallery, the university, and producers.

Over 25 per cent more of the Art Gallery permanent collection on public display.

Over £13m capital investment attracted to Council cultural assets.

A focus on crafts and craft businesses.

A focus on the provision of facilities for artists and crafts people, which includes working and living space.

A combination of public and private funds attracted to the Quarter.

The Cultural Quarter remains largely in the control of the Council and has grown from an ad hoc development into an approved Quarter by the planning department.

This is not an amateur or community arts-led development, except that these needs are met through the redevelopment of the Library, Art Gallery, and Theatre.

No formal evaluation of the Cultural Quarter has taken place.

reporting through the normal committee structure. In reality, the Wolverhampton Cultural Quarter has grown opportunistically, with little planning. The Chief Cultural Services Officer has indicated that it would have been preferable to plan the Quarter from the outset.

What is of particular interest in the Wolverhampton approach is a recognition of its industrial past, that is small businesses, which were craft-oriented. In one sense the town is investing in the creative industries as the new craft-based small businesses of the future which complement other activities, and relates to digital technology companies being located in the science park. There seems to be an overarching coherent policy approach, combining existing Council cultural assets with major institutions such as the University, with over 22,000 students, of which many are training to enter the creative industries as the University has a substantial Faculty of Art and Design. It is possible to view the Cultural Quarter as a hub for production, presentation, and sale of cultural goods and services by reinvesting in existing cultural assets and supporting Council services.

5.4 Cultural Entrepreneurship, Newcastle Arts Centre

This model demonstrates how a focus on a particular geographical area by a cultural entrepreneur and collection of buildings provides a catalyst for the establishment of a Cultural Quarter.

The development of the Newcastle Arts Centre on Westgate Road, Newcastle tells a story of local entrepreneurship, a single-minded dedication to create better performance space for the arts and to revive the arts with a strong flavour of the locality. It is an art-initiated mixed-use development in listed buildings. A crucial factor was the training for the local labour force, which was funded by the Manpower Services Commission (MSC), the forerunner to the Training and Enterprise Councils. The success of the development lies in local government involvement, civic pride, and making maximum creative use of central government funding. It is important to note that the funding came from a variety of sources not directly connected to the arts.

The Arts Centre development raises the key question: when is an arts organisation seen as an investment asset rather than as a drain on public funding? – the sustainability argument. The project, which was instrumental in attracting interest and thereby investment in Newcastle's West Village, demonstrates how the arts can contribute to and benefit from urban regeneration, and rely less on traditional cultural funding sources.

The need for facilities for artists in the community led Mike Tilley and Norma Pickard to search for premises that were highly visible and accessible to the public at large. They wanted a place not only with traditional Art Gallery facilities but one where practising artists could create and display their work, where the public could use the studio and workshop facilities on an ad hoc basis, and where the artists and the public could interact. The centre was to be both a working and a leisure environment.

They chose a complex of buildings in Westgate Road that had lain unused for nearly ten years, and were consequently in a derelict condition. The buildings were in a run-down part of town where businesses had been closing down for years, and with little prospect of commercial regeneration. The fact that the buildings were "listed" and subject to restrictions on development made it a very risky venture. Tilley and Pickard therefore faced an uphill battle to secure financial support. However, they believed that the space would accommodate both commercial and arts facility uses, with the income from the commercial uses helping to cross-subsidise the arts uses. The premises also afforded the requisite high visibility for the project, and augmented other schemes, notably the refurbishment of the Tyne Theatre and Opera House, which were helping to upgrade the area.

The execution of the project depended on the creation of a package of measures in which the construction, final use of space, and financial support were all bound together. The plan illustrates the type and arrangement of the development. The buildings facing Westgate Road would be let as retail units on the ground floor and offices and flats on the top floor. It subsequently proved necessary to redesign some of the upper floors, as the intended provision of residential accommodation was not initially grant-aided. Hence, they are now office accommodation let to professional tenants. The easternmost building houses the arts centre proper. Within this building the ground floor arcade is the reception/gallery linked to Forth Lane, and with entrances at both ends offering an attractive route between Westgate Road and Pink Lane. This area provides access to performance areas on the ground floor and to studios, workshops, and offices related to the arts centre on the other levels. A courtyard allows for open-air exhibitions and performances as well as being a centre of circulation through the scheme. Movement into the court is also possible from Westgate Road through an existing alleyway below no. 71. The intention therefore was that the buildings should become part of the city's movement patterns and make a positive contribution to the fabric of the city, not only by creating new routes and areas which would be interesting in their physical form but also by providing spaces where activities and events could be generated.

Work began on site in 1981. The first tenant (a restaurant) moved into the complex in 1982. There are now various commercial and professional craftsmen and tenants although the final stage of the project still remains to be completed. The execution of the work has been very heavily influenced by the way in which the financial package was worked out. Because funds were at a premium and cashflow slow, a cost efficient strategy had to be devised. This was achieved by the following tactics.

The contract was turned into a very labour-intensive exercise, but one which employed as few conventional and specialist contractors as possible. Workers were employed directly by the Newcastle Arts Centre, but under the auspices of a government job creation scheme. The project gave the young and long-term unemployed an opportunity to learn new skills. The advantage to the project is that the funding has come from the Manpower Services Commission. The disadvantage of this scheme is that the majority of workers are trained on site, but shortly after completing their training they move *off* the job. No worker under the scheme can be employed for more than a year. Despite these constraints, there was a competent workforce with high standards of workmanship. Other tactics included:

- The salvage and re-use of materials from the site. The overbuilding, which was demolished, was taken down carefully to save the materials used.
- Generating income and an early cash flow from the commercial uses. The revenue from commercial occupiers generates over £50,000 annual rental income, which covers all the mortgage interest, and part of the capital repayment and refurbishment.
- Mixed uses would permit a wider range of funding sources by making the arts centre eligible for non-arts directed funding schemes.
- The phasing of work. This allowed for more careful preservation of the buildings and excavation of the historic site. It also allowed flexibility in the design to accommodate problems encountered during renovation and redevelopment.

The initial package of grants came from the Inner City Partnership (Economic Development Grant), Conservation Grants (because of the listed buildings) from a partnership of the Tyne and Wear Joint Conservation team, City of Newcastle, and English Heritage, and the Manpower Services Commission (an annual amount for training and administration of workers). All these funds were for a percentage of repair and renovation costs and sometimes, like the Conservation Grant, materials only. The grants did not cover the purchase of the building. However the trustee Savings Bank showed an interest in the project, and offered a mortgage on the property once the bulk of the first phase of the development costs, approximately £750,000, had been secured by funds and grants from public sources. The only part of the project so far to receive financial support because of its connection with the arts is the Newcastle Media Workshops. They obtained a capital grant form the Arts Council of Great Britain, supplemented by money from Northern Arts. Newcastle City Council provided some additional funding under a special scheme because the studios were using upper floors of buildings.

The premises were originally on the market at £250,000 but were eventually purchased for £110,000. The TSB lent £117,000, with the benefit of a three-year Interest Relief Grant, which was given to Newcastle Arts Centre by the Inner City Partnership to cover the interest on its mortgage for the first three years of operation. The arts centre paid the interest to the bank and was then reimbursed by the Inner City Partnership. In effect, the city and the DOE paid the interest on the mortgage for that period of time so the bank's risk was minimal.

In 1986 the Newcastle Arts Centre experienced cash flow problems and the bank refused to extend the mortgage, despite significant progress. The project was now partially let and trading, and showed an equity over the original loan. This refusal slowed

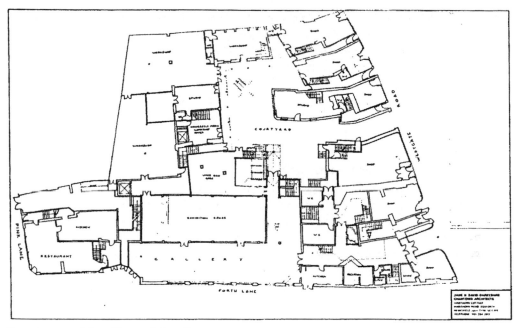

Floor plan, ground floor, Newcastle Arts Centre.

progress markedly. Eventually the City of Newcastle intervened and acted as broker between the Newcastle Arts Centre and the Northern Rock Building Society, which subsequently re-mortgaged the property for £270,000. Reasons for the cash flow crisis were the delays in obtaining approval for grant aid, up to eighteen months, and more extensive decay than the original survey revealed.

The enterprise and dedication of Mike Tilley and Norma Pickard resulted in an attractive and much needed arts facility. This is also an example of the importance of creative individuals responding to an explicit need, and provides an alternative model to the more recent local authority-led development found in Sheffield or Wolverhampton. Since 1982 the project has contributed to training and/or employment for 500 people. The arts centre has helped, together with the Tyne Theatre and Opera House, which is also situated in Westgate Road and being developed simultaneously, to revitalise a very moribund area of the city. The establishment of The Newcastle Initiative (TNI), launched in June 1988, which was a campaign led by leading figures in business, the academic community and government to revitalise the city provided further interest in the arts facility. Its aim was to provide a steady growth in employment, an improved urban environment, and the maximum possible contribution to the economy of the whole North East region. As a result of TNI support the area has been renamed the West City Theatre Village, and designated as one of its five flagship projects for Newcastle's revitalisation. Bill Hay, Chief Executive of The Newcastle Initiative recently said of this area:

It could be Newcastle's equivalent to Greenwich Village. We see it becoming an area where you can go out and enjoy yourself in safety and style. We see the opportunity not only to redevelop in terms of business, but also see the return of people living in the area, through new housing.

It should be noted that TNI's perception of this broader role for the Newcastle Arts Centre was influenced by information from Northern Arts (the local Regional Arts Association) on the economic potential of a cluster of arts organisations in a location historically linked with entertainment. Northern Arts' input argued for the value of information as well as financial broking in the regeneration of British cities.

Clearly the aim is to build on the work of those with the original vision. The project illustrates that when public funding sources can grasp an arts organisation's vision as complementing the socio-economic needs of its environs, they can accomplish two objectives; funding the organisation's development, whilst at the same time creating a catalyst for regenerating the area in which it is situated. The project shows how successful an arts-initiated and property-led rejuvenation can be in providing both arts facilities and urban regeneration, and as a result attract Cultural Quarter zoning.

5.5 The Jewellery Quarter, Birmingham

About a mile north-west of Birmingham City Centre, there is a Quarter where a large number of small jewellery-related firms have clustered for over 150 years: this area is well known as the 'Birmingham jewellery quarter' (BJQ). Over the years, the area has experienced various waves of changes, housing development, and industrial ups and downs. Nevertheless, it still accommodates a dense concentration of jewellery workshops, factories, retail shops, residential houses, and jewellery-related organisations. Thanks to this critical mass of jewellery-related activities, it promotes itself as one of the main jewellery centres in the United Kingdom after London and Sheffield, as well as being a vibrant Creative Quarter around a national historic site.

The BJQ was at its zenith at the turn of twentieth century in terms of employment, with over 30,000 employees overall. World War I, and then World War II, affected the industry in such a way that it never really recovered. Besides, other external forces contributed to its decline, including restrictions on precious metal suppliers, post-war purchase tax, the general decline of the manufacturing industry in the United Kingdom, and more recently, overseas competition from low cost countries and production capacity in the Far East, South East Asia and China. The BJQ has made structural adjustments in response to market and technology changes, including technological innovations and large-scale mechanisation to reduce costs, as well as the further development of the retailing sector. However, since World War II artisan and manufacturing jobs have shrunk from about 35,000 to just below 5,000 in 2002 (De Propris and Lazzeretti 2009).

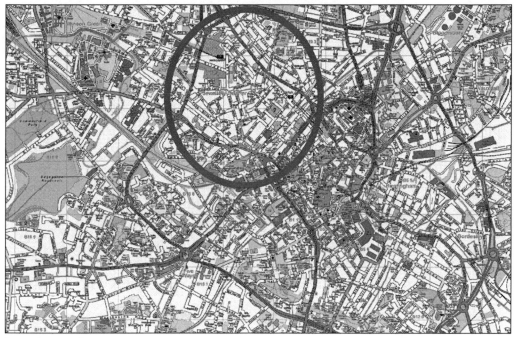

Birmingham jewellery quarter.

A current analysis of the size of the jewellery industry in the BJQ shows that Birmingham still remains the second main producer of jewellery in the United Kingdom. The BJQ still hosts a jewellery cluster.

In total, by 2006, there were still around 500 jewellery manufacturing, retail, and wholesale businesses in Birmingham and employment accounted for 16 per cent of UK total industry (Annual Business Inquiry, ONS and IDBR, ONS for 2003–2006).

The Jewellery Industry

In order to understand the Birmingham jewellery cluster, it is necessary to include the composition of the value chain in the jewellery making process and the following diagram shows the main jewellery and related tasks. From this it is evident that jewellery making is highly specialised and over time firms have become expert of one or more tasks. This explains the small size of firms and the customised nature of the business.

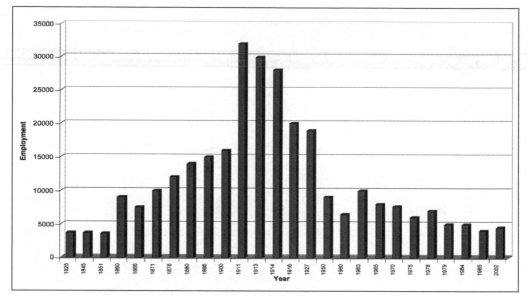

Employment in the jewellery cluster in the Birmingham Jewellery Quarter.

Currently the jewellery cluster in the BJQ remains the concentration of jewellery businesses that once expanded across the whole BJQ area. The rest of the BJQ now hosts a variety of businesses such as software/business consultants, law firms, bars, restaurants and elegant apartments, as the area has become increasingly popular in part due to its proximity to the city centre.

Creativity and Innovation Capacity

The jewellery industry has clustered in the BJQ since the turn of the twentieth century, when it developed as a geographical concentration of industry-specific production activities. It was characterised by the presence of small firms, artisans, and workshops. Firms were specialised and benefited from internal and external economies and the production process was characterised by an external division of labour which created the well-known Marshallian "industrial atmosphere". Finally, economic activities were imbued in a community network as people worked and lived in the same place.

The ability of the Birmingham jewellery cluster to maintain its grip on demand was, in the past, due to innovations in treating precious metals, such as electroplating or mechanised chain moulding; as well as product design and fashion setting. The geographical proximity of similar specialised businesses supported this by generating virtuous circles of competition and cooperation. More recently, the mass production of affordable jewellery

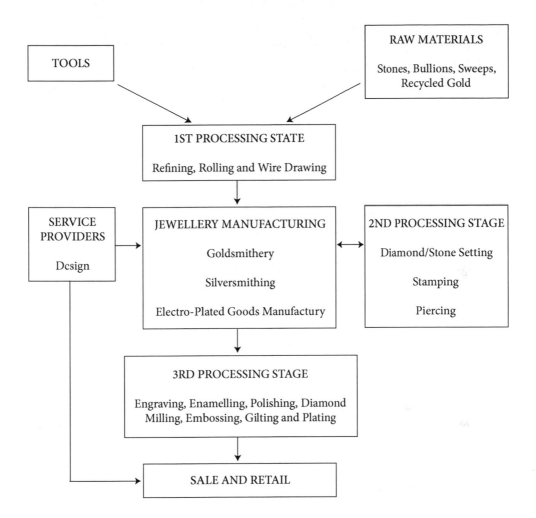

has become increasingly monopolised by Chinese and Indian producers, so Birmingham jewellery firms have no other option but to aim for the "top end" of the market. Indeed, to maintain their competitive position in the domestic market and to export, jewellery firms have to keep up with technological progress, but more importantly to offer pieces of jewellery that are highly innovative and rich in creative content.

The market repositioning of the Birmingham jewellery district is not unusual. Indeed, many traditional manufacturing industries whose competitive advantage had been eroded by price competition from low cost producers have moved away from mass production to concentrate on technology and design.

Creativity, Space and Networking

Around 25.9 per cent of the businesses[1] rely on their own creative capability, either in-house research and development (R&D) facilities or in-house designer-makers for technology and/or design ideas; meanwhile, one-third (33.3 per cent) of businesses source technology and/or design ideas flexibly from both internal and external channels. Finally, about 18.5 per cent of businesses do not have their own technology capacity, but mainly depend on external sources for technology or design, including external designer-makers, client firms, supplier firms, and education/research institutions. "Client firms" are mostly cited as one of the main external sources. Some businesses also mentioned that they pick up new design ideas from trade fairs, magazines. and international exhibitions. A small proportion, 7 per cent of businesses, source technology/design ideas from education/research institutions, linked to dedicated training institutions located in the BJQ, such as the School of Jewellery, part of Birmingham City University.

Generally, firms with increasing turnover have some form of creative capacity either in-house or externally: in fact two-third of firms with increasing turnover has either in-house or external creative capacity. In particular, designer-makers are well recognised in the jewellery industry as being important sources of creative design and ideas and, therefore, contribute to the competitiveness of firms. Businesses that access designer-makers are more likely to perform better, with 38.5 per cent using designer-makers either internally or externally, have increased turnover over the past five years. What this shows is that combining creative designers with manufacturing and commercial operations in a spatial context that is a Quarter is advantageous to firms that want to grow and be competitive.

Detailed sources of technology and/or design ideas.

	Frequecy	%
In-house R&D facility	33	30.6
In-house designer-maker	48	44.4
External designer-maker	14	13
Client firms	21	19.4
Supplier firms (component supplier or service provider)	18	16.7
Education/research institutions	9	8.3
Trade fairs/global networking, head office, demand, books, magazines, international exhibitions	5	4.6

Policy and Regeneration

Since the 1940s the BJQ's slow decline has attracted the attention of policy makers. Policy support packages for the redevelopment and regeneration of the area have been put into practice. The focus of the early plans concentrated on the repair of old workshops and the building of new premises for jewellers (for more information, see Smith 1989; Mason 1998; Pollard 2004). Since the 1970s, in recognition of the cultural value of the Quarter, attention has been paid to preserving nineteenth-century buildings. Different parts of the Quarter, such as "Key Hill" and "the Jewellery Quarter" (1980) following "St Paul's Square" (1971) were declared as conservation areas (Smith 1989; Haddleton 2005). In the meantime, a range of buildings were upgraded and rehabilitated under various sources of public or private funds (Smith 1989). Such public sector-led regeneration efforts continued into the 1980s and 1990s.

One of the latest initiatives, which has been influential in the evolution of the Quarter, is the 'Jewellery Quarter Urban Village project' – a Jewellery Quarter regeneration partnership created in 1998 by Birmingham City Council, Advantage West Midlands, the Prince's Foundation, the Jewellery Quarter Association, British Jewellers Association, the Developers Forum and other partners (Birmingham City Council 2005). The objective of the project has been to

> seek to achieve a more responsive and intelligent approach to the integration of new homes, shops, commercial, employment and community uses, while protecting the existing jewellery manufacturing and retail base. (Warburton 2005, p. 1)

Under the project, the restrictive land-use policies were lifted, residential units developed, the business base diversified, and leisure and tourism activities promoted. This is consistent with Birmingham city's reinvention economic plan in promoting itself as the *"meeting place of Europe"* (Henry et al. 2002). The effects of the plan, however, have been subject to critique since this urban regeneration plan has strongly contributed to the "aestheticisation" (Pollard 2004, p. 173) or gentrification of the Quarter, which may ultimately damage the economic (and social) base of the Quarter's jewellery manufacturing networks.

At the same time, Advantage West Midland, a government regional development agency, launched a development strategy aimed at supporting industrial clusters in the region (drawing on the DTI (2001) report on clusters in the UK) and in particular identified a set of high-value added industries that were grouped under the label "high value added consumer good" clusters, which also comprised jewellery (AWM 2005). More recently, this set of clusters has been re-branded as "interior and lifestyle" (AWM 2008). This is in line with the DCMS recent emphasis on creative industries. According to the 'Creative Industries Mapping Document' (DCMS 1998), the creative industries include: advertising, architecture, arts and antique markets, computer and video games, crafts, design, designer fashion, film and video, music, performing arts, publishing, software, television, and radio. In the more recent sector breakdown of the above creative sectors, jewellery can be found in the craft sector (Frontier Economics 2009).

It is clear from this that the jewellery cluster in the BJQ is a creative cluster, i.e., as an agglomeration of manufacturing and retailing businesses in a creative industry like jewellery. But walking around the Quarter today only some of it seems to reflect this aspiration. The jewellery cluster now stands at a "critical juncture" (De Propris and Wei 2007; and Pollard 2004), with real opportunities for renewal ahead as a creative cluster.

Note

1. Based on research carried out by De Propris and Wei as part of a British Academy-sponsored project by means of a firm survey in May–July 2005 in the jewellery district in the BJQ. Questionnaires were posted to all 412 jewellery and jewellery-related firms located in the quarter; with 108 valid responses, corresponding to a 26 per cent response rate. The sample comprised mostly small-sized firms, with 77.8 per cent of the respondents are micro-firms with one to ten employees (including proprietors), and only 2.8 per cent of firms in the sample have more than 50 employees (8.3 per cent for 11–49 employees). Their main production activities range from jewellery manufacturing related activities (52.6 per cent) to designer-making (12.3 per cent), wholesale, importing and retailing of jewellery (28.7 per cent), business service provider to jewellery firms (0.6 per cent), supply of specialist tools and machinery (1.8 per cent) and other activities (4.1 per cent). Such a combination of manufacturing and commercial activities reflects the increasingly diversified business base. In particular, it shows how relevant the share of wholesale and retailing activities currently has.

Chapter 6

Features and Benefits of Cultural Quarters, Internationally

Ann Galligan
Alison Holmes
Louise Johnson
Monika Mokre
John Montgomery
Simon Roodhouse

The selected international case studies introduced in this chapter are included to demonstrate that the cultural and creative industry quarter model is not confined to the United Kingdom. Examples found in this chapter are drawn from North America, Australia, Austria, and Ireland. Dublin, Temple Bar, is often cited as an important example alongside Sheffield, and there is increasing interest in the Vienna MuseumsQuartier as a state-led cultural regeneration solution. The Pawtucket Rhode Island example illustrates the importance of political will power and beneficial tax regimes, whilst Geelong provides an example of capitalising the indigenous cultural infrastructure. The size, scope, and context vary, however there are underlying commonalities of physical refurbishment of buildings, rejuvenation of run-down areas of cities, and housing the arts and heritage solutions.

The selected examples are illustrative of differing approaches to Cultural Quarter development although they all share a common interest in supporting the redevelopment of an area, buildings, and creative activity. It is the way they go about this and where the emphasis is placed which is of interest. In particular, the Vienna MuseumsQuartier has been chosen because it provides an excellent example of the use of graded buildings for cultural gain and economic advantage.

6.1 The Museums Quarter, Vienna, Austria

This project is a Cultural Quarter located in a particular geographical area of the city which acts as a focus for cultural and artistic activities through the presence of a group of buildings devoted to housing a range of such activities, and purpose-designed or adapted spaces to create a sense of identity, providing an environment to facilitate and encourage the provision of cultural and artistic services and activities.

It is a dynamic international scheme that sets out to raise the profile of the city as an international cultural tourism centre; in fact the city and state wanted to establish themselves as the seventh most important centre in the world.

Although Vienna has a substantial international reputation for music, it has not been able to promote other cultural dimensions, including museums and contemporary arts and design. This is what makes the MuseumsQuartier so interesting. It is visionary, dynamic, exciting, and at the same time resolves a range of local cultural rehousing issues.

Arial views of the Vienna MuseumsQuartier.

Austrian Cultural Policy Influences

The Austrian government, in office since February 2000, has been emphasising the need for new economic structures for culture, the arts, education, science, and even social affairs. Severe cuts of public subsidies have been a consequence of this policy, which has also impacted on institutions within the MuseumsQuartier – though the political intention to build and maintain this Quarter mainly out of public funds remains beyond question. However, the claim that "creativity should more and more become part of economics" (Franz Morak, Austrian Secretary of State for the Arts) introduces a radical break with traditional Austrian cultural policy and poses serious problems for artists and arts institutions in Austria.

To understand this situation it is necessary to describe two main features of Austrian arts policy:

• Austria defines its national identity to a high degree in terms of artistic and cultural values. To other countries and foreign citizens it presents itself as a "cultural nation". Foreign observers are often astonished by the huge public attention artistic events attract – but this interest is very superficial, with the engagement centred on events such as festivals, international concerts and, of course, cultural scandals.

- A second characteristic of arts policy in Austria has been until recently the extremely close relationship between politics and the arts. The arts have been almost 100 per cent financed by public means; private sponsorship has scarcely any importance at all. That's why the artists depend to a very high degree on the benevolence of politicians and bureaucrats.

The roots of this situation are historical. The prosperity of the Habsburg territories was an important reason for the flourishing of the arts, as well as for their dependence on state support.

Economic historians suggest that considerable portions of the Habsburg territories, and the Austrian lands in particular, which included Vienna, were highly prosperous at the end of the 18th century, at least in relative terms. Their per-capita incomes were probably well ahead of those of Brandenburg (Prussia) and very likely higher than that of France. Only England and the Low Countries may have been in a superior position. Prosperity brought great wealth to well placed members of the nobility and the small group constituting the upper bourgeoisie of Vienna and the nearby territories, among them Hungary and Bohemia (including Prague). They spent liberally, running their courts and mansions in a lavish style which included the services of many composers and performers. (Baumol and Baumol 1994)

Furthermore, culture and the arts have traditionally been a means to promote the political ends of the Austrian state:

Already at the time of the monarchy cultural policy was not only patronage. Art as the highest means to build up a state as an outstanding possibility of appropriating history, should help to ensure the unity of the diversifying national interests. The huge buildings of the 'Ringstraße' built in the second half of the nineteenth century ... bear witness to these considerations. (Österreichisches Zentrum für Kulturdokumentation, -orschung und -vermittlung 1992)

The generous public support for the arts as a characteristic of cultural policy has survived the end of the monarchy. "The state's support for culture continued in its own management, the long-term practice of the royal court" (Pleschberger 1991, p. 63).

It would be extremely attractive to ascribe the end of this kind of cultural politics to the political changes actuated by the change of government in 2000; as a matter of fact new ways of financing the arts have been in discussion for at least a decade now. The recent history of the MuseumsQuartier can be seen to coincide with this discussion: missions for this Quarter have been constantly oscillating between the idea of a "cultural manifestation" of Austria and the striving for the largest number of visiting tourists as possible. But the concept of bringing "creative industries" into the MQ in order to generate at least a moderate income from rents has gained momentum under the new government, creating further pressure on small under-funded cultural initiatives. As there is hardly any knowledge in Austria on how to find sponsors and sell artistic products at the moment, lip service is paid to the creative industries, whilst in reality the big and traditional museums that are the most prominent parts of the Quarter continue to be financed by substantial public subsidies.

So, up to now the new market orientation of cultural policy has not been much more than a catchword and a veiled menace for cultural initiatives. The close relationship between politics and the arts described above led to a situation in which rules of accountability and measurability were never clearly defined, but were replaced by negotiating processes between officials and representatives of cultural institutions. For observers from outside Austria it is surprising how little information is available on hard facts such as revenue, visitor numbers etc. Decision-making on public support for the arts is usually based exclusively on artistic judgements (often of a specialised jury). In this way, a broad room for arbitrariness is opened, as aesthetic quality is not really a category that can be measured. On the other hand, the broad room for negotiations enhances the flexibility of Austrian cultural policy, which can be good for artistic innovations.

The MuseumsQuartier is a typical outcome of this policy, with a commitment to state funding based on the value of the arts to Austrian society as an intrinsic part of life. It does seem problematic that no performance indicators are given to the highly subsidised institutions that will be part of this project, and that the MQ Company is able to run an annual deficit (Waldner, CEO, MQ Company).

A Description of the MuseumsQuartier

The MuseumsQuartier is a "brand name" for a particular physical single cluster site, the Imperial Stables, which at present comprises about 40 diverse cultural organisations[1] and culturally related activities occupying 53,000m^2 of useable space. This includes two new museum buildings, and two discrete theatres with seating capacity of 1,200. Additional exhibition space is available for hire, along with offices, workshops, and ateliers. This short-term space has been grouped together under the brand name Quarter 21. Many of the smaller cultural organisations are included in Quarter 21,[2] (see note 2 for a description of Quarter 21), described as "a structure of self-responsible, constructively competing content-entrepreneurs, a modular-action platform for independent small institutions, culture offices and temporary initiatives" (Waldner, CEO, MQ Company). Alternatively it can be described as the vehicle for a cultural industry cluster, with a focus on creative activity, new and multimedia technology.

Common facilities are also incorporated into the overall scheme, such as signposting, an information centre (infopool), toilets, seating areas, and public courtyards. In addition to these institutions there are also private tenants, restaurateurs, and shopkeepers, as well as those who have rented space over the years and have their homes there.

A typical smaller cultural organisation found in the MuseumsQuartier is Basis Wien, a documentation centre with an online database on contemporary art in Austria that also aims at presenting and discussing contemporary art. Basis Wien relies on grants from the state government and the City of Vienna. It found itself in a major financial crisis in summer 2002, when funding of both bodies was reduced, as well as paid out very late, and a mainly EU-funded project was therefore at risk. Its precarious financial situation also places the organisation in a weak negotiating position when determining its future with the MuseumsQuartier Company. However, contrary to other smaller and critical institutions such as Depot and Public Netbase that have been driven out of the MuseumsQuartier, Basis Wien could come back to its quarters within the MuseumsQuartier after having spent more than a year in an interim location.

The Leopold Museum, which perceives itself as a national museum and is funded almost entirely by the state government, forms one of the key MuseumsQuartier landmarks. It is a private foundation set up to care for and display the collection of Professor and Mrs Leopold, comprising over 5,200 items. The Foundation is the single most important collection of the Austrian twentieth-century artists Egon Schiele and Gustav Klimt, and was established in 1994 with the purpose of preserving Professor Leopold's collection and retaining it in Austria. The collection, valued at 6.5 billion ATS by Sothebys New York in 1994, was handed over to the Foundation by the Leopold family on condition that the state and the National Bank of Austria (a sponsor) paid them 2.2 billion ATS in fourteen instalments up to 2007 (Parnass). In addition the state agreed to provide premises in the MuseumsQuartier, cover the costs of the new building, supply the Foundation with an annual budget for purchases, and will also cover the Foundation's annual operating deficit.

The Foundation board of governors, which is responsible for the all aspects of its work, comprises four members appointed personally by Professor Leopold, and four members appointed by the state, drawn from the Ministry of Education, Science and Culture on the one hand, and the Ministry of Finance on the other hand. It is not difficult to see how closely this is related to government and the incestuousness of the Austrian cultural establishment.

All members are remunerated and serve for five years with the exception of Professor and Mrs Leopold who are life members. The board has established a Directorate and approved the appointment of Professor Leopold as the Museum Director for his lifetime. Incidental to, but an example of the closeness of the Museum to the development of the MuseumsQuartier, was the appointment by the board of the then director of the MuseumsQuartier Development Company to the Foundation as the Business Director for six months. Both Directors were given powers to conclude contracts on behalf of the Foundation approved by the governors (Interview, Romana Schuler). This is not untypical of the Austrian approach to managing the arts, and enables a small cultural establishment under the political auspices of the city and state to shape and control cultural provision and programming.

The Influence of a Building and Location

The MuseumsQuartier cluster of cultural activity forms part of the historic city centre, and is expected to strengthen the existing provision, primarily museums such as the Kunsthistorische Museum (Museum of the History of the Arts) and the Natural History Museum situated in the immediate neighbourhood, by adding a more active and lively contemporary dimension. At the same time it is intended to provide an up to now missing link between the Imperial Palace, with its museums, and the narrow meandering streets of an old suburb at the rear of the stables. It is easily reached by the metro and tram system. The vision is to create a major cultural focus in the historic city centre for visitors.

The Imperial Stables, a seriously decaying national heritage site, presented a significant physical and restoration challenge in the sense of marrying in a single location the needs of a wide variety of organisations with the severe limitations of important but decaying eighteenth-century buildings.

The ornately decorated Winter Riding School, formally designed, reflecting the tradition and expectations of the empire at that time, now contrasts with the comparatively austere functionalism of the adjacent Kunsthalle of the City of Vienna, Leopold Museum, and Museum of Modern Art. The exterior of the Kunsthalle is entirely built of red brick, and truncated at both ends. Inserted at either end is a gleaming metallic cantilevered surface. The Kunsthalle is an independent structure that is, however, placed very close to the longitudinal front of the Winter Riding School, and whose brick roof overlaps the ridge of the latter.

The exterior of the Leopold Museum is a white stone cube. It is contrasted by the leaner dark grey stone block of the Museum of Modern Art Ludwig Foundation, Vienna.

The juxtaposition of the historical and contemporary is a surprising and successful feature which epitomises an underlying philosophical approach to the development, that of integrating the past with the present. It is, however, a characteristic of the Quarter that it is only visible from the inside. Externally the new structures cannot be seen; the main front of the building is the original eighteenth-century facade. This solution is the result of a long fought-over compromise between those who wanted the Viennese City Centre to retain its historic form and those advocating contemporary architecture.

There are at least six restaurants, cafes, and bars, with some cafes open until 4:00 am. In addition there are museum bookshops in the Leopold Museum, Museum of Modern Art Ludwig Foundation, Vienna, and the Kunsthalle, a large art bookshop with an attached café in the main entrance, leased out directly by the MuseumsQuartier Development Company. The chairman of the MuseumsQuartier Development Company describes this as "the landlord with his own shop in his own home" and does not perceive this activity as contrary to the facility management purpose of the company or an exploitation of a unique competitive position. In all cases these facilities are sub-contracted to private operators who compete with each other for business and with similar facilities in the individual museums. Little attempt it seems has been made to avoid duplication and overlap, in order to provide the visitor with choice and maximisation of income for the operators. It seems that competition is viewed in this case as healthy and an example of diversity and autonomy at work. However, these activities are an important source of revenue for the MuseumsQuartier Development Company and the museums, and will ultimately rely on a substantial regular flow of visitors throughout the year if they are all to succeed.

Other facilities include a general bookshop, the infopool, a visitor centre, toilets, seating areas, clear signposting, and special tours for groups in German and English. The MuseumsQuartier Development and Operating Company provide all these facilities.

A State Instrument: The MuseumsQuartier (MQ) Company

The MuseumsQuartier Developing and Operating Company, the umbrella organisation, was set up in 1990 to manage the MuseumsQuartier on behalf of the state and city governments. It is a limited company with shareholders, a board of directors and a Chief Executive. The federal government established the terms of reference as:

1. *The objective of the enterprise is ... the planning, construction, maintenance, the administration of the real estate and the management of the MuseumsQuartier ...*
2. *The company is ... entitled to all businesses and measures that are necessary and useful to achieve the aim of the company. The competences of the museums ... are not affected by this entitlement.*
3. *Above all the following activities can be carried out by the company:*

   - *Planning, management and realisation of investments to create the MuseumsQuartier, including the acquisition of areas necessary for the MuseumsQuartier;*
   - *To make available and keep ready rooms, equipment and services for the institutions of the Republic of Austria, above all for the collections and museums of the Republic;*
   - *The acquisition, planning, preparation, organisation and carrying out of exhibitions and events, as well as the organisation and carrying out of related fringe events and leisure time programmes;*
   - *The letting and leasing of rooms in the MuseumsQuartier;*
   - *In connection with the MuseumsQuartier the running of cinemas, distribution and marketing of movies as well as production, showing, distribution and marketing of videos;*
   - *Advertising and P.R. as well as publications for the MuseumsQuartier;*
   - *Visitor services by arranging visits of artistic and educating events etc, also in commission of third parties;*
   - *Running of an information service.* (Grundsatzliche Uberlegungen zur Unterricht und kulturelle Angelegenheitenan den Misterrat vom 26th September 1996)

This company is wholly owned through a share distribution by the state government and the Vienna City Council, the landowners.

The MQ Company has extensive powers, which go well beyond that of typical facilities management functions for a particular site. It has a clearly defined creative programming role.

The letting arrangements, a key remit of the MQ Company as facility managers, are inevitably complex in such a large scheme. The major institutions, for example, are independent organisations with substantial funding from government. However, the city and the state are the primary MQ shareholders, and the main contracts are let to them; they in turn sub-let the contracts to the organisations they fund. Consequently through this mechanism the city and the state determine the tenants for the MuseumsQuartier. In the case of the smaller organisations the contracting takes place through the Quarter 21 administration, which is also managed by the MuseumsQuartier Company. In every case the contracts include a service charge to include keeping the site clean and tidy, which – in combination with the rents – provides a major source of revenue for the company.

Organisational Simplicity, Confusion and the Creative Dilemma

The adopted organisational structure for the MuseumsQuartier is based on a land ownership model, with a limited company, the MQ Company, as the umbrella organisation responsible for the site and its operation including the renting of space (Gesellschaftsvertrag der MuseumsQuartier – Errichtungs – und Betriebsgesellschaft mit beschtankter Haftung 29th March 1999). The company rents space to the nearly 40 cultural organisations such as the Leopold Museum and the Museum of Modern Art Ludwig Foundation, Vienna. (These organisations are autonomous, with their own boards of management and constitutions.) These stakeholders require all the rentable space on the site to be let in order to minimise the annual deficit and enable the company to generate surpluses, which can be used to cross-subsidise the rent for the poorer and smaller cultural organisations.

At one level the organisational relationship is that of landowner and tenant; however, structural disjuncture occurs when the MQ Company engages in cultural promotion and presentation activities or attempts to control the autonomy of the individual organisations through the introduction of common ticketing and telephone systems, as it believes it can. The Mission Statement of the MuseumsQuartier emphasises this:

> ... by seeking as much autonomy as possible and pursuing as many common interests as necessary. The MuseumsQuartier strives for the degree of joint facilities needed for the successful operation of the complex as a whole. (Gesellschaftsvertrag der MuseumsQuartier und Bertriebsgesellschaftmit beschnkter Haftung 29th March 1999)

This has resulted in a loss of independence for tenants and increased competition between tenants and the landlord, leading to a reduction of efficiency and a predictable lack of cohesion. This general situation causes confusion and at times friction over roles and responsibilities, with the independent cultural organisations guarding their autonomy as much as possible and resisting stakeholder funding pressures to conform. These complexities are amplified with the Quarter 21 concept, which is a mechanism to enable the MuseumsQuartier Company to directly control the smaller spaces by choosing the tenants through a selection procedure for the Quarter 21 spaces owned, managed, and let on a short-term basis by the MuseumsQuartier Company. Consequently there seems to be a blurring of the MQ Company role as facilities manager with that of cultural patron, and promoter. This becomes all the more obvious if one takes into account that the implementation of Quarter 21 not only brought new institutions to the MuseumsQuartier but drove out other institutions at the same time. Public Netbase, the Institute for New Culture Technologies, and Depot Art and Discussion – both small institutions that participated in activities against the Austrian right-wing government – were not given acceptable leases within the Quarter 21, although they had been active in the MuseumsQuartier already during construction works.

The management structure of the MQ Company has no formal constitutional relationship with the occupants of the Museums Quarter, which is surprising given the size and nature of the site as well as the number and diversity of tenants. For example there are no representatives from the twenty tenants on the MQ Company board of directors, although there is a formal subcommittee, which includes all tenants chaired by the Director of the MuseumsQuartier Company, who reports to the board. In addition no tenants association or equivalent independent organisation exists to act on their behalf and represent the collective interests of the tenants.

The management model for the MuseumsQuartier is hierarchical, with the company controlled by the state and the city, which indirectly determine the strategic policy and operational decisions. This involvement goes well beyond the conventional facilities management role, incorporating the active engagement in promotion, ticket sales, and programming. Although the organisations in the MuseumsQuartier are constitutionally independent the majority are directly or indirectly funded by the state or city. Consequently the level of autonomy to act independently of the MQ Company is severely curtailed. This situation became especially problematic in the years 2000–2002 when the city government was social-democratic while Austria was governed by a coalition of Christian-Democrats and the extreme right Freedom Party. The habitual competition for public recognition between these two bodies was thus enhanced by their political differences.

Individual programming of events such as exhibitions remains a competition between individual tenants and the MQ Company. Whilst there is a desire to recognise "richness in diversity" by the MuseumsQuartier Company, the demand for cohesion and synergy seems to be the preferred policy.

> — the absolute freedom of art, by which art can attach itself freely to any substance it chooses in order to exercise the imagination on it, has made of the new artist a tabula rasa. Infinitely susceptible to new shapes because no shape can be regarded as final, he is in a state of perpetual self-transformation, engaged in what Hegel quaintly calls unendliche Herumbildung, an infinite plasticity. (Aesthetik II)

The difficulty with a hierarchical structure and control management system is that they fetter the creativity of tenants because creative activity is often about breaking rules, extending boundaries, and challenging conventions. Hegel describes breaking rules and challenging conventions as the means to arrive at new ways of seeing and interpreting the world, that is new knowledge.

The questions then for the MQ Company are whether through the existing management structures creativity can be fostered, and whether the Company can live with the consequences of the outputs that may be at times unpopular and controversial, as Hegel aptly describes. This poses less of a problem for the MQ Company in its relationship with the large state- or city-funded organisations such as the Leopold Museum, where the creative controversy will often rest with the interpretation by the curatorial staff of the collections. However, the conceiving, making, production, and presentation of the contemporary arts present entirely different challenges to the MQ Company managers. There does however seem to be an implicit policy that those chosen to occupy space in Quarter 21 are expected to operate as businesses, by paying rent and meeting their annual operating costs, rather than focusing on creative activities.

The MuseumsQuartier Company understands its role as a developer, facilities, and promotional manager, not least because this is enshrined in the terms of reference and mission determined by the state government when the company was set up. The facilities and promotional management roles have been the priorities for the initial twelve to eighteen months as the site becomes fully operational. However, the management of artistic programming of the site has also commenced with Quarter 21, and the engagement in creative programming stemming from the progressive commissioning of the "common" exhibition and display spaces.

The Stakeholders, State Trusts, Foundations, and Related Legal Structures

The critical stakeholders of the MuseumsQuartier are the Vienna City Council and the federal government. Not only do they own the site but they also have the controlling interest in the MuseumsQuartier Company, and fund directly or indirectly the majority of the organisations occupying the site. The annual subsidies going to the different institutions are estimated at around 14.5m Euros (= $14.3m) if neither the subsidies for the Vienna Festival of 150m ATS nor the annual rates for the purchase of the Leopold

Collection are taken into account. These stakeholders have a multiplicity of interests – the development of an important site in the historic city centre, the perpetuation of major cultural institutions, and support for contemporary arts practice, which are all connected with the promotion of Austria as a world cultural centre. The civil servants see it from the city and the state perspective as a mechanism for re-positioning Austria in the modern world by celebrating the past and showcasing the contemporary.

The Leopold Foundation, one of the major tenants, is a private foundation with a board of governors, 50 per cent of which are state nominees. Although there are aspects of the Foundation structure that reflect the particularities of the Austrian legal system it is recognisable as a model found in other parts of the world. The state Trust model, a similar convention to the Foundation, is used in the MuseumsQuartier by the tenants, and is one used by governments as a means of exercising devolved control, for example Sheffield Museum and Gallery Trust .

In particular national museums have been established as state Trusts with a board of trustees which are autonomous of government, although government approves all the appointments to the board and receives an annual revenue grant from the state. It supposedly gives the managers of the museum or cultural organisation greater freedom to manage, and the Austrian government more flexibility to choose how and at what level to fund the organisation for "agreed" purposes.

Other legal structures that have been adopted are limited companies, which is the preferred model for the MuseumsQuartier Development Company. The association model is popular with smaller cultural organisations as it is relatively easy to establish at low cost, and has little direct government interference, although it is possible for the state, through grants, to influence their governance.

This diversity of legal structures generates additional complexities for the MQ Company as the facilities manager, requiring different tenancy agreements that recognise the legal independence of each organisation. The common factor, however, is that either the state and/or the city of Vienna fund most, if not all, of the cultural organisations of the MuseumsQuartier directly or indirectly.

Financing the MuseumsQuartier and Its Inhabitants: A Public Sector Dinosaur?

The capital cost of converting the stables into workable space and building two new museums is estimated to be over $200m, which has been provided by the city and state governments both as grants and as guarantors for the banks (to facilitate cash flow), who have lent the money to the MQ Company. It has been recognised by the City Council in particular that the MQ Company vehicle was the most efficient devolved mechanism available to city and state for the purposes of a major capital project, and subsequently leasing the rentable space (Boris Marte, Buero des Stadtrates fur Kultur der Stadt Wien).

The revenue needed to operate the site and provide the facilities as well as service the debt is derived from the rents of the occupants. It is expected that the rental income and the service charges will, when the site is fully let, cover all the costs incurred by the Company in repaying the capital debt and servicing and maintaining the site. However, the city and state governments provide the subsidised rentals for the poorer cultural organisations by allowing the Company to run an annual deficit.

There is very little private sector involvement in the MuseumsQuartier, and the commercial activity seems to be centred on the selling of food and drink and books. All venues sell tickets and this, on average, amounts to 10 per cent of the annual revenue for these organisations. Sponsorship is evident, and the MQ Company is actively looking for sponsors; unfortunately, a coordinated strategy with the tenants is not well developed. In addition it is recognised by the federal government that sponsorship is difficult to attract in Austria, as there are few major international companies, and the traditional source of patronage, the aristocracy, is no longer in a position to fulfil this role. From whichever financial perspective the MuseumsQuartier is considered, the city and the state governments are the biggest and most important capital and revenue funders. In reality the federal government is Austria's primary cultural patron, replacing the aristocracy and supported by City Councils (Ministerialrat Dr Rudolf Wran, Bundesministeriuim fuer Bildung, Wissenschaft und Kultur). In general there seems to be little pressure on the managers of the MQ Company to attract visitors because the bulk of the income is derived from the leases, and that is largely guaranteed by the city and/or state governments. In its first full year of operation the MuseumsQuartier attracted 1,116m visitors. Visitor numbers thus only slightly exceeded the forecasted 1.1m, based on a conservative calculation of the 1999 performance of the key museums and centres. However, when this study was undertaken national and international critical acclaim matters, and MuseumsQuartier visitor numbers do not seem to be a critical success factor in financial or cultural terms.

At the time of writing, it does not seem as though the managers in the MuseumsQuartier are under the same pressures as colleagues in North America, Italy, France, the United Kingdom, or Australia in attracting more and more visitors and alternative revenues. For the MuseumsQuartier cultural manger emphasis is placed on the importance and significance of the cultural product and/or service in national and international terms. Artistic critical acclaim is seen as the primary performance indicator.

Cultural Programming, a Question of Control?

With the number and diversity of cultural organisations involved in the MuseumsQuartier, all with a direct interest in programming as the central focus of their work, it is no surprise to find limited cooperation, particularly if artistic critical acclaim is the primary performance indicator. Jealousy and mistrust between the organisations, and collectively with the MuseumsQuartier over-programming, is evident, largely as it relates to the core identity and purpose of the organisations themselves; in other words, their rationale for existence. Although at an informal operational level there is evidence of information exchange, the mechanism for formal interchange and exchange of ideas, plans and future activities, has noticeable limitations as a communication tool. In particular, the representatives of the institutions are only able to make recommendations for action, which can be accepted or rejected by the MuseumsQuartier board and management.

This safeguarding of the individual organisational identity through the protection of programming is unsurprising, although there is an inevitable danger in duplication, overlap, and confusion. Consequently, there is little in the way of formal joint exhibition and event planning, as it is expected that as programming is a "creative" activity organisations and individuals will build up their own relationships over time, which may lead to future collaboration. At present there is no incentive to collaborate, and particularly with the MuseumsQuartier. The diverse and ad hoc nature of the programme offerings is perceived as a strength and the Quarter's attractiveness to the visitor. This is underlined by the federal government, "which values the freedom of the arts", sees no need for "artistic" cooperation and does not wish to interfere directly in the affairs of individual cultural organisations, even though it funds them (Ministerialrat Dr Rudolf Wran, Bundesinisterium fur Bildung, Wissenschaft und Kultur).

This "richness in diversity" approach has conveniently sidestepped other complications such as joint education and marketing programmes. In the case of education, the large museums, the children's museums and creativity centre, as well as the Architektur Zentrum Wien, all have a direct interest in children and relationships with schools. A similar pattern can be detected for public lectures and discussions. Staff are employed on behalf of their organisations to develop and deliver educational and marketing programmes, with no formal interaction or channels of communication to facilitate the sharing of practice, ideas, and information between the tenants and the MuseumsQuartier Company.

Marketing and Branding the MuseumsQuartier

The one obvious area of common interest and mutual benefit for all concerned in the MuseumsQuartier is marketing, including branding. Yet confusion abounds, and fragmentation exists between the individual organisations and the MQ Company over roles and responsibilities. When preparing the case, there seemed to be a general lack of internal communication between the tenants and the Company – a central tenet of marketing – with no agreed marketing strategy, which includes all parties and their activities. The Leopold Museum, for example, has its own marketing plan without reference to the Museum of Modern Art or the Kunsthalle. Similarly the Vienna Festival plans seem to have little relevance to the Architektur Zentrum Wien programme, Quarter 21, and the Children's Museum activities, let alone the museums and galleries. The Company, however, accepts responsibility for marketing and branding of the Quarter as a location, but sees the marketing of programmes is an "individual" matter left to the tenants themselves regardless of how confusing this may be to visitors.

The Company expecting to "arouse the curiosity of the old and new target groups" (MQ Company Marketing Plan 2001) with an annual expectation of attracting 1.1m visitors, with the Leopold Museum as the star attraction with around 250,000 to 300,000 visitors a year.

For all this there has been some limited consultation and discussion between the MQ Company (location and branding marketers) and the tenants (specific brand image/communication concept marketers) about how they want to be represented in the marketing literature produced to promote the location. This is indicative of the structural fault lines that have resulted in a lack of effective communication channels. Although there is an established logo for the MuseumsQuartier, described as "simple, practical, effective, consciously non-artistic" (MQ Briefing Information 2001), it has not yet been enthusiastically adopted by the tenants, and used only partly in their literature and general marketing.

Many of the organisations generate temporary exhibitions and tour these shows nationally and internationally, with associated lecture programmes and education services for children, all of which need marketing. There is little evidence of working collaboratively, a lack of understanding of the benefits of supporting each other in strategic partnerships, and the MQ Company's failure to promulgate these concepts. For the Company to do this requires an overall strategy to be developed, agreed by all concerned, resourced, and realised. There is a general consensus that the MuseumsQuartier and its marketing activities are expected to increase visitor numbers for the tenants, and that this growth is largely through international tourists. Much of the evidence and understanding of the existing audience is derived from tenant ticket sales. For example, the Kunsthalle, with around 160,000 visitors in 1999, has identified that 80 per cent of them are under forty years old, 51 per cent come from the city and 24 per cent are overseas visitors. There are an equal number of men and women, with a high number of students. The Museum of Modern Art Ludwig Foundation, Vienna, attracted between 110,000 to 150,000 visitors in 1999 to its two sites in the city, and expects to at least maintain 150,000 visitors in the new premises in the MuseumsQuartier, with a higher proportion of overseas tourists. The Vienna Festival is well established and with the new and expanded facilities predicts paying audiences of around 200,000.

The smaller organisations are largely serving local, regional, and national cultural markets, often associated with practitioners, critics, and curators. It is expected that the MuseumsQuartier will act as a "honey pot" for practitioners and a visible focal point for international collaboration. How this is to be measured remains unclear, and whether this reflects the nature of creative practice is yet to be seen. For all this there remains deep distrust between the tenants and the Company, and between tenants themselves, and consequently there is a reticence to share what is perceived as sensitive "commercial" information about visitors.

The Last of the Big Spenders or an International Exemplar?

What is perhaps the most surprising aspect of this project is the willingness of the Austrian government at national and city level to commit substantial levels of capital and revenue funds on cultural activity in a time of public sector constraint. This can be regarded as a bold and welcomed example to the world or the last vestiges of an old empire, just as France and the United Kingdom have been required to reinvent roles as a result of the loss of empire. The close interrelation between the state and the arts can be understood as a legacy of Joseph II, the son of Maria Theresia, who started this tradition (Marchart 1999). Whatever else is said regarding this project the management challenges are considerable. The key to future success is how the MuseumsQuartier reinvents itself after the building works are complete and the business of attracting visitors comes to the fore, along with the need to make Quarter 21 work as a centre for the development of creative businesses.

Is this, however, the ultimate cultural palace? The Quarter can be described as the ultimate cultural palace as far as the city and the state is concerned, but the problem lies in the perception of the cultural tourist, which has yet to be seen. Although the Quarter has set out to combine the business of presentation with practice epitomised by the establishment of Quarter 21 alongside the Leopold Museum, it has yet to be proved whether this combination will work. There are no formal mechanisms for genuine interchange between tenants to encourage interaction between presentation and practice. There is also a danger that the practice activity is seen as a showpiece for the public which has never worked in the past and is likely to drive creators elsewhere. What also follows from this is whether the management and related structures are capable of encompassing the essential anarchy of artistic practice. The indications are that the structures that have been put in place are set up to enable the state and city to exercise control and hence aesthetic judgement, public patrons, Public Netbase and Depot being cases in point. Is this a desirable model for the wellbeing of cultural activity in Austria?

What is difficult to understand in the Quarter is whether the original intention of saving a national heritage site and meeting the housing needs of a number of cultural organisations has been overtaken by a desire to engage in the new cultural agenda, the creative industries. Consequently, the need for a long-term, negotiated, agreed, and realistic strategy has never been stronger, and a shared vision has yet to materialise. Disappointingly, there is little evidence to suggest that this development will make a tangible difference to the individual practitioner in the city, except for those who are lucky enough to be chosen to occupy ateliers as artists in residence or rent space in Quarter 21. If anything there are emerging concerns that cultural resources from the city and the state will be jeopardised as the Quarter 21 develops.

Despite this development making best use of an important set of buildings, and answering the housing the arts crisis, it is doubtful if any measurable expansion of the activity in the city is likely to occur as a result. However, there is little doubt in the early stages the Quarter will be an attractive focal point for cultural activity.

In a wider context, however, the MuseumsQuartier has already changed cultural activity in Vienna as it is clearly attracting cultural initiatives to the surrounding area. Small galleries and arts mediating institutions settle down around the MQ, complementing in this way the small creative businesses in the area behind the MQ. Whilst the success of the MQ itself still has to be proved its animating effects on its surroundings can already be seen.

Vienna MuseumsQuartier Features and Benefits

A grand vision for an old city to reassert itself as a major cultural centre in the world. The solution to resolving accommodation crises for cultural organisations in Vienna. The use for a major grade one listed building in the heart of the city, which has remained derelict for many years.

A visionary architectural approach combining graded property with twenty-first century designed architecture, to provide a dynamic, exciting, and vibrant environment;

A galleraria, with shops, bookstores, restaurants, cafes, and cultural production and presentation all on one site.

A combined and concerted approach to marketing the MuseumsQuartier for the benefit of individual organisations.

A unique centre for creative industries production, Quarter 21, and major cultural icons such as the Leopold Museum.

The critical mass approach to attracting visitors, locally, nationally, and particularly internationally.

A public sector-led and controlled development, incorporating City Council and state- funded cultural organisations that spent $200m capital on the project.

Tension exists between highly creative organisations, and the regulatory framework necessary to operate the Museums Quarter by the management company, which is owned and by the city and state.

The major investment over the long-term to establish Vienna as an international contemporary cultural centre, not just a centre known for its music.

The interactions between the different organisations within one physical location has yet to be worked through.

The establishment of the Management Company with clear marketing responsibility and identity for the Museum Quarter is innovative, and generating the general profile, which benefits the individual organisations.

The reputation of the organisations can be enhanced by being associated with the Quarter, and in particular the smaller organisations stand to benefit from this clustering, far more so that the large organisations. In the case of the larger organisations, benefits are likely to accrue from increased international visitors and an enhanced profile on the world cultural stage if the MuseumsQuartier is effectively marketed as a location.

Jobs have been and continue to be created in the Quarter, and a set of buildings have been brought back into use, along with the first glimmers of increased creative industry activity in the immediate vicinity. There is a potential through Quarter 21 to develop creativity and businesses, as well as "artistic endeavour", which may provide a catalyst for further expansion of creative businesses in the city if the management system is flexible enough in the future.

6.2 The Geelong Cultural Precinct, Australia

Introduction

In 2007 it was announced with much fanfare that the Australian city of Greater Geelong and the Victorian state government would jointly fund the development of a new Master Plan for the Cultural Precinct[3] of the city. This move built on over 150 years of investment in key cultural institutions in particular a regional Art Gallery (first opened in 1890), a major parkland (developed from 1872), the Central Library (1959) and Heritage Centre, a performing arts centre (1980), and an Old Courthouse Building. In addition, the city wanted to reconceptualise its image, reorient its fractured manufacturing economy, reactivate its city centre and reinvigorate its social fabric by investing heavily in the creative arts. The Cultural Precinct designation has a particular history in this regional city of 120,000 inhabitants which colours its form and role. The new approach to, and expansion of, the city's Cultural Precinct also marks a shift in attitude to the arts from primarily consumption to a greater emphasis on creative activity and the key cultural institutions being more about production, economic opportunities, skills, and community wellbeing.

History of Geelong and Its Major Cultural Institutions

Located 75km south-west of the Victorian capital city of Melbourne, the state's second city of Geelong began as a wool port and agricultural processing centre before becoming a major car and truck manufacturing city by the mid-twentieth century. With an array of related industrial operations – oil refining, aluminium smelting, car components, and glass-making – as well as a significant textile and clothing industry, the city was hard hit by the decline of Australian manufacturing from the 1970s (Rich 1987; Fagan and Webber 1999).

Table 1: Components of the Geelong Cultural Precinct (Sources: Begg 1990, organisations' websites).

Building/Spaces	Initial Construction	Modifications
Johnstone Park	Originally Western Gully watercourse to Corio Bay. Made into a park in 1872 to enhance the Town Hall. Named after a former mayor, it gained a wooden bandstand in 1873.	In 1872, the park was divided when the railway was extended. 1887 it was reduced further when the Gordon Technical College was built. 1919 War Memorial built. Belcher Fountain relocated to the park in 1912 and moved in 1956, 2006 and 2008.
Geelong Town Hall	Foundation stone laid in April 1855 when the southern wing was built.	1917 completed with the original design. Minor additions to the rear.
Geelong Art Gallery	The Art Gallery Society initially used the Town Hall from 1895. The Gallery was opened in 1915 on the western side of Johnston Park between the Town Hall and the former fire station (now Library). Initial building had a portico and vestibule facing the park and G.M. Hitchcock Gallery.	1928 Henry P. Douglas Galley 1937 H.F. Richardson Gallery 1938 J.H. McPhilling Gallery 1956 and 1971 expansions
Geelong Regional Library	Formerly a fire station; 1959 current building	Adds the Geelong Historical Records Centre (now the Geelong Heritage Centre) in the 1970s. 2009 Proposed to be a new revamped Community Cultural and Learning Hub, geared especially to accessing and using new technologies for the young but also community-wide.
Old Court House Building		1994 becomes the Court House Youth Theatre and Café. Home to "Back to Back" theatre. 2010 planned refurbishment with A$6.6 investment from the state.
Geelong Performing Arts Centre (GPAC)	Site chosen in the 1970s had a number of existing buildings: Temperance Hall built in 1858–1959. Demolished in 1978 for GPAC. Mechanics Institute opened in 1856. Destroyed by fire in 1927 it was replaced by the Plaza Theatre, now incorporated into GPAC with retail shops on the Ryrie St frontage. Steeple Congregational Church – opened in 1857 and altered in 1910 with the Band of Hope building now part of GPAC.	2009 plans to refurbish the Ford Theatre with a A$3m allocation.

With the systematic opening of the Australian economy to foreign competition from 1973, the industrial base of Geelong contracted dramatically, with high levels of unemployment and abandoned plant as companies either closed, moved or replaced labour with new technology (see Johnson 1990). Initial responses within the city were to create new industrial and business estates, offer relocation packages, and revitalise its central business core around retailing. The latter strategy was developed further in the light of successful waterfront restoration projects in the United States and United Kingdom, by introducing development plans for the "City by the Bay" and "Steampacket Place". Along the Geelong waterfront, through a mix of urban design, public art, building restorations and re-use, tourist attractions and facilities, the entire city was reoriented towards its bay-front and a new consumption economy focused on tourism, recreation, and spectacle (Johnson 2006, 2009a and 2009b).

Whilst deemed successful by many, for others there was still scope to further develop the arts foundation of the city through a bold bid for a southern hemisphere Guggenheim Museum. With Bilbao as its model, over the late 1990s and into the new century, key business men, the regional tourist authority, and local government worked with the state government to commission feasibility studies and designs as well as to court the interest of the Guggenheim Foundation and its mercurial director, Thomas Krens. Amidst significant expenditure and heated debate within Geelong about the proposed cultural icon project, the idea imploded, primarily because of financial problems with the Guggenheim operation in New York and the scale of funds needed locally to support it (see GBN 2000; Carr 2002; Johnson 2009a and 2009b).

But the value of the creative arts in realising a host of regional objectives was not seriously undermined by this experience. On the contrary, with the obvious success of public art along the waterfront, the city growing rapidly and restructuring successfully towards community, business, recreation, and personal services, it seemed that the possibility of being not so much a Cultural Capital but a magnet for the Creative Class, as theorised by Richard Florida, was an achievable goal (2002, 2003, 2005). And it is in this context that the proposal to redevelop and extend the Civic and Cultural Precinct was viewed.

With the failure to lure a Guggenheim Museum, Geelong adopted a Florida-inspired agenda that located the arts within an overall package of promoting the city to both its residents and investors. As a result, an array of city and regional strategic plans positioned the creative arts and cultural heritage as one of seven fundamental "pillars" of the region and proceeded to map their importance, incorporate the views of their practitioners, and identify priorities for further development. A key "Lighthouse Project" was designated from within the Arts and Cultural Heritage Pillar Group and this involved converting a relatively un-coordinated set of cultural institutions into a Cultural Precinct. Such a move could only occur because of the historical legacy of parks and civic buildings that had been created close to the city centre over the previous centuries. As table 1 indicates, the components of what became this precinct have much longer histories as centres of artistic and cultural activity.

The Cultural Precinct

With the failure of the bid to secure a Guggenheim for the waterfront then, the city shifted to a broader quest to value the creative arts as a key pillar of the region and, after a lengthy consultation process, through the redesign and expansion of its Cultural Precinct. To date more than A$500,000 has been devoted to its master planning and over A$9m committed by the Victorian state government to extend and refurbish GPAC (Aust$3m) and the Courthouse Youth Theatre (Aust$6.5m). All of these institutions as well as, the Geelong Art Gallery, the Historical Records Centre, Back to Back Theatre and Geelong Library, are to be moulded into an integrated precinct (GPC Masterplan Project Update Vol. 3 and 4). These developments are located within a broader arts and cultural strategy to "increase appreciation of diversity, arts and culture", and are absorbing the lion's share of inner city development resources but providing "a vibrant heart of cultural activity in the G21 region" (G21 Region Plan 2007, pp. 64–65). The refurbishment also signals a move for the institutions involved from presentation and consumption to being more about production and dissemination. This change of emphasis also involves reconceptualising the arts in terms of broader social and economic outcomes.

Historically this area, located close to the CBD of the city and overlooking a major park, had accommodated a major Art Gallery and, more recently a performing arts centre, public library and historical records office (see table 1). The area is also the location for other important civic buildings, a nineteenth-century Court House and the Town Hall. Consequently it has been known as the Civic Precinct for much of its history. However, by the early 2000s, the idea of focusing one part of the inner city on the creative arts gained currency. Thus in 2003 the G21 Region Strategic Plan noted as one of its "regionally significant projects", the "development of a Regional Cultural Precinct that recognises opportunities for ... existing and new infrastructure to support the arts, conferencing, research, learning and telecommunications" (G21 Strategic Plan 2003, p. 10). As a "Lighthouse Project" for the region and one supported by the Arts and Cultural Heritage Pillar Group as well as a host of stakeholders, development of the Precinct came to represent the importance of the arts and their spatial concentration to Geelong's future economic, social, and cultural development. Such an emphasis has not been without its critics, who point to the enormous concentration of resources on already established and well-funded institutions at the expense of smaller, emergent and often more innovative organisations. There has also been a questioning of the spatial concentration on the inner city at the expense of investment in other parts of the region. Thus, for example, the councillor for the working-class and multicultural northern suburbs of Geelong has asked rhetorically why there are not plans to develop a Cultural Precinct there. Arguing that new immigrant groups to the area lack spaces to gather and express their cultural identities, she looks askance at the energy, dollars, and planning emphasis placed on inner city facilities which cater for already well-heeled patrons (Corio-Norlane Research Forum 2009).

Despite such reservations, however, development of the central Cultural Precinct is proceeding apace. The concept plan involved a review of existing facilities as well as opportunities presented by the redevelopment of the nearby Western Wedge – a blighted zone in transition extending from the central railway station to the waterfront – and work on revitalising the retail core of the city. Thus the 'City of Geelong City Plan 2008–12' includes a film and TV strategy, a major events strategy, central Geelong place management, CBD retail strategy, and the 'Geelong Cultural Precinct Master Plan' (Positive Solutions 2009). The resulting project involves an enhanced Public Library integrated with the Heritage Centre, performing arts centre and Art Gallery, the recognition, upgrade and integration of other existing cultural and heritage facilities including the old Court House (currently used as a youth theatre) and improved links between key heritage buildings and transport services (G21 Strategic Plan 2003, p. 21). The anticipated benefits of the project reflect the Pillar Group concerns which are economic development, health and wellbeing, lifelong learning, telecommunications, research, recreation, and transport. There is an expectation that this culturally-led project can deliver:

- Opportunities for greater regional community engagement in the arts, culture and heritage and lifelong learning which will have a positive impact on community wellbeing;
- Fostering of tourism and economic development opportunities;
- Nurturing of the capability of artists and providing them with improved opportunities and training within the region;
- Facilitation of improved identification, management and presentation of the region's heritage assets; and
- improved community capability with respect to research and telecommunications (G21 Strategic Plan 2003, p. 21).

Table 2: Usage and Visitation Rates at Key Cultural Institutions in Central Geelong 2004–2009 (*The Wool Museum and Costa Hall are not within the proposed Precinct, but are close by. Source: Paton 2009b)

Institution within the Cultural Precinct	Visitation rates in:	
	2004/5	2008/9
Geelong Art Gallery	42,707	51,832
Geelong Regional Library	248,901	211,507
Courthouse Youth Arts Centre (total of audiences and participants in workshops)	(2005/6) 1,034	4,116
Geelong Performing Arts Centre (GPAC)	152,428	147,700
Geelong Heritage Centre	9,347	6,748
National Wool Museum*	25,173	37,935
Costa Hall* (Part of Deakin University but administered by GPAC)	57,737	69,498

Public sector investment is therefore seen as stimulating the regional economy, growing the number of tourist visitors, providing contemporary facilities for a growing city population (expected to reach over 300,000 by 2031) as well as collaborative cultural opportunities (Positive Solutions 2009, p. 5). In other words, this cultural precinct is to deliver enhanced levels of artistic activity, capability, and training as well as greater access; higher levels of community wellbeing; expanded lifelong learning; support tourism and boost economic development. In addition to this extensive list is the facilitating of heritage management and improved research and communications. It is an ambitious agenda which has general support but by necessity has been scaled down into a more modest set of proposals which focus on refurbishing and extending the cultural institutions that currently occupy the designated precinct area. As a result the overall aim is to grow and enhance existing cultural investments, to broaden their appeal, update their infrastructure, and expand their reach from being primarily about consumption by a narrow social group to involve more locally generated production (Paton 2009a).

This project comes at a time when the cultural consumption of the key institutions has stalled. As table 2 indicates, it was only the large Costa Hall, the Courthouse Youth Arts Centre and the Geelong Art Gallery that have successfully and consistently increased participant numbers from 2004/5 to 2008/9.

Thus despite extensive outreach and engagement with metropolitan performances, GPACs attendances are declining along with visitation rates at the regional library and heritage centre (Paton 2009a). This decline may be due to the long-term lack of investment as there is an agreed need amongst arts professionals in the region to physically update these facilities. For example the gallery cannot house let alone display most of its collection; the library is sorely lacking in the new necessary technologies to be useful as an information hub while GPACs age is clearly registered on its building. The need for investment in the various institutions in this precinct is therefore acute. However, such a local set of objectives, which consume large amounts of capital, sit uneasily with the larger agenda demanded by city planners for the arts.

The overall objective is for the reinvigorated precinct to reflect the much loftier ambitions that the creative arts have held in this city for over two decades. Such ambitions are echoed in other cities around the world as they consciously reinvent their images, social lives, and economies around the arts (see Johnson 2009b). Thus the redevelopment of this precinct is expected to grow the cultural life of the city; in particular its artists and audiences through more high quality activity; its infrastructure through refurbishment and expansion to provide amongst other things spaces and opportunities for local cultural identity expression. In addition, the Precinct is expected to improve the social fabric through higher levels of participation, greater social cohesion, development of new audiences, better urban public spaces, and support for the local economy by growing training and employment prospects as well as visitation rates and tourism. All these benefits are deemed necessary to repositioning Geelong as a desirable place to live, work, and visit which in turn can underpin and support the inward investment of new

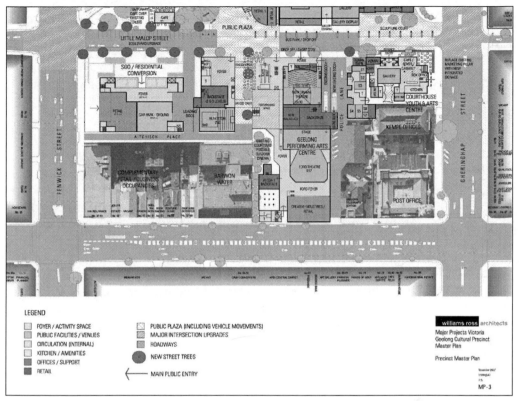

Figure 1: Master Planning the New Geelong Cultural Precinct (Source: Victorian Major Projects, copyright Victorian Government).

firms and people as well as the retention of the existing population, especially those with higher education qualifications (Positive Solutions 2009).

The 'Geelong Cultural Precinct Master Plan' not only ensures spatial unity through urban design, pedestrianisation, and public art (figure 1), but also through other plans for common marketing, the sharing of box office and cleaning facilities, and a coordination of major events, public space usage, and an array of retail, and eating spaces. The aim is to generate more cross over audiences to make going to the theatre or gallery a less formal affair. All of this will occur in street and eating places, not just in the arts spaces. The key institutions in the Precinct are also expected to generate more artistic production. The further aim is therefore to both activate the existing consumption facilities and support the creation of cultural product with rehearsal spaces, workshops, and outreach activities. Such ambitions are integral to the planning of the Precinct, but so far funds have only been allocated to refurbish the main theatre, GPAC. So whilst the overall Cultural Precinct Plan is highly ambitious – encompassing production not just consumption, impacting on the whole city as well as the arts – its realisation is very much a long-term project, dependent on the ongoing allocation of substantial amounts of government funding.

6.3 Pawtucket, Rhode Island, United States, Turns to Artists for Its Revitalisation

Arts and Cultural Quarters, or cultural districts as they are called in the United States, are readily gaining recognition as important policy tools for community planning and redevelopment, particularly for once-vibrant, older industrial cities. Policy tools are instruments or plans of action undertaken by a municipality in achieving social, economic, political, or aesthetic goals with a clearly delineated outcome in mind. They include designated areas as arts and cultural districts or enterprise zones and in implementing strategies such as rent control, tax breaks, and tax stabilisation and subsidies for individuals, developers, and corporations. Pawtucket, Rhode Island employed all of these tools in its effort to fill empty real estate and to renew the face of its once vital downtown. The city began achieving goals by turning to artists and other small creative businesses and entrepreneurs as partners in an effort to rejuvenate its city core. The city also realised that many of the same strategies it had used to attract other small business to its downtown could be applied to the creative sector and, in doing so, rediscovered how location, innovative technology, individual creativity, as well as just plain true grit can play a role in urban vitality.

Pawtucket, Rhode Island

Pawtucket, population 73,142, is located in the north-east corridor of the United States approximately four miles north of Providence, Rhode Island and 40 miles south of Boston, Massachusetts, in one of the most populous and travelled sections of the United States. Pawtucket rose to fame as the "birthplace" of the American industrial revolution when Samuel Slater left England in 1793 on an entrepreneurial mission to make his mark in what was then the new creative economy of water-powered mills. Slater built and operated the first cotton spinning machine in the United States in Pawtucket on the banks of the Blackstone River, a mighty spigot spanning two states that would fuel much of the growing textile industry in this area. The idea caught on and fuelled the growth of similar commerce throughout America.

As a result, Pawtucket soon became a major industrial force in the United States boasting over 70 mills that employed hundreds of workers. During its heyday, the city was a hub of enterprise, with fabric, yarn and other related goods as its signature wares. Yet by the middle part of the twentieth century, Pawtucket had witnessed an exodus of many of the vibrant, large mill businesses that had become its hallmark as the manufacturing capital of Rhode Island. Whilst the city still had a strong business presence in some of the mills outside its downtown, occupied by such companies as major toy giant Hasbro, its downtown was dying and its industrial and tax base was shrinking. Thus, the city realised that it needed a new economic development strategy to turn itself around. Yet like many older post-industrial cities, it found there were few new, large-scale businesses to attract. As a result, Pawtucket, like nearby Providence, Rhode Island's capital city, chose to think "outside the box" in developing an urban renewal strategy featuring an arts and cultural district to jumpstart its revitalisation with artists and other creative workers as its main clientele.

Pawtucket's Rebirth

There were three main stages involved in Pawtucket's rebirth. The first was in the city seeing the empty and under-utilised mills as a resource and an asset rather than a liability, and using preservation and historic tax credits as well as tax stabilisation treaties as tools to fill these mills with artists and small arts businesses. The second phase was in designating 307 acres in its downtown as a cultural district and borrowing on an innovative tax strategy from neighboring Providence that exempts artists who live and work in the district from sales and income tax on original works produced within its borders. Finally, the city codified these moves through an inclusive planning process that resulted in them being added to Pawtucket's Comprehensive City Plan. The city also formally designated Herb Weiss, a member of the Department of Planning and Redevelopment, as a the liaison to both businesses and the arts community and put him in charge over overseeing the relationship with both artists and developers. This was a crucial move in uniting the two, often adversarial groups, under the common cause of creating safe and affordable live/work spaces for artists and profitable ventures for developers and the city. With the political support of Mayor James E. Doyle behind this effort, the municipal government took a direct, hands-on approach to attracting artists and small arts businesses to the city, and as a result, became a local, national, and international model of an arts-friendly, forward-thinking, creative industries approach to city planning that incorporated a number of key components explained in the following paragraphs.

The Mills as Assets

The key to Pawtucket's revitalisation was in seeing its vacant and under-utilised mills as assets, not as liabilities. Rather than an urban renewal policy of demolishing unwanted properties to make room for the new that so decimated much of the historic richness of many urban New England communities, such as New Haven, Connecticut, Pawtucket sought to capitalise on its existing buildings, reframing and redesigning them for a twenty-first-century economy. Yet whilst recognising the aesthetic and historic value of its mills,

Pawtucket never lost sight of its hard-scrabble, working-class roots and regarded the mills as under-utilised work spaces and recognised the potential of artists and small arts and creative business as part of its urban renewal and workforce development strategy; not simply a component of its non-profit, arts policy funding commitment. Rather, it saw the arts as part of a spectrum, ranging from the non-profit community-based festivals and neighbourhood programmes, to the new wave of freelance and small arts businesses, which was instrumental to the city's total arts and cultural policy and key to its financial turnaround. Pawtucket also developed policies that worked to keep creative workers living and working in the area for the long haul, not as described in the Richard Florida (2002, 2005) model of viewing artists as itinerate, sometimes unwilling agents in achieving some larger urban renewal vision. As Pawtucket and its city officials are proud to say, Pawtucket "talks the talk and walks the walk" for artists and small arts businesses and always saw artists as small businesses with long-term potential for the city's growth.

The results of Pawtucket's strategy are apparent as more than 70m properties and complexes currently house live/work artist studios, offices, and manufacturing firms. They employ almost 1,000 individuals in a US state with almost 13 per cent unemployment in 2010. Whilst the city has not remained unscathed, it is clear that without such a strategy to attract artists and small arts business for the long haul that Pawtucket would not be in the position it is in today. The city estimates that its arts initiative will ultimately fill over 2m ft^2 of space in the commercial buildings and mills with arts live/work lofts, studios, performance spaces, and small businesses throughout the city. In large measure, this new mode of thinking about cultural districts transformed the way in which the arts and artists were perceived by policy makers, investors, and even artists themselves, placing the emphasis more on their economic role as arts businesses as much as recognising them for the their traditional aesthetic and societal roles. This "second wave" of cultural district thinking defines the arts as an individual as much as a collective enterprise, with creativity at its core. In many instances its goal is to attract artists and other creative workers in filling urban spaces such as lofts, abandoned and under-utilised mills, tenements, and other light industrial buildings, as well as other urban settings such as Brownfield sites (Galligan 2008). Examples of some of the mill projects in Pawtucket are included below.

a) Blackstone Studios

In 1985 internationally recognised restaurant designer Morris Nathanson and his wife, Phyllis, bought the vacant mill once home to the Rhode Island Cardboard Box Company and began the process of seeing mills as potential live/work spaces for artists and small arts businesses. They transformed 25,000ft^2 of unoccupied space into Blackstone Studios, creating thirteen living spaces and studios. It is important to note that Blackstone Studios was the one of the first legal live/work loft conversions created in Pawtucket and the state. Whilst there had been some artists who set up living quarters in artist studios illegally, the Nathansons worked with the city's Planning Department to make their venture legal and in compliance with all aspects of the city's building and fire codes. This initiative heralded the

Photographer, Sal Mancini.

beginnings of a sound working relationship between artists and the city that laid down the basis for future public/private collaboration with the city, local artists, and arts businesses. Since that time, the Nathansons have sold 25,000ft^2 of vacant adjoining mill space for twelve creative sector additional studios and perhaps more importantly have served as an inspiration to other artists and developers.

b) Riverfront Lofts
Then next major development in re-visioning the mills as assets came when Boston-based developer Ranne P. Warner invested $1.5m in redeveloping Riverfront Lofts adjacent to

Blackstone Studios in 2001. This rehabilitation project converted the former Lebanon Mills into over 110,000ft² of live/work space as part of 59 new condominium units. The impact for the city was enormous. Before renovation, the empty mill brought the City of Pawtucket $17,000 in property taxes. In 2008, the city collected $250,000 in taxes. The developer took advantage of Rhode Island historic preservation tax credits and was granted a ten-year real estate tax phase-in. Units in this mill range from $150,000–$600,000, so tax incentives and treaties were an important component in the realisation of this project.

c) Bayley Lofts

Another Pawtucket success story is Bayley Street Lofts, located in what was the former Parkin Yarn mill. Long vacant, it now houses 25 live/work "condos" in a five-storey brick building. It offers twenty units at market rate and five units at a discounted more affordable rate for first-time buyers, further buoyed by the current economic stimulus incentives in the United States. Its developers also took advantage of Rhode Island historic tax credits.

Photograph by Frank Mullin courtesy of Hope Artiste Village.

d) Hope Artiste Village

There are a number of examples of highly successful mill developments outside the city's formal downtown arts and cultural district as well as studios rehabilitated by area artists as mentioned above. Hope Artiste Village is near the Providence line and includes an eclectic mix of arts businesses, artist live/work lofts, restaurants and other residences in one of the largest mill renovation projects in Rhode Island history. The historic mill of 600,000ft² that once housed a candy factory now includes office suites that are at 80 per cent occupancy and the rest under construction. It features eleven live/work artist lofts and inside retail space that suggests an arcade-like atmosphere where artists and small arts and creative businesses work inside glass doors where shoppers can stroll in an indoor environment. This set-up was so popular that the highly successful farmers' market sets up in the corridors on Saturdays during the winter, giving further exposure to the retail shops in the complex. The final phase could potentially include 134 residences. It now houses over 80 small businesses, creative sector companies, and artists, employing almost 300 people.

e) Properties Developed by Richard Kazarian

Richard Kazarian, a nationally known antique dealer and designer, has brought much energy to Pawtucket's redevelopment effort. He first purchased the former U-Pick Shoe Store located in the downtown area and converted 2,190ft^2 into a home/studio. He has been instrumental in buying, selling, and converting similar space into antique and auction properties, including a former Elks Club.

f) Other Examples

Inspired by these successes and the friendly arts-business climate create by the city and its planning department, more private mill developments large and small began to spring up. They include the silk-screen company that houses twelve artists in studios in 22,000ft^2 of space at a former cotton yarn mill on Fountain Street. A former five-and-dime store also became home to a number of working artists as did a host of buildings along Main Street in the downtown area. Another example of effective development is a former furniture store in the downtown area converted to live/work space by an architect/designer team. Another artist bought the former, long-vacant Rhode Island Hospital Trust Bank building and converted it into artist studios. In addition individuals have developed studio space within the city, including well-known artists Gretchen Dow Simpson and Mimo Gordon Riley, amongst others.

Incentives for Development and Growth

Pawtucket has fostered growth by attracting large and small-scale project developers as well as encouraging individual artists and small business to buy or rent properties. It has done this by creating a database of all available commercial and industrial property that is updated quarterly, by assisting developers obtain tax credits and treaties, and in providing key information about zoning, housing, and fire safety codes. The Planning Department has also taken a personal interest in the artists and creative businesses that move into the city and have often helped them locate space and move into it, as well as promote them as part of the city's thriving working artist community.

Yet none of this would have been possible without an innovative funding strategy to assist developers and potential artists and business. This included tapping into federal, state and local incentives to make the redevelopment of the mills a reality. As the mills were deemed historic properties, developers were able to obtain both federal and state historic preservation tax credits to finance their renovation. This is important for two reasons: first, many banks were unwilling to provide financing for mill restoration as it was both costly and risky as many had been vacant for a long time. Second, historic tax credits could be sold to third parties and converted to cash and this made them very attractive to large corporations and businesses that needed tax deductions and to developers who needed money to finance their projects. As such, developers could sell the credits for a percentage of their actual cost, thus giving them the needed capital for the renovations. Pawtucket has been highly effective in promoting these programmes and assisted developers in securing them.

A second tax strategy used by the city was to offer individual developments tax stabilisation treaties ranging from three to ten years. By offering such a gradual phase-in real estate property tax, it allowed buyers to take the risk of buying property in the mills that would otherwise be prohibited. It also transmitted the message that Pawtucket wanted artists as long-term tenants and that they would be treated like any other small business. Yet perhaps the most innovative and successful state tax incentive Pawtucket employed was in creating an arts and cultural district in its downtown that gave artists who lived and worked in the district a waiver from paying state sales and income tax from the creation of original works they sold.

The Creation of the Cultural District

In 1998 Pawtucket went to the Rhode Island General Assembly to lobby for the creation of a 307 acre district. At that time there were approximately only 90 arts and cultural districts scattered across the United States. Since then, thirteen commercial buildings, many vacant, unused and under-utilised in the historic downtown core, have been purchased by artists or creative sector companies. This bold attempt at urban renewal would create the largest cultural district in America. It would also take advantage of one of the most innovative tax incentive policy tools, sales and income tax breaks for individual artists pioneered in the United States by neighboring Providence, Rhode Island's capital city.

After learning of Dublin's Temple Bar's experiment with tax incentives for artists and other creatives who lived and worked in the district (Roodhouse 2006), the Mayor of Providence crafted a plan to do the same, virtually creating a brand identity for the city that accentuated the richness of Providence's artistic past as he sought to entice the new type of arts and creative workers heralded by Richard Florida to live and work in its downtown artists' districts. To accomplish this, he promised an exemption from sales and income tax to all who created original works within the district's boundaries. But the "artist zone" never truly materialised as the rents in the district were well out of the reach of most working artists. In fact, less than a dozen took advantage of the tax credit and most artists actually wound up living and working outside the downtown, even though Brown University and the Rhode Island School of Design were producing first-rate workers within walking distance of the designated district.

On the other hand, Pawtucket had a wealth of vacant space and could attract artists from Providence, Boston and elsewhere with reasonable rents and easy access to major universities and East Coast hubs. Realtors could afford to charge far less for light industrial space that was conducive for many artists. In addition, as the Pawtucket Department of Planning and Redevelopment was a partner in this effort, artists had less fear of illegal live/work arrangements and the risk of eviction from such illegal lofts.

In 1999, Pawtucket was granted permission by the State Legislature to create a 307-acre arts and entertainment district in its downtown. At that time, the district was one of the largest in the United States, encompassing 60 city blocks and 23 mills. As in the case of Pawtucket, many cities and towns have since expanded the scope of cultural districts from an arts organisation-based model to include live/work spaces for artists and small arts businesses. This second wave of cultural district development includes artists as well as collective arts enterprises. As mentioned, creativity and innovation is at the core of the second wave cultural districts. As such, cultural districts act as magnets in attracting artists and other creative individuals, filling spaces such as lofts and under-utilised buildings and light industrial spaces in vacant mills and factories (Galligan 2008).

Designated as a model economic development project, the state provided significant tax incentives to Pawtucket artists selling or creating original art, and who lived and worked within the district, and to galleries established within the district's boundaries. The law also exempts artists living and working with the district from state income tax on earnings generated from their creative work as an artist, writer, dancer, composer/performer, sculptor, painter, photographer, actor etc. To be eligible, a certificate of residency or location must be obtained from the city, with the final approval determined by the Rhode Island State Department of Taxation and the Rhode Island State Council on the Arts.

As in the case of Providence, many of the hundreds of eligible artists for these tax breaks in Pawtucket never took advantage of them. Whether this process became too involved and required too much bureaucracy for most, or whether artists thought it was not worth the effort in terms of sales and income, therefore more symbolic than real for most artists, is not clear. As Jason Shupbach, the Director of the Governor of Massachusetts' Office of Creative Industries, has argued in the past, tax incentives such as these are brilliant marketing tools as they show that the city cares about artists and their work, and that their business matters to the city. They also create a sense of an artist-centric area that is perceived as welcoming and where creativity and new works and ideas are being produced. As a result of all of the city's effort on behalf of individual artists, with or without tax breaks, Pawtucket was named in 2008 as one of ten great places for working artists in the United States by *Art Calendar Magazine*, a clear recognition of the effort the city has made to make artists welcome and successful.

Pawtucket's District Is More Than Just for Working Artists (the Armory Arts Center)

Pawtucket is a recognised leader of the "second wave" cultural district, but it still regards itself as a dual-purpose arts and cultural district, and hosts a very successful multi-week, annual arts festival. In addition, it has lured a number of successful arts organisations to the city such as the Sandra Feinstein Gamm Theatre, the Stone Soup Coffee House, and Mixed Magic Theatre. It has a traditional granting programme for artists as well as the successful Pawtucket Artists Collaborative, a park, and a minor league baseball team. The cornerstone of the city's traditional arts and cultural district development has been the rehabilitation of the old armory and drill hall in the centre of the city. The city sold it for $1 in 2001 to the Pawtucket Armory Association and it is now home to the successful Gamm Theatre and the city's visual and performing arts high school.

The Role of Political Will

Pawtucket's Planning Department may be unique in offering "one-stop shopping" services to artists, but none of this could have happened without municipal involvement and political goodwill on the part of the Mayor and his key department heads. One of the most important political voices involved in the process of transforming the mills from liabilities into assets was Pawtucket's Mayor James E. Doyle. Mayor Doyle championed the strategy of attracting artists to the city and made it a priority to make his Department of Planning and Redevelopment responsive to artists and developers alike. After the city's once thriving textile industry dried up, the Mayor was left with abandoned mills and little economic recourse and having the mills unoccupied and falling into disrepair made them potential fire and public safety hazards and targets for vandals. The Mayor charged the department's Planning Director Michael Cassidy and its Economic and Cultural Affairs Officer Herb Weiss with creating policies and an outreach programme to developers and artists alike that would ensure its success. They also reached out to other city departments such as housing, public safety, the police, and the fire inspector to formulate a plan to coordinate their efforts. As a result, the city has been highly successful in meeting artists, zoning, and taxpayer needs in rebuilding this community. Mayor Doyle's efforts in this regard have earned him recognition by the US Conference of Mayors and by the Rhode Island Arts and Business Council.

Whilst his predecessor was the one first attracted to the Providence experiment with tax incentives for artists who lived and worked in a designated area, it was Mayor Doyle who championed the strategy of attracting artists to the city and made it a priority to make his Department of Planning and Redevelopment responsive to artists and developers alike. In many ways, this "policy window" of opportunity for the city (Kingdon 1997) occurred when problems such as under-utilised mills, solutions such as the availability of artists and small arts and creative businesses looking for affordable space to fill them, and the Mayor's desire for change met to put Pawtucket on its current course.

The Ongoing Planning Process

Pawtucket made great gains in establishing its arts and cultural district and in forming a nascent arts community within its borders. It did so however without a conscious plan. In 2003 the city took a major step in creating a long-range plan for continued economic and civic engagement with the arts. Encouraged by the results of the city's initial experiment with an arts district, Mayor Doyle, with the guidance of the Planning Department and the 20/20 Committee (comprised of business and community leaders) set out to create a strategic plan for continued growth. The intention of this plan was to articulate ways Pawtucket could further realise its goals of urban revitalisation, economic growth, workforce development, and civic engagement via the arts and creative workers. It also recognised the potential of the "creative economy" by capitalising on the region's great wealth of artists and other workers in the various sectors now recognised under the creative economy umbrella. It also took advantage of the knowledge base and potential employment potential of the local colleges and universities, including ivy-league Brown University, the Rhode Island School of Design, Johnson & Wales University, and Providence College, all just miles away. The main thrust of the report was to encourage the city to continue work with artists and small arts businesses in further strengthening its economic base. A second recommendation was for Pawtucket to continue to promote itself as a great place for artists to live and work. The third goal was for it to think more regionally in developing alliances with nearby cities and universities in order to capitalise on regional strengths and resources. Parts of this multi-year plan were incorporated into Pawtucket's Comprehensive City Plan. This has formalised the city's relationship with workers in the creative sector in charting its future course.

Conclusion

There are many unique aspects of Pawtucket's relationship with artists and other creative workers. First, this partnership is being developed as a long-term investment rather than a short-term intervention to restore the city's vitality. Instead of using artists as instrumental agents of urban renewal (often dubbed the SoHo Effect based on the experiences of artists in Lower Manhattan), Pawtucket is seeking to develop a long-term, sustainable relationship with artists and the arts. In what can be referred to a new policy paradigm, the city is moving beyond artists' traditional role as a quick fix for urban blight, and is welcoming them into the fold as desirable partners in the city's long-term recovery.

Second, Pawtucket recognises the need to consider artists who are opting to live and work within its confines as professionals and as viable small businesses. As such, the city is employing many of the same economic development strategies it would with any other small business venture such as tax credits and assistance with real estate, licenses, and zoning. With the forces of technology, globalisation, and instant communication and new networks of distribution, who artists are and how they work are often radically different than in previous decades. This is in keeping with worldwide shifts in the workforce that now includes much of the arts as a key component of the creative industries. Whilst other components of Pawtucket's economy such as manufacturing are shrinking, the arts as part of the larger service sector are growing.

Finally, Pawtucket's strength was in looking at the mills as it assets, not as its liabilities. Whilst rehabilitating vacant and under-used mills was part of the city's economic development strategy, Pawtucket never lost sight of its goal of preserving its historic mill properties, and as a result, was able to recognise the potential of using federal and state historic preservation credits to assist in this endeavour.

6.4 Temple Bar, Dublin, Ireland

Temple Bar, Dublin is often quoted as an engineered building-led regeneration solution with an explicit cultural focus. It can be described as a Cultural Quarter that is part of

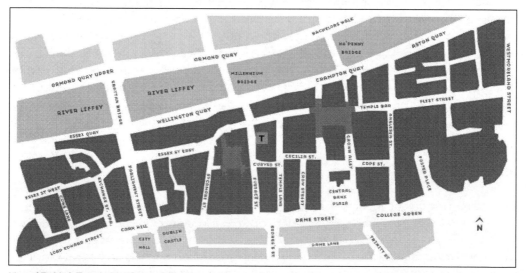

Map of Dublin's Temple Bar, Cultural Quarter.

Temple Bar, Dublin.

a larger strategy integrating cultural and economic development objectives, usually linked to the regeneration of a selected urban area. It is also a complex cluster of activities – networks embedded in a particular place, located on a 28-acre site in central Dublin sandwiched between O'Connell Bridge to the east, Dame Street to the south, and the River Liffey to the north. Temple Bar is in fact one of the oldest parts of Dublin, dating back to 1259 when an Augustinian Monastery was built there. In the seventeenth century a William Temple, Secretary to the Earl of Essex and a Provost of Trinity College, built his home there, giving the area its name – a bar was the name for a walkway by the river. The area today dates largely from the eighteenth century when cargo was loaded and unloaded on ships docking at the Quays on the south side of the Liffey. With the building of a new Custom House in the nineteenth century the old Essex Quay at Temple Bar fell into disuse, and the area became a centre for the clothing trade – tailors, drapers, cap makers, furriers, and woollen merchants.

Although Temple Bar is only a few yards from O'Connell Bridge, Trinity College and Dublin Castle, close to Dublin's main shopping area, the late twentieth-century city developments had all but passed the area by. Temple Bar had as a result become a backwater. This situation was not helped because the state bus company (CIE) proposed to redevelop most of it as a new transportation centre, linking bus and rail. As a result CIE began to buy up property in 1981, paving the way for demolition and redevelopment.

Paradoxically, this triggered a fall in property and rental values, which encouraged a process of revitalisation. Activities which could afford only low rents on short licences – or no rent at all – moved into the area. These included artists' studios, galleries, recording and rehearsal studios, pubs and cafes and restaurants, second-hand and young designer clothes shops, books and record stores, as well as a number of centres for a range of "third sector" organisations. They added a new dynamic to the area, and existing businesses such as printers, cutlery shops, and seedy hotels that had not yet been bought out or evicted by CIE. During the mid 1980s networks of enterprises became established, and linked to larger cultural players such as the Project Arts Centre and the Olympia Theatre. In this case planning blight had encouraged organic renewal of an urban area through low-rent arts activities.

Despite the derelict buildings and lack of investment in the area, Temple Bar had acquired a reputation as a place of discovery and vitality, where a wide range of social and economic exchange took place. It was frequently referred to as "Dublin's Left Bank", on account of its relatively high density of people living and working there, a mixture of architectural styles, close proximity to the quay, narrow streets, and a lively atmosphere deriving mainly from culture activities – recording studios, video companies, artists studios, theatres and pubs, cafés and restaurants.

These businesses and arts organisations formed the Temple Bar Development Council in 1989, and began to lobby for the area to be regenerated as a Cultural Quarter. It was recognised by the Council that their culture could be lost by wholesale redevelopment of the area or by adopting a property value-led approach to urban renewal. Although investment was desperately needed to prevent the building stock falling into greater disrepair great care had to be taken not to destroy the sense of place that had already been created by the mix of businesses there.

The strategy adopted to achieve this was a combination of culturally led urban renewal, physical renewal, urban husbandry, and local enterprise development, particularly in connection with the cultural industries and evening economy. An early strategic development framework for the area was prepared in 1990/1 and recommended:

- Adoption of a stewardship ethos and management approach to knitting back together the urban area;
- Adoption of twelve cultural projects to act as urban "chess pieces", localised strategic interventions to create activity and interest – these include a Film House, sculpture gallery, photography gallery, music venues and the old Olympia Theatre;
- Provision of business grants and loans to help young cultural and other entrepreneurs set up in business; this was accompanied by a survey of existing businesses in the area;
- A major training initiative in business skills and the various cultural industries, but also in catering and venue operation;
- Promotion and stimulation of an evening economy;
- A major initiative to improve permeability and pedestrian flow through the area, involving the creation of two new public spaces, outdoor venues, niche gardens, corners to sit and watch the world go by, culminating in the design of two new public squares;
- A major programme of public art and cultural animation, designed to reclaim and give meaning to the area's public realm;
- An overall approach to property management and upgrading based on balancing the need to improve the area's environment with the need to retain existing activity;
- The introduction of vertical zoning linked to the provision of grants and tax relief status;
- Design of new buildings by young Irish architects, with the accent on modern design within the context of the historic street pattern;
- Major marketing and information campaign using good modern design.

This strategy, the 'Development Programme for Temple Bar' (1992) was largely implemented by Temple Bar Properties Limited (TBPL), a state-owned development company established in 1991 that was distinct from the Temple Bar Development Council.

The state-owned company engaged in acquiring properties, refurbishing them, and negotiating rents with occupiers. In addition, it undertook development schemes on its own volition or as joint ventures with private owners and developers. To do this, it was granted an initial IR£4m from the EC and borrowed IR£25m privately, with a state guarantee. Monies generated from rental income are ploughed back into the property renewal programme and environmental action, and used to cross-subsidise cultural projects. In the final analysis a total of public funding for Temple Bar was some IR£40.6m, the bulk of which (IR£37m) was spent on the Cultural Development Programme 1991–2001. A further IR£60m has been borrowed and repaid through TBPL's commercial programme. Throughout the period 1991–2001 the private sector is estimated to have invested over IR£100m in the area.

TBPL was established as a small company with a limited shelf life initially of five years (extended to seven, and then ten). Its role was to ensure that the future development of Temple Bar corresponded to the set of cultural planning, urban stewardship, mixed-use planning, and urban design principles enshrined in the strategy established in 1992. Most of the physical development programme for the area was completed by 2001. Since then, Temple Bar Properties Limited has continued to manage certain key property holdings as well as putting on various events.

TBPL executed its various functions with twenty staff, just under 75 per cent of whom, including the Managing Director, the Cultural Director and Marketing Director, were women. The company was structured into three divisions, which at first sight seemed unusual:

- The Property Division, which was to acquire, improve, let, and manage TBPL's own portfolio, collect rents and intervene in the assembly of sites, the process of urban design, and to work on schemes and proposals either on its own or with individual landowners and developers;
- The Cultural Division, whose role was twofold: one, to secure the implementation of twelve key cultural development schemes in Temple Bar; the other to organise a programme of cultural animation, events, festivals, and concerts;
- The Marketing Division, whose brief was to conduct public participation exercises and internal marketing to people already in the area, but also to devise and implement an area placemaking strategy to raise the Temple Bar profile nationally and internationally.

In addition, TBPL and Dublin Corporation adopted a set of urban management principles for improving city diversity and mixed-use building on the Corporation's own 1990 Temple Bar Action Plan for urban renewal. These principles formed the backdrop for the existing street-by-street and block-by-block design guidance and new development schemes. As a result, over the first seven years TBPL commissioned a high-profile architectural framework and urban design competition; devised an economic development strategy to encourage and support entrepreneurship in the cultural industries; created two new urban squares, including the east-west route through the area; adopted mixed-use zoning to achieve diversity and stimulate the evening economy, urban culture, and street life; and initiated a major area marketing and information campaign.

In 1992 there were 27 restaurants, 100 shops, half a dozen arts buildings (some of them falling down), sixteen public houses, two hotels, 200 residents, 70 cultural industry businesses, and 80 other businesses in Temple Bar. However by 1996, when most of TBPL's own development schemes had been completed, there were five hotels, 200 shops, 40 restaurants, twelve cultural centres and a resident population of 2,000 people. By the end of 1996, there were an estimated 2,000 people employed in Temple Bar, an increase of 300 per cent.

The final major commercial development undertaken by TBPL was the Old City, designed to create a significant retail and residential cluster in the area between Parliament Street and Fishamble Street in the western end of Temple Bar. Situated around a new pedestrian street, Cow's Lane, the development consists of 191 apartments, 24 retail units, a crèche, and landscaped gardens.

Temple Bar Properties Ltd, as a property development company, ceased trading in 2001. By that time, Temple Bar was home to some 3,000 residents, 450 businesses employing close on 2,500, and twelve high quality cultural venues. The whole area had become a showcase for urban design, architecture, design, and style.

This success brought its own problems. By the mid 1990s Temple Bar had developed a reputation as the "Stag Night" capital of Europe. Research commissioned by TBPL revealed that these visitors – largely groups of young women and men from England – were beginning to cause other visitors to stay away. This problem was addressed by a coordinated management response by landlords and hoteliers in the area, essentially by refusing accommodation to large same-sex groups. By 2001 Temple Bar was coming under criticism for being too trendy, too popular, too facile. Pete McCarthy's travelogue *McCarthy's Bar* (2001), for example, contains the following complaint on the "ruthless redevelopment and marketing of Temple Bar":

> *Continental café culture has arrived, a forced planting of non-indigenous chrome counters, almond-flavoured latte and seared yellow-fin tuna in balsamic lemongrass and rhubarb jus. Japanese-besuited media ponces sit in windows sipping bottles of overpriced cooking lager, imported from Mexico, and other top brewing spots, to the banks of the Liffey. Plain, unadorned, authentic pubs, previously unchanged for decades, now reek of new wood and paint, as they're gutted and refurbished to conform to the notion of Irishness demanded by the stag nights from Northampton and conference delegates from Frankfurt who fill the streets, interchangeable inter smug fat smiles and Manchester United replica shirts. (Cited in Montgomery 2003)*

It is the case that success in Temple Bar has brought many more visitors, who party and enjoy the contemporary culture derided by McCarthy, whose nostalgic clinging to the past seems to ignore the economic and cultural benefits to businesses and people in what was a run-down area. This is an argument about what type of culture has been established as a result of the redevelopment of Temple Bar. It clearly has absorbed and encouraged a spectrum of cultural engagement rather then a narrow traditional state-sponsored arts practice. There is also the temptation to assume that the redevelopment of Temple Bar was plain sailing, with straightforward instalments of commercial property development. This view conveniently overlooks the area's other future as a glorified bus depot. Moreover, it is not readily understood that the recession of the early 1990s and the high interest rates at that time almost led to an early liquidation of TBPL. The later boom in Ireland's economy certainly played a large part in the success of Temple Bar, but in the early days there was no boom, simply risk.

TBPL retains responsibility for managing various matters in the area such as a Green Plan including waste management for the area, additional street cleaning, and the ongoing maintenance and security of Meeting House Square and Temple Bar Square. TBPL continue to programme outdoor cultural events and markets, all of which are free to the public. A traders' group (TASQ) has been formed to coordinate marketing of the area and to provide additional street cleaning. TBPL is also responsible for managing three writers' studios and an International Visiting Artists' Apartment.

What is important about the Temple Bar experiment is that it was designed from the outset to regenerate a run-down area, substantially in a part of the city centre. The cultural component was used as a significant generator to attract private investment over time. The key trigger for this Quarter was access to European Union capital funds to kick-start the development. It has resulted in a physical regeneration of the city, and

---

Dublin's Temple Bar, Features and Benefits

A public private sector partnership triggered by European Union capital funds.

A broadly based Cultural Quarter, with live/work provision.

A regeneration project using culture as the "life" of the Quarter.

A successful model of mixed development, including bars, cafes, restaurants, and hotels.

A sense of place and identification.

Places for people to meet, eat, drink, and socialise in the winter and summer.

The success of this Quarter can be measured in economic terms: 3,000 residents, 450 businesses employing close on 2,500, and twelve high quality cultural venues.

a Cultural Quarter in the Raymond Williams sense, with an international reputation for its bars, restaurants, and entertainment. It is the atmosphere generated by bringing together cultural activity and establishing the live/work community that provides the heart to this Quarter.

It can be measured as a success, in terms of regenerated buildings, new build, jobs created, and business location. It is more difficult to determine how effective the Quarter has been in developing creative businesses from the micro, to small and medium over time. Although there has been considerable public sector involvement this Quarter has not been built around landmark cultural features, but rather twelve small cultural initiatives, nor has it incorporated City Council cultural services. It can be described as a buildings-led regeneration project which is culturally based, reflecting a Williams cultural interpretation rather than the narrower creative industries or arts focus.

6.5 Grand Opera House, Belfast, Northern Ireland

Cultural Quarters have often sprung from an existing cultural presence, linked to a public sector initiative, and the Grand Opera House, Belfast is an example of this approach. The Grand Opera House is in reality a theatre, although its origins were as an opera house, leading to a bingo hall and ultimately a cinema before being renovated. It is an important listed building in the city centre.

This project acted as a catalyst for rejuvenating the centre of Belfast by stimulating the night time economy at a time when people were persuaded to stay at home in the evenings because of the terrorist bombings. It was a Northern Ireland government initiative, one that the local authority chose not to undertake because of its own political focus.

During the 1970s the IRA attempted to achieve its goal of a united Ireland by wiping out the economic existence of Northern Ireland through a bombing campaign aimed at economic targets. This acted as a deterrent to the outside investment on which the North is so substantially dependent. The bombing was directed at any establishment considered a commercial success, thus central Belfast was a prime target. City centre shops and businesses suffered. The security barriers erected in 1973 enclosing the heart of the central business district may have made the centre safer but they did not make it more pleasant. It was not uncommon for people who used to shop regularly in the city centre to say they had not been in central Belfast for over five years. This situation concerned the Northern Ireland government, who began to look for ways of reinvigorating the city centre, despite the bombings. The Grand Opera House became one of the main planks of this, as well as contributing to the economic regeneration of the immediate area where the Theatre was located. One of the main ways in which this occured was through the increased demand for catering facilities to fulfil the pre- and post-show eating and drinking demands.

The history of the Opera House involved its sale in 1972 by Rank Odeon, who had bought it in 1961 and converted it into a cinema. The buyer was a property developer who proposed to demolish the building and erect an office block on the prime city site. But Kenneth Jamison, Director of the Arts Council of Northern Ireland (ACNI), and Charles Brett, founder member of the Ulster Architectural Heritage Society and a member of ACNI's Board, had both identified the Grand Opera House as a building that should be preserved. They, together with Arthur Brooke, the then Permanent Secretary of the Department of Education (which is responsible for funding ACNI), were the three key people instrumental in the saving and refurbishment of the Grand Opera House. Arthur Brooke had recently chaired a working party that had considered measures to return nightlife to the city centre.

The combination of an influential and sympathetic ear in government, the desire to conserve a building of architectural importance, rejuvenate the city centre nightlife and maintain a large-scale theatre presence in Belfast, led to the Opera House being listed, bought (in 1976) and restored for ACNI by the Northern Ireland Department of Education. Once the initial priority of architectural preservation through listing was attained the two other priorities were tackled: to secure adequate financing and to solicit further support from the public sector.

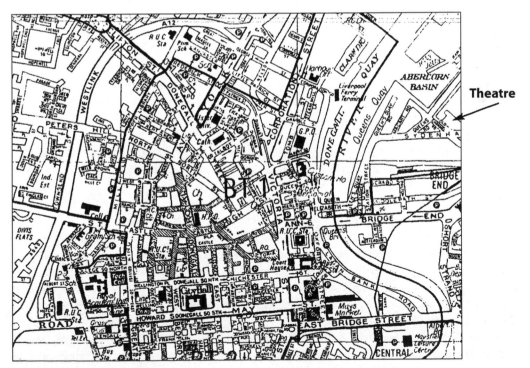

Site of Grand Opera House, Belfast.

Because the Opera House had been seriously neglected, it was purchased and renovated at much less expense than would be required to build comparable new facilities. Starting in the summer of 1976, restoration proceeded in three phases, thereby accommodating the Department of Education's capital programme and making maximum benefit of end of fiscal year funds. The three stages, costing a total of £3,315,000, consisted of wind and weatherproofing and other external repairs; repairing foundations; restoring and refitting the interior, as well as modernising the stage and its equipment.

Unfortunately the agreements on the restoration of the Opera House did not include a written agreement between ACNI and the Department of Education on funding the future programming of this venue. ACNI assumed that the Department would increase the ACNI's annual grant by £500,000, allowing it to run the Theatre directly. Instead of increasing ACNI's funding, the Department reduced the Council's annual grant because of the need to divert funds to secure the Province's industrial base, particularly the DeLorean car works. This reduction in funding placed ACNI and the Grand Opera House in a difficult and sensitive position. Trapped by high public interest in the reopening of the Opera House and the reality of limited government funding, ACNI felt it only had one option. In order to open the Opera House it was necessary for them to reduce other clients' grants. In September 1980 the Grand Opera House reopened with its first production in its new role as Northern Ireland's premier large-scale theatre.

The long-term result of this lack of written agreement on an annual operating grant between ACNI and the Department of Education, as well as the fact that there are no other sources of funds for the Opera House, except ticket sales and sponsorship, means that the Theatre regularly has an annual deficit. The financial success of the Theatre depends on its annual programme, which is difficult to control because it relies on existing touring productions; the capacity constraints of the building (990 seats), and limited grant aid. The increasing costs of importing productions from the rest of the United Kingdom aggravate this financial burden. Furthermore, sponsorship is restricted by the size and financial fragility of the business community.

At the same time as ACNI was restoring the Opera House the city centre was the focus of redevelopment by two groups: a working party of elected City Council representatives and the business community presided over by Chris Patten, the then Minister responsible for Northern Ireland, and a group composed of representatives from the larger stores in the city centre. Their priorities were to improve public transport, especially off-peak service, upgrade the environment, and pump-prime the redevelopment of the area. In autumn 1980 these groups had their first major breakthrough with the introduction of late-night shopping.

As well as this business-orientated redevelopment, Belfast had another major development focus, the area around Queen's University. This part of the city was the traditional centre of Belfast's arts world and the home of its major theatres and cinemas.

Given this area's political neutrality, it was (and is) the one spot seen as having a safe nightlife throughout "The Troubles". Since 1980 this area has further benefited from many new restaurants and restored pubs.

The city centre and the University area are connected by one mile of Great Victoria Street, nicknamed "Bomb Alley" in the 1970s. Since the redevelopment of the Opera House, which is located on this street, and the subsequent growth of restaurants and pubs around it, this area is now locally known as the "Golden Mile" (see map) and has evolved into an informal Cultural Quarter. From the outset, it was the intention that the Opera House should be a major provincial theatre with outstanding national and international arts related events, as well as housing local activities such as the Ulster Drama Festival, Ulster Youth Theatre, and Opera Northern Ireland. It has succeeded in doing this and recently announced a major expansion of facilities.

Despite the beauty and success of the existing Theatre, it suffers from a severe lack of space, particularly in the front of house and backstage areas. The new development will encompass an L-shaped site around the Grand Opera House to include the following:

- Lift access to different levels for people with limited mobility;
- Wider choice of seats for those with limited mobility and wheelchair confined;
- An education suite for all ages, comprising a 150-seat studio theatre and dedicated foyer that can be used for performances, workshops, master-classes, and rehearsals to supplement the outreach programme;
- New public areas, including foyers, bars, a café, and function rooms;
- Improved backstage facilities and wing space to provide more room for large-scale modern productions;
- Improved and extended accommodation for visiting companies, including dressing rooms for 100 people and a band room for 60 musicians;
- Air-cooling and improved ventilation in the auditorium;
- Increased and improved toilet facilities, doubling current facilities;
- New offices for staff and visiting companies.

As well as meeting this ACNI objective, the Grand Opera House has provided an anchor for connecting the nightlife in the city centre with that in the University area, thus creating a Cultural Quarter. This is an example of culturally-led regeneration based around the need to invigorate the Belfast nightlife, save an important building, and maintain a major theatre presence in the city. The result is an informal Cultural Quarter.

The Opera House does raise an important issue: the importance of including operational and management considerations at the planning stage. If a cultural capital investment project is used to improve the cultural infrastructure, economy and image of a city it is essential to consider how future programming is funded.

The project also demonstrates how an art facility can contribute to a more lively culturally orientated city centre, thereby helping regenerate the economy by attracting people to the city centre, encouraging new restaurants, wine bars, and bistros to open in the vicinity, as well as creating a sense of safety and at the same time bringing an important historic building back into use.

Grand Opera House, Belfast, Features and Benefits
Focused on one important architectural building.

Close to the University.

Champions for the project.

A major theatre brought back to life.

Evening economy stimulated.

Counteraction to the "bombings".

Secondary activity established, such as cafés and restaurants.

Notes

1. Organisations Involved in the Vienna MuseumsQuartier (except the organisations of Quarter 21; see Note 2):

   - the Architektur Zentrum Wien (a centre for exhibitions, presentations, and debates);
   - the Art Cult Center – Tabakmuseum;
   - Basis Wien – art, information, and archive;
   - the Kunsthalle Wien (an exhibition venue for international contemporary and modern art);
   - the Leopold Museum (which includes the largest collection of works by Egon Schiele);
   - the Museum of Modern Art Ludwig Foundation Vienna (which houses one of the largest collections of modern and contemporary art);
   - the Tanzquartier Wien (a centre for modern dance and performance);
   - the Theaterhaus fur Kinder (a theatre for children aged four– to thirteen years which includes dance, musicals, puppet theatre, and opera);
   - the Vienna Festival;
   - wienXtra (a children-oriented information centre);
   - Zoom (a creativity centre and exhibition space for children engaged in art, culture, society, and science).

2. An explanation of the Vienna Quarter 21 Mechanism.
   This mechanism is intended to address the question of the small, underfunded cultural organisations and how contemporary creative activity is incorporated into the MuseumsQuartier. The elements of the Quarter 21 are:

- A forum for cultural theory;
- Studios for artists;
- Platform for crossover activities;
- Cultural joint office;
- Digital media area (internet café, independent media centre, media studios, platforms for music and film);
- Arena, reading room;
- Creative industries (start-up offices for design, film, photography, e-music, fashion, new media/IT, literature/book stores, art publishers);
- Commercial users (bookshops, bars, and cafes).

The users are expected to take responsibility for their work, the outputs and to pay the rent for the space in the Quarter 21. The MuseumsQuartier Co. manages the general infrastructure and space such as the visitors centre, arena, conference rooms, courtyards, and the square in front of the building. In addition it operates the lease contracts for the users in Quarter 21 as it does for all other parts of the site; however, in this case, there are three categories of lease: cultural (heavily subsidised), semi-commercial (subsidised), and commercial (no subsidy).

The management of the MuseumsQuartier has established an advisory board, "Network 21", which recommends to the Chief Executive which users should be offered a lease contract in the Quarter 21 and in which rental category. The Chief Executive can either accept or reject the recommendations and reports his actions to the board. It also has a wider remit to advise on content and programming for the common spaces.

Once chosen, users rent a space of the size they can afford and this is maintained on their behalf by the company as part of the lease agreement. Any alterations to the space are also the responsibility of the company, and the consequent costs incorporated in the rental charge.

General technical equipment is provided and maintained by the company. Users must prove they have the financial means to meet their operational costs including all rental charges whatever the lease category.

Institutions currently included in the Quarter 21:

- Electric Avenue
- institut fünfhaus
- MEDIENQUARTIER21
- monochrom
- quintessenz
- SPOILER
- transeuropa
- A9-forum transeuropa
- FOUND FOR YOU
- Kiesler-Zentrum Wien
- KulturKontakt Austria
- polyklamott
- Kulturbüros
- -> AICA
- Büro für Kulturvermittlung
- Culture2Culture

- DUB
- EIKON
- ImPulsTanz
- Klangspuren
- MKA
- Schlebrügge
- springerin
- Galerienverband
- Ovaltrakt
- math.space

4. Cultural Precinct is the term used in Australia to describe a cultural or creative industries quarter.

Chapter 7

Putting the Principles into Practice: A Cultural Quarter for a Proud Northern Town

T his chapter takes forward the principles and the practice of Cultural Quarters and applies them to a typical northern English town to provide a practical example of public sector planning for a Cultural Quarter including the factors which influence decision-making. The underlying principles for Cultural Quarters are as follows:

Activity: economic, cultural, and social
Form: the relationship between buildings and spaces
Meaning: sense of place, historical and cultural

Consequently, an essential prerequisite is the understanding of the local and wider regional cultural policies and practice; local governance, as well as any history leading up to the current position.

This approach is illustrated by providing a practical example: Bolton, a typical northern industrial revolution town. Bolton can be usefully compared with the Wolverhampton case study in terms of size, population, history and approach to developing the quarter in that the local authority plays a key role, however, beyond that there are noticeable distinctions. It does not seem to follow the cultural entrepreneur model found in Newcastle; however, it has resonances with the Belfast Grand Opera House and Vienna MuseumsQuartier examples as a public sector. cultural building-led revival.

The focus on Bolton provides us with a useful and realistic cultural, social and cultural policy insight, illustrating the levels of complexity a local authority is expected to engage in. This highlights the need for a champion to provide the vision, drive and leadership; a cultural entrepreneur. Examples of this are the Newcastle Studios and the Grand Opera House, Belfast.

This approach assumes another principle, that a Cultural Quarter is introduced to complement and build on existing infrastructure and interests. However, prior to considering the political, geographical and infrastructural context the history of Cultural Quarter development in the town should be recognised.

The Cultural Quarter approach in Bolton can be traced back to the establishment of Le Mans Crescent in the 1930s, which was designed to include the Museum, Art Gallery and Aquarium in the town centre as a public benefit. Included with this was a library, theatre and lecture facilities. However, the Crescent also includes the Magistrates' Court and office facilities for social services.

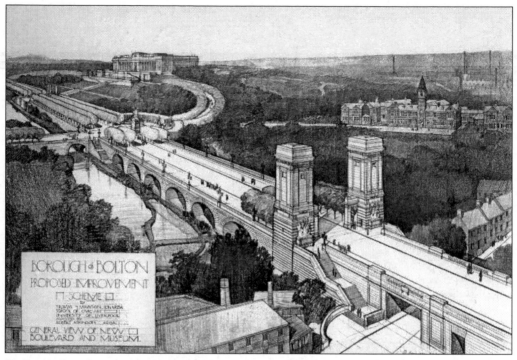

The Town Hall and Queens Park. Reproduced with the kind permission of David Mawson, formally of Feilden & Mawson.

Le Mans Crescent was originally designed to house the Museum, Art Gallery and Aquarium, the architects being Bradshaw Gass and Hope. One can only assume that there was always an original vision to provide substantial cultural facilities associated with the Town Hall as a major civic centre. Drawings of an early visionary Leverhulme concept by Thomas Marson BMP are included, illustrating the tree-lined boulevard planned for the rear of the Town Hall, and a scheme to link the Town Hall with Queens Park, an early Cultural Quarter. The tree-lined boulevard never happened.

There is a history of attempting to develop cultural provision in Bolton stemming from the 1960s, largely focused on establishing an arts centre, loosely modelled on the Arts Council of Great Britain formula promoted throughout the 1970s. (Hutchison 1977)

In the 1990s another attempt was made to establish a Bolton arts complex, based on proposals by the Arts About Manchester consultancy to combine marketing, branding and the coordination of the Octagon Theatre, Albert Halls, Central Library, Archives and local studies, the Museum, Aquarium and Art Gallery programmes.

The most recent attempt at establishing a Cultural Quarter was undertaken in 2003 with a submission by Bolton Metropolitan Borough Council of the document 'Le Mans Cultural Quarter Creative Heart', Community Soul, outline proposals to the Department

The Town Hall and Tree-Lined Boulevard. Reproduced with the kind permission of David Mawson, formally of Feilden & Mawson.

Le Mans Crescent, Bolton, 2004.

for Culture Media and Sport for PFI credits, March 2003, with an addition, The Vision – 'Business Case, a Whole but not a Palace, Creative Heart, Community Soul', December 2003, to the Department of Culture Media and Sport for PFI credit funding. A further report was commissioned – Bolton town centre cultural development potential, Le Mans Crescent and Cheadle Square scoping exercise for Bolton Metropolitan Borough Council, Bradshaw Gass and Hope, January 2003 – to support this submission.

7.1 Politics: The Wider City Region and the Manchester Shadow

Bolton is one of several cotton and wool mill towns, such as Rochdale, Bury and Oldham, which circle the city of Manchester, forming Greater Manchester. The influence of the city on the periphery is significant. Consequently, city cultural policy, including the establishment of Cultural Quarters, directly impacts on the towns in the outer circle, the city region. In Greater Manchester the Manchester Northern Quarter (close to the centre of the city of Manchester) is recognised as the example of Cultural Quarter provision. It is difficult to relate this development to other cultural centres, for example, the Salford Quays initiative. Salford Quays is a classic example of an urban regeneration project to bring back into life the Manchester Ship Canal and docks area by the reclamation of land. A master plan for development from 1985 to 2002 included one-third commercial offices, one-third residential and the remaining third leisure. In addition it required the creation of a flagship project that would be highly visible, and this fell within the leisure component of the plan, with the establishment of the Salford Centre for Performing Arts. This centre subsequently became the Lowry project, which includes the Lowry building that houses theatres, galleries, including the display of the largest L. S. Lowry collection in the world, an interactive gallery, bars, café, restaurant. conference and hospitality facilities. It has two auditoriums, seating 1,730 in the Lyric Theatre and 466 in the Quays Theatre. In addition there is the Lowry Plaza which is a triangular public space to act as a focal point for people arriving at the centre over the Lowry Bridge. It is in Cultural Quarter terms, a very large arts centre.

Both projects attempt to address regeneration of a physical area through cultural engagement with differing origins. Brown, O'Connor and Cohen describe the Manchester Northern Cultural Quarter, (Brown, O'Connor, and Cohen, 2000) as:

In the case of the Northern Quarter, it is situated at the northern edge of Manchester City Centre and is a major shopping and market area since the mid-nineteenth century. When city centre rents rose in Manchester during the property boom in the 1980s, the availability of cheap rents, flexible letting, high vacancy in small properties encouraged the migration of small cultural businesses to relocate in the area from the late 1980s onwards, this was also fuelled by the enterprise allowance scheme. The area was also popular for entertainment and pleasure up to the 1970s and as a consequence of this and the migration of new cultural businesses became a focus for the Manchester music scene. The area includes major independent record retail outlets such as Eastern Bloc and Piccadilly records; cutting-edge music venues and clubs, new risen music orientated bars such as adroit 201, fashion outlets as spatially flex powers and numerous offices and workshops in use by micro cultural businesses.

They also point out that the grouping of around 200 cultural businesses in this area did not result from city-led concerted cultural industries of Cultural Quarter strategies, unlike the Sheffield City Council approach. However, a recent report on the Northern Quarter for Manchester City Council indicates that there were a range of issues that required attention in the Northern Quarter such as derelict buildings, crime and antisocial behaviour. The leader of Manchester City Council confirmed that it is important to strike a balance in the Northern Quarter. The Council wants to nurture the creativity that exists in the area but at the same time develop the huge potential the Quarter has to offer, being so close to the heart of the city centre. This epitomises the public policy Cultural Quarter expectation; of regenerating an area, contributing significantly to the local economy and being creative, lively and exciting, a risky place.

It is worth noting when considering activities in Manchester that the Northern Quarter, although well known, is not the only Cultural Quarter in the city. Manchester's cultural strategy identifies three Cultural Quarters: Oxford Road Corridor, a national centre of excellence in research and teaching in cultural disciplines, provides some of the city's key cultural attractions; the Northern Quarter, with a cluster of creative enterprises in a mixed economy of shops clubs and bars; and Spinningfields, which has the potential for development as a national centre of excellence in media industries linked to Granada and new technology expertise. This strategy may identify such Quarters but does not explain how the city intends to coordinate these activities and harness the creative energy to generate a significant contribution to the local economy and communities in which they reside.

In its city cultural strategy Manchester claims to have the strongest arts and museum community outside London, with Manchester Art Gallery, the Museum of Science and Industry, Manchester Museum, Whitworth Art Gallery, Peoples History Museum, Cornerhouse Contemporary Arts Centre and CUBE Architecture Centre. However, references to other cultural provision such as the library service are limited to John Rylands, Chethams, Portico and the Central libraries.

It also asserts that the UK's largest regional concentration of media and creative industries can be found in the city. These developments are mechanisms for the social, economic and cultural aspirations of the city; however, the policy interfaces between local, regional and national cultural interests in particular are confusing and remain difficult to articulate at a local level.

For the purposes of contextualising the Bolton Cultural Quarter project, it is necessary to understand the policy stance taken by Manchester City Council (www.manchester. gov.uk/regen/culture/strategy 2004):

Culture is an integral component of the new economy and a major force in regional growth, attracting students, visitors and investment. Manchester is the major location in the North of England for cultural industries and for visitor attractions and is the gateway to the Northwest as a tourism destination. The city is the core of a wider city region which includes the Lowry, Imperial War Museum North, Manchester United Football Club and Lancashire County Cricket Club.

This *wider city region* concept is further developed in terms of the claims and ambitions incorporated in the strategy for the region as follows:

Manchester is the cultural hub of the Northwest region and this strategic role is now recognised by regional and national agencies. Manchester's cultural attractions record 10.5 million visits in a year. These visitors are drawn from the city itself with a population of 439,000, from Greater Manchester with a population of 2.5 million and 6.3 million people who live within a 30 mile radius. For major events, there is potential to attract people from a population of 11.2 million who live within 50 miles of the city.

The Cultural Strategy for England's Northwest recognises the contribution of Manchester and Liverpool to the region's image and economy. The Association of Greater Manchester Authorities (AGMA) supports cultural activities that enhance the international reputation of the conurbation. Manchester Airport PLC has taken a lead in encouraging commercial sponsorship for the arts in Manchester and the surrounding region.

It identifies the key opportunities as:

- *Recognition of Manchester's role in the Cultural Strategy for England's Northwest and in national and regional strategies for sports, arts, heritage and tourism will be a first important step towards securing investment which matches the city's achievements and supports its future ambition.*
- *National and regional arts, sports and heritage access programmes offer opportunities to support community involvement.*

The strategy is organised around a number of core themes, which are again worth noting for the purposes of understanding the problems facing Bolton in establishing a Cultural Quarter in the city region. These themes are described as:

The Cultural Strategy builds on the city's achievements and takes account of the opportunities and challenges. It has two main ambitions:

- *to secure full recognition of Manchester's role as a cultural capital;*
- *to increase and broaden participation in cultural activities.*

The cultural strategy is organised around five themes:

- *Cultural Capital;*
- *Cultural Learning;*
- *Culture for All;*
- *Cultural Economy;*
- *Marketing Culture.*

In the case of the cultural economy theme the opportunities identified by the strategy include:

- *The North West Regional Economic Strategy identifies the growth potential of tourism, media and creative industries. This provides a context for putting in place appropriate mechanisms to support the new creative, knowledge and leisure economy;*
- *The Department of Culture, Media and Sport (DCMS) green paper 'Culture and Creativity: The Next Ten Years' sets out a framework for supporting culture and creativity through partnership with the Department of Trade and;*
- *Industry (DTI) and Department for Education and Skills (DfES).*

There are similar problems encountered by other towns and cities, around London for example. The London shadow operates over the south-east, yet places like Brighton have built further on their cultural heritage and cosmopolitan mix to retain the distinctive and independent social and economic community which is increasingly attractive to Londoners.

Manchester Shadow Features and Benefits

- An ambitious cultural policy based on the concept of the city region;
- A discipline-led, sub-sectoral approach to Cultural Quarters;
- The proximity of a regional cultural hub to Bolton;
- Good international communication connections;
- A lack of policy connection between established Manchester and Bolton Councils-led cultural provision with the Cultural Quarter developments;
- Europe's largest University conurbation, with a substantial faculty of Art and Design and large numbers of graduates wishing to enter the creative industries;
- The potential benefits of the Manchester effect, which is attracting international tourists and supporting the Bolton profile;

- The city of Manchester provides additional cultural consumers for producers in Bolton;
- The danger of the Manchester shadow, denying resources at sub-regional and regional levels for cultural activity in Bolton and other old cotton and wool towns;
- It remains unclear how economically driven the cultural policy and Cultural Quarter development is in the city of Manchester;
- Arts centres such as the Lowry Centre are not Cultural Quarters but cultural anchor developments in regeneration projects.

7.2 Local Policy Frameworks

Bolton is typical of many towns in that it has largely been directly or indirectly led by local authority plans and strategies to address local social, economic and cultural issues, often driven by regional and national government requirements for funding. These are as follows:

- The Bolton Community Plan 2003–2012;
- The Bolton Education and Culture Plan, 2003–2006;
- The Bolton Local Cultural Strategy, 2003–2008 (2002);
- The Bolton Arts Action Plan, 2002;
- The Town Centre Action Plan 2004 (appendix 1);
- The Bolton Economic Strategy 2004–2008 (February 2004);
- The Learning and Skills Council, local area review, 2004.

These and other policies are expected to add up to Bolton's local strategic partnership vision, 2004.

> *Ensure that Bolton will become a great place to visit and in which to live, work, learn and to do business.*

Several of these policies have combined to provide a framework for supporting the establishment of a Cultural Quarter in Bolton. In particular, the town centre action plan identifies the need for a Cultural Quarter as an integral component of the regeneration of the town centre and states:

Developing a Cultural Quarter
   The majority of the town centre's cultural attractions are focussed within the spaces provided by the finest quality buildings within the town centre around Le Mans Crescent. This concentration of heritage-related buildings and spaces present an opportunity to develop a cohesive strategy linking the development of cultural and arts provision to the enhancement of the heritage of the town centre.

This interest in the economic potential of cultural provision and activity is echoed in the Economic Strategy for Bolton through its mission:

Bolton, working towards a robust, modern, competitive, innovative and knowledge based economy, with opportunities for all and a community that is able to take them.

There are three core themes of the strategy, which include increasing economic investment, improving economic performance and addressing social exclusion. In order to increase competitive potential the strategy suggests the need to:

Change the industrial composition of the Borough, moving from an over-reliance on declining and low value-added sectors to the knowledge based economy with a high proportion of businesses in growth sectors (including the cultural industries).

The town centre is identified in this context as a priority project and it is suggested that:

The attractions of sites in the West of the Borough contrasts with the relative paucity of opportunity in and around Bolton town centre. While consolidating its retail position the future development of the town centre is seen as key to the objective of the economic strategy. The town centre is critical both as an alternative business location but also as a key symbol of the aspirations of the town and its quality of life.

What begins to emerge from this is the recognition by policy-makers at a local level of the usefulness of cultural manifestations in furthering economic development, enhancing the quality of life and promotion. There is, for example, a concern in the strategy about the image of the Borough, and a key priority is to establish, amongst key partners, an image for the Borough which reflects and supports its economic aspirations. The image should root itself in the past industrial heritage but also look to a different economic future. In the context of the town centre it is suggested that the emerging town centre strategy provides the opportunity to redefine the way the Borough is viewed, by generating a step change within the area. There is

The need to be more forward-looking which should be reflected not only in our marketing material but also in the way high-profile areas such as the town centre are redeveloped.

In addition, there are regional cultural planning agencies with an interest in cultural activities in Bolton:

- Government Office for the North West;
- Northwest Development Agency, engaged in the development of a regional creative industries cluster strategy, *England's North West: the strategy towards 2020, 1999;*

- North West Cultural Consortium, which has developed the cultural strategy for England's North West, 2001;
- North West Arts Council of England, and the arts strategy;
- North West Museums Libraries and Archives Council, regional strategy;
- North West Tourism Board, strategy;
- North West Sports Council, strategy;
- The North West Regional Assembly, cultural strategy.

Finally, there are national agencies with policies in local matters such as:

- MLA, the National Council for Museums Libraries and Archives with Renaissance in the regions; the new vision for England's museums, 2001 and developing the twenty-first-century archive; and action plan for UK archives, 2001–2002, 2001;
- The Department of Culture Media and Sport, Green Paper, Culture and Creativity; the Next Ten Years, 2001;
- The Office of the Deputy Prime Minister.

Perhaps the most significant of the plethora of strategies influencing Bolton is the identifying and meeting of local needs and aspirations in regional, national and international contexts.

Subsequently, the establishment of a Cultural Quarter at a local level inevitably requires engagement with a government-sponsored agency landscape which is multi-layered, complex, confusing and resource intensive, as the Bolton example illustrates. However, some basic messages can be distilled from these policies that are specific to Bolton.

Key strategic Policy Issues

- Town centre redevelopment and regeneration;
- Bolton's regional, national and international profile;
- Generation of jobs, graduate retention, and business development;
- Post 16 educational attainment.

7.3 The Bolton Cultural Policy Concept

The acceptance of the Cultural Quarter concept has been assisted by the willingness of the Council to develop and establish the Bolton local cultural strategy, (Bolton's Cultural Strategy 2001/2) introduced in 2001. Bolton has shown no great pretensions in its cultural ambition. Today, however, it has developed and introduced a local authority cultural strategy on behalf of the Department of Culture Media and Sport, defining local culture as:

Culture embraces a wide variety of meanings and values for people. The definition of culture used in this strategy falls into two dimensions:

- *Culture as an essential part of everyone's life, the cultural activities, the making, doing and enjoying;*
- *The culture of the Borough, the way of life in Bolton and what influences it.*

This provides an insight to the quality-of-life dimension referred to in the Bolton's Local Strategic Partnership Vision, 2004, and assists in understanding what the Council in partnership with local cultural organisations considers culture to be:

- Visual, performing, broadcasting and media arts e.g. theatre – national, regional and local, dance, cinema, music and painting;
- Sports e.g. watching and participating;
- Museums;
- Arts e.g. art galleries, art workshops and creative industries;
- Play e.g. parks and playgrounds and informal play opportunities;
- Parks and open spaces;
- Libraries;
- Heritage e.g. Bolton's industrial background and cotton mills, the Mass Observation photography project of the thirties and nineties, and Bolton's multicultural dimension;
- Built environment e.g. the Town Hall, Victoria Square, Le Mans Crescent and Reebok stadium;
- Countryside e.g. the West Pennine moors;
- Identity and image e.g. Bolton as a mill town, Mass Observation photography project, Bolton Wanderers Football Club;
- Shared memories e.g. local disasters and major events;
- Relationships e.g. family, schools, clubs;
- Beliefs e.g. religious, political.

This inclusive definition of culture as a way of life mirrors the conceptual frameworks of Williams and Bourdeau and the consequent reinforcement of coherence and convergence – the arts and heritage in culture and culture as a manifestation of society – a richness in diversity paradigm.

Bolton may have adopted such an approach in order to rekindle a shared community identity and vision for the future as a result of declining industry, unemployment and an uninspiring quality of life.

These towns are not alone in the UK or elsewhere in the world where economic activity has declined or substantial population change occurred, or social upheaval experienced. For example, Toronto has produced a creative city work print (Toronto Culture 2001), which describes cultural activity in the city, and a direction for developing a cultural strategy. It makes the best of existing assets and realises the social, economic and financial benefits by ensuring that Toronto is recognised as a world centre for cultural activity, including the creative industries. For example, it describes relationships in a number of respects but particularly,

> *The city needs to change its relationship with our major cultural institutions, from the donor/ beneficiary to partners in creative city building.*

The Workprint document summarises the approach in the following way:

> *All of these questions really boil down to one: how do we transform ourselves into a productive, creative, attractive global city with a sharply delineated, vital identity?*

It is evident that the Bolton cultural concept encompasses far more than the traditional arts and heritage. It facilitates engagement and interaction with many, if not all of the components such as the built environment, beliefs, play and shared memories that come together to create a culture – a genuinely inclusive and democratic approach. This is in stark contrast to the national policy where there is no interest in culture as the unifying concept determined by consumers and creators, not by government or its agencies. (Jowell 2004)

For example, the museum becomes the focal point for reflection and interpretation of past cultural activities as a means of informing the future: *culture as industry, reflecting the past and encouraging the new.* It tells us about our past cultural and industrial history and relationships through the nature of practice in the past and present. If we begin to consider placing our activities, including interpretation, in this broader spectrum of interrelationships there is a basis for sustainability, engagement with the environment and subsequently a justification for public funding interventions. However, with the arts and heritage as integral components of the cultural community, actively engaging culture as industry provides the most effective and powerful future strategy for Bolton.

Culture as an industry challenges the traditional role of the large cultural institutions as is symbolic of the community and how that society wishes to present itself to others. It also questions the chosen mechanism for reflecting back to society approved cultural traditions and practices to remind us corporately of our history and sense of place. (Roodhouse 2002)

Whilst all of these functions are valuable there is a tendency for such institutions to absorb the largest share of any public funding available for culture. This issue can be addressed by establishing these institutions as businesses, in the creative industries sense like any other, and for public sector intervention to be targeted specifically at what investment is needed to "grow" the business.

With the arts and heritage as integral components of the cultural community actively engaging culture as industry provides the most effective and powerful strategy for the establishment of a Cultural Quarter.

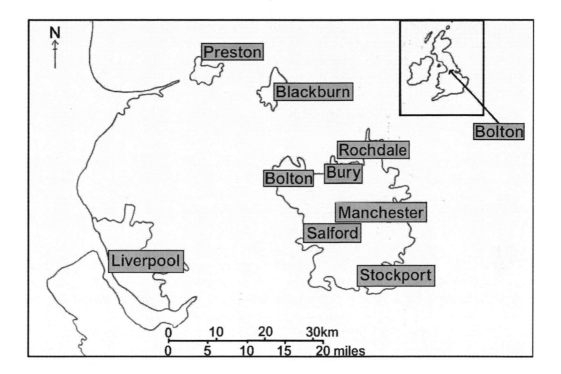

Understanding the spatial, demographic and infrastructure factors is essential to any consideration of a Cultural Quarter in terms of the Cultural Quarter principles of form or place and activity, as they deliver the basic platform for spatial and business development. When integrated with an assessment of cultural and related activities it determines what is feasible and deliverable for that particular locality. The Borough of Bolton in the North West of England is one of ten boroughs that make up the Greater Manchester conurbation. With a population of 261,037 it is bounded by Lancashire and by the Greater Manchester Boroughs of Bury, Salford and Wigan. Bolton has a total area of 13,973 hectares, of which 6,230 hectares is built-up land. It is 11 miles north of Manchester City Centre. There are just over 108,085 households in the Borough.

In the Index of Multiple Deprivation 2000, seven of the Borough's twenty wards are within the 10 per cent most deprived wards in England. The seven wards – Burnden, Central, Derby, Farnworth, Halliwell, Harper Green and Tonge, are home to 98,000. Based partly on these statistics and earlier indices, Bolton has attracted special funding under the City Challenge, Single Regeneration Budgets programmes 2, 3, 4 and 6, together with a significant allocation of funding through the National Strategy for Neighbourhood Renewal. There are, however, areas of significant prosperity within the Borough.

Bolton is a multi-racial Borough. The 2001 Census of Population showed that over 28,671 people classified themselves as belonging to a non-white ethnic group – nearly 11 percent of the population. In Greater Manchester only Manchester City, Oldham, and Rochdale have greater proportions of ethnic minority groups. By far the largest ethnic minority group in the Borough is that of Indian origin, with a significant population from Pakistan. Just less than three-quarters of the ethnic minority population live in the inner wards of the Borough, which are Derby, Central, Halliwell, Burnden and Daubhill.

Bolton town centre is of sub-regional importance within Greater Manchester and South Lancashire. It is the "Jewel in the Crown" of the Borough and the key economic driver within it. Its continuing success is vital to the economy of the Borough of Bolton in that it provides employment for over 19,000 people and has a retail catchment of 760,000 (2001). It is the centre for commerce, culture, civic functions, entertainment and heritage, and has an increasing resident population.

Bolton is a compact town with a transport network strongly focused through radial routes on the town centre. There are ever increasing delays on the road network caused by increasing car ownership and use. Bolton is well connected to the regional motorway network via the M61. Bolton town centre has the substantial number of around 12,500 car parking spaces, with 5,800 of these being public spaces provided by the Council and private sector. Public car parking associated with shops and supermarkets add a further 2,200 car park spaces.

Bolton railway station provides frequent services to Manchester, and is the busiest station in the conurbation outside Manchester City Centre. It is well connected to other regional centres including Wigan, Preston, Blackpool, Windermere and Blackburn.

Bus services operate at frequent intervals along the majority of radial routes into the town centre and are "town-centre terminating", hence reinforcing the town centre as being an important destination. The bus station is presently located on land between Moor Lane and Blackhorse Street. There is also a bus station adjacent to the railway station on Newport Street, which, despite the smaller size of the Newport Street bus station, leads to no hegemony for one bus station location or the other.

7.4 Bolton Public Sector Cultural Provision

Before moving towards consideration of approaches to a Bolton Cultural Quarter it is necessary to establish an empirical baseline, which includes an understanding of the relevant public sector services and private sector activity. This section includes the brief explanation of public and private sector services engaged in cultural and creative activities. It is not comprehensive, but focuses on key providers. However what it does demonstrate is the importance of the local authority as the key provider of public cultural services, the planning authority (it decides where and what development takes place) economic lead, and local political voice through its elected councillors.

Museums and Archives

None of these services are statutory local authority functions. However, the Public Libraries and Museums Act 1964 obliges every local authority "to provide a comprehensive and efficient library service". This principally covers the Local Studies part of the service. The Local Government Act 1972 states that "a principal council shall make proper arrangements with respect to any documents that belong to or are in the custody of the council or any of their officers". The Archives service is subject to inspection from the Public Record Office as a recognised place of deposit for public records and the Historical Manuscripts Commission. The Museums Service attains nationally recognised minimum standards set by the Museums, Libraries and Archives Council for Museum Registration, and the Professional and Ethical Standards that are set by the Museums Association. The Aquarium is licensed under the Zoo Licensing Act.

The services are concentrated in the main Le Mans Crescent site, but include:

- Central Library and Museum, housing
  - Central Museum and Art Gallery
  - Aquarium
  - Archives Local Studies Unit
- Hall i'th' Wood Museum
- Smithills Hall Museum
- Westhoughton Library local history exhibit area
- External museum store (large collections of local social and industrial history, geology, costume and others)
- Archives and Local Studies stores in
  - Market Hall basement
  - Town Hall basement
  - Horwich Library (Bolton MBC departmental records)
- Local Studies Collections in Key Libraries
  - Horwich
  - Farnworth
  - Westhoughton
  - Harwood

An emergency Bolton local studies collection exists at Greater Manchester County Records Office. In addition the Service operates Schools Museum loans.

The history of these services is worth noting; not least that Le Mans Crescent was specifically designed to house the Museum, Art Gallery, Aquarium and Library:

1852 Bolton adopted the Libraries and Museums Act
1853 Bolton Public Libraries start collecting all types of published and unpublished material of local significance

1884 Chadwick Museum opened to the public in Queen's Park

1890 Art Gallery opened in Mere Hall (since closed)

1902 Hall i'th' Wood Museum given to the town by Lord Leverhulme

1938 Smithills Hall Museum was purchased for the town

1939 New Museum and Art Gallery opened, together with a Central Library in Le Mans Crescent, its present location

1966 Friends of Bolton Museum and Art Gallery founded

1972 Bolton Central Library approved as place of deposit for certain classes of public records under the Public Records Act 1958 and 1967

1974 Bolton Metropolitan Borough established an Archive Service, which collected material for permanent preservation

1990 Bolton Archive Service and the Local Studies Section of Bolton Central Reference Library were combined to form the Bolton Archive and Local Studies Unit

1990 Designated Archive and Local Studies Searchroom provided on the ground floor of the Central Library

All three museums have full Registration under Resource's Phase 2 Museum Registration Scheme.

All of the services are operated directly by Bolton MBC, except Smithills Hall, which was operated by the Council until April 2001. Since then the Smithills Hall and Park Trust have run it under a Service Level Agreement with Bolton MBC. The Council provides the Trust's funding but the building and its contents remain in Council ownership. Visitor numbers for the service are as follows:

Museum:

1st April 03	11,821
May 03	11,798
June 03	10,378
July 03	14,526
August 03	14,506
Sep 03	9,929
Oct 03	16,295
Nov 03	15,697
Dec 03	10,942
Jan 04	13,949
Feb 03	19,837

Aquarium:

1st Jan 03	5,330
Feb 03	7,738
March 03	5,545
April 03	6,808
May 03	6,185
June 03	4,916
July 03	8,067
August 03	9,597
Sep 03	4,525
Oct 03	7,364
Nov 03	6,753
Dec 03	4,721

Museums and Archives

None of these services are statutory local authority functions. However, the Public Libraries and Museums Act 1964 obliges every local authority "to provide a comprehensive and efficient library service". This principally covers the Local Studies part of the service. The Local Government Act 1972 states that "a principal council shall make proper arrangements with respect to any documents that belong to or are in the custody of the council or any of their officers". The Archives service is subject to inspection from the Public Record Office as a recognised place of deposit for public records and the Historical Manuscripts Commission. The Museums Serice attains nationally recognised minimum standards set by the Museums, Libraries and Archives Council for Museum Registration, and the Professional and Ethical Standards that are set by the Museums Association. The Aquarium is licensed under the Zoo Licensing Act.

The Library Service

The Bolton library service has the following provision:

- A network of 14 libraries based in and reflecting Bolton's very different communities;
- The majority of libraries in reasonable condition;
- A new mobile library in services since March 2003;
- The public finance initiative involvement with the Castle Hill Centre, which will result in the relocation of Tonge Moor library with the primary school and services for young people;
- Rapidly developing electronic services promoting access.

The Hub for the network is the Central Library, which is located in Le Mans Crescent. This library is open nearly 60 hours a week and attracts between 3,000 to 3,500 people every day. In 2003/04 it issued over 700,000 items and proved to be the busiest of all of the Borough libraries. It is also recognised as one of the busiest in the Northwest region. In total, the Central Library holds approximately 250,000 items in stock and is the second most important reference library in Greater Manchester. In particular, there are specialist collections, which include:

- British standards;
- Music scores;
- Car workshop manuals;
- Classic fiction, predominantly out of print or last copy material;
- A significant children's library.

In addition, the Central Library is part of the People's Network, with twelve PCs available for public use; however, this is restricted by the lack of learning space accommodation and equipment. The Department for Culture Media and Sport, in partnership with Resource now the Museums, Libraries and Archives Council have established The People's Network, which is the first significant step to allow libraries to fulfil their potential in the digital age. Much reinvestment funded through the New Opportunities Fund has enabled almost all public libraries in England to establish a UK online learning centre by the end of December 2002, as well as providing library staff with computer training and learner support skills. A further £50 million programme is creating online content. (Holden, J., & Leadbeater, C. 2003)

In particular, this network is expected to provide access to other government services, creating new links to local services, and improve access to online information services as well as creating content, hosting communities online, accessing national content and working with organisations such as Learn Direct to provide online learning.

In addition, the library service provides a modest temporary exhibition space for community, voluntary, local authority and statutory requirements. This includes, for example, community events such as boundary commission changes, local authority consultation, art group events, and working with the Museum, Art Gallery and Aquarium to develop local services.

There are over 100,000 items available for loan which are not on open shelves at present.

There are constraints on the library through the lack of space within the buildings, particularly the Central Library, for the range of services needed to be offered, especially meeting the digital citizenship needs in Bolton.

Community Arts

Community arts are particularly important in Bolton, and were championed by the former Council Arts Unit. This was a small team, which acted as a contact centre for the arts in the Borough. In particular it was able to provide information about the arts and creative industries, including contacts, plans and projects. In this capacity it represented the views of the Council, regarding the arts in Bolton, fulfilled an information and brokerage role, as well as providing advice and support for any arts activity, artist, art organisation or arts businesses regarding funding opportunities. It also acted as an advocate for the arts in the town. In particular, through its support for community arts, participation in artistic activity increased, with over 1.7 million people taking part in arts activities a year, and over 1.2 million attendances each year at arts events. This represented a threefold increase in numbers since 1993. The Arts Action Plan describes much of the work that the Arts Unit, now incorporated into the Arts and Community Services Team, undertook.

There are over 25 agencies giving advice and support, as well as running arts activity in the Borough, for example, the Artist In Schools agency and the % for Art team, the Arctic and the Octagon Theatre's Activ8 theatre, Community and Educational Programme team, as well as over 70 amateur groups covering, drama, opera, music and fine arts.

The Arts Unit has facilitated participation in these activities by working through Council departments and services. It also supports community arts facilitators located in different agencies, including the University of Bolton.

Creative Industries and the Enterprise Unit

The Bolton Borough Council Enterprise Unit focuses on the creative industries, social enterprise and other enterprise growth sectors, providing specialised business support and strategic management and development of incubation workspace. The Enterprise Unit provides the support network for Bolton's creative industries, one of the country's fastest growing economic sectors. As part of Bolton Metro's Regeneration & Economic Development Division they provide hands-on support for those wanting to start a creative business. They now have a client base of over 600 creatives in the Borough comprising micro and macro businesses and community arts groups.

The Fuse Studios is an integrated business support and accommodation initiative based at the Enterprise Centre, Washington Street, for creative industries in Bolton. Using derelict space within a former mill, fifteen low-cost incubator units have been created, together with a shared office/resource facility. Six half-bays have been designed to house those that need a flexible space with abundant natural light. Seven closed industrial units are ideal for those working in ceramics, wood or metal work, sharing access to two kilns and a printing press. Two office spaces are available for those working in industries like Graphic Design. The Enterprise Unit is currently developing a further five units, which will be an innovative space for those working within the realms of digital media. (cidt@bolton.gov.uk 2004)

The Enterprise Unit host Wired City events, local informative and informal networking events, where guest speakers from some of the region's up-and-coming businesses share their experiences and answer questions. Digital Media clients have the opportunity to meet other creative businesses, share issues, opinions and thoughts on their business sector, as well as the chance to explore opportunities for collaboration.

Continuing Professional Development is a pilot programme developed jointly with Bury and Wigan MBC's to increase the knowledge and skills of people working in the creative industries, especially pre-start-up and new start-ups, so that those businesses survive and grow and contribute to a thriving creative industries sector. This is a personal programme tailored to each individual and/or enterprise and using a range of learning mechanisms including mentoring, action learning, advice surgeries, research and reading as well as seminars and courses.

The creative industries is one of the fastest growing sectors of employment in the UK, and to mark this the Unit has produced a video to target school leavers and graduates who may want to embark on a career within this sector. 'Making Creativity Work' explores numerous vocations within the creative industries, and highlights support networks. The video follows three case studies: Nazeera Atcha, a Community & Visual Artists from Bolton; Stephen Morris, a Fashion Designer from Westhoughton; and Munaf Ibrahim, a Graphic Designer from Bolton.

7.5 Further and Higher Education, With Some Reference to Schools

Bolton has a well-established higher education institution. The University of Bolton is strongly vocationally focused and makes a significant contribution to the local economy and community. It has over 7,000 students, with a significant range of undergraduate and postgraduate courses in the creative sector, and has recently established the Creative Industries Group. In 2004 the University opened a Design Studio on the Deane campus, very near the town centre. The Design Studio combines technology and creativity in an imaginative way and provides education and training programmes as well as support to local and sub-regional industry.

Bolton Community College, created by merging Bolton College with Bolton Council's Community Education Service, provides excellent learning opportunities for people of all ages including school leavers, adults returning to learning, employees and trainees. The College offers more than 500 courses at many centres across the Borough of Bolton ranging from introductory courses to Higher National Diplomas. To help people in their studies many of the college centres offer childcare facilities and student support and advice services.

Bolton Sixth Form College is the only Sixth Form College in Bolton and provides a bridge between school and higher education and employment. The College offers independence within a framework of guided self-discipline.

More than 75 per cent of Bolton Sixth Form College students progress to higher education. Bolton Sixth Form College students successfully apply to universities within the region and throughout the country, with special provision for those students wishing to apply to Oxford and Cambridge universities. This progression to University is achieved both by A level and AVCE students. The College also has an Academic Fellowship "Fast-track" scheme, available for students who anticipate getting mostly A grades at GCSE.

Three of the seventeen Bolton secondary schools have specialist arts status, and consequently are important to any town centre Cultural Quarter development. These are Harper Green Community Secondary School, Smithills Community Secondary School and Turton Media Arts College.

7.6 Bolton Cultural Industry Statistics

There is a general paucity of primary data available on the cultural industries in the northwest region. However, the North West Regional Intelligence Unit commissioned two research projects in the cultural industries, which provide background information.

The first report, 'Benchmarking Employment in the Cultural Industries' (Graver, A. & Harrison, J. 2002) provides an analysis of secondary data from a variety of sources and concludes that there are:

- 393,000 people employed in the cultural industries;
- Almost 3/5 of employment is in tourism – 225,000 people;
- There are 146,000 people employed in creative industries, and 43,000 in sport and leisure;
- The cultural industries account for over 12% of all employment in the region. The breakdown is 7% in tourism, 4.5% in creative and 1% in sport;
- There are over 36,000 cultural enterprises in the region;
- Over a third of the workforce in the creative industries are self-employed compared to 5% in tourism and 9% in sport.

Tourism businesses make up by far the largest proportion of business units – and 47.9 per cent of businesses in the cultural industries and almost 8 per cent of all businesses in the northwest.

It suggests that Bolton employs 10,846 people in the cultural industries, which represent 9 per cent of all employment in the area.

The second report, 'Benchmarking the Health of Cultural Businesses' (Experian Business Strategies and Burns Owens Partnership 2003) sets out to provide a better and a deeper understanding of the way cultural businesses operate in the region in order to guide future decision-making, in particular focusing on the performance and needs of small and micro businesses. It is also expected to provide a tracking mechanism for the development of cultural businesses over time using comparable quantitative indicators. Whilst this report is generally useful as background information to the performance of micro and small cultural businesses in the region, it is unhelpful at a local level because the data cannot be disaggregated to provide useful information at a local level. It does not, for example, include public sector services or supported provision, and the cultural industries are divided into three new groupings which do not reflect the generally accepted sub-sector categories derived from standard industrial classifications used in the DCMS regional cultural data framework.

Consequently there is little primary data available about the cultural industries in Bolton and it will be necessary at some stage to undertake a baseline analysis rather than relying on secondary data and estimates. However, the estimate of the number of creative businesses in Bolton taken from the Bolton Borough Council Enterprise Unit is 515, broken down into sub sectors in the following table:

Broadcast Media:	5	Textiles:	10
Ceramics:	6	Visual Arts:	75
Sculpture:	9	Music:	130
Community Art:	22	Performance:	17
Craft:	33	Theatre:	13
Digital Media:	32	Photography:	21
Graphic Design:	47	Literature:	23
Film/Video Production:	20	Publishing:	6
Fashion Design:	9	Miscellaneous:	21
Interior/Furniture Design:	16		

Source: Bolton Metropolitan Borough Council, Enterprise Unit, 2004.

What is apparent from this description of the geography, demographics and public services in a relatively small town (in UK terms), is the importance of the local authority, not only as the major provider of cultural services but also in terms of direct and indirect influence on education provision. Local authorities are, however, recognised by the Arts Council of England as the major deliverer of cultural services at a local level. They are also well placed to access funds from national government and the European Union as the delivery agent at local level, accountable locally. However, for all this, local authorities suffer from a demanding and extensive committee structure for decision-making, conflicting priorities between statutory and non-statutory (culture) responsibilities and, above all, direct political influence. Often there is little freedom to manage, with an inflexible hierarchal structure. This has resulted in more services being put into Trust. The Sheffield Gallery and Museum Trust case study in chapter 2 is an excellent example of this and provides a valuable insight into the cultural management issues of a local authority. It points the way to an increasing interest in partnership working. It also demonstrates the spectrum of existing and potential stakeholders required to be engaged in the development within the local authority itself. When this is combined with private sector businesses, professional services such as architects and developers, master planning and management are essential.

Chapter 8

Key Influencing Factors in Establishing a Cultural Quarter

In establishing a Bolton Cultural Quarter in an old cotton town with a long and proud history, a spectrum of factors inevitably need to be recognised, understood and incorporated in any emerging model. This chapter describes these factors in detail, to illustrate the complexity of developing a Cultural Quarter around the principles of culture as business, a sense of place and meaning, as well as capturing activity, but above all else the need for specific solutions which reflect local circumstances.

8.1 The Town Centre Factor, an Architectural Inheritance and Zoning

The town centre has progressively declined in economic importance and, as a consequence, action is required to restore the significance of the town centre as a nucleus of social and economic activity. This has been confirmed in a recent survey and ranking of shopping centres in the UK, (Experian 2004) on behalf of the British Council of Shopping Centres.

On this basis, a number of mid sized centres present real opportunities for further urban regeneration. These include Warrington, Hanley (Stoke-on-Trent), Stockport, Maidstone, Doncaster, Northampton and Bolton.

However, Bolton has inherited impressive nationally recognised architectural gems such as the Victorian Town Hall and Le Mans Crescent, but needs to consider what legacy is being created for future generations. Bolton is known for its Town Hall, which Pevsner praised as one of the best Victorian examples, but what is the architectural contribution to be made today which will stand the test of time and attract critical praise as a major contribution to raising the town's profile? Examples of new architectural contributions which have as a consequence raised the profile of the area are the Guggenheim Museum in Bilbau, Spain, or the new Art Gallery in Walsall, West Midlands.

Zoning is an increasingly popular mechanism employed in town centre development by those responsible for economic and planning regulation as it provides an effective means of clustering related and compatible activity in a designated spatial area. It is used, for example, in the Wolverhampton Cultural Quarter.

There are zones being generated in and around the town centre which need to be considered in the establishment of the Cultural Quarter, particularly how the zones relate to each other. The zones are:

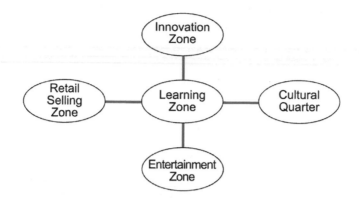

The key principle for a Cultural Quarter is that any designated cultural zoning is specifically linked and overlapped with learning and innovation zones. In other words, the zones bleed into and interact with each other in a supportive mechanism rather than boundaries and frontiers. It is important that Cultural Quarter activities, networks and infrastructure interact and support other sympathetic zones, as well integrating with any transport proposals.

It is anticipated that the proposed Bolton town centre activity zones described in the following diagram, which typifies many planning authorities, will not act as barriers, as mentioned earlier, and reflect the interaction described.

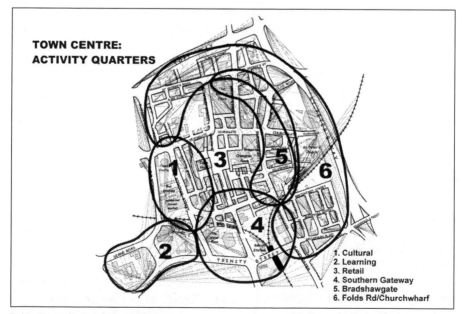

Bolton Town Centre Activity Zones.

8.2 Creative Business Growth as a Contribution to Wealth Creation

There is recognition that creative businesses form an integral part of the local economy and culture, whether they are publicly or privately funded as suppliers of products and services to local and sub-regional markets, as explained in cultural statistics for Bolton. (Roodhouse 2000) Consequently these businesses deserve to be recognised, supported and promoted in the interests of broadening the economic base of the town, generating added value jobs and retaining graduates. The Borough has made a start on this with the establishment of the Creative Industries Development Team (Enterprise Unit) at the Enterprise Centre which provides work space and business support to a limited number of organisations.

Cultural products and services are consumed locally, and this demand requires to be met. One interesting aspect of the 'Benchmarking the Health of Cultural Businesses' report is that there is substantial demand for cultural goods and services at a local level generally across the region.

8.3 The Existence and Use of Council Cultural Assets

It is possible in the case of Bolton, to suggest that the "family silver" has never been taken out of the vault, and that it is time for the town to demonstrate its sense of place and represent to the world a meaningful representation of the town and its people.

For example, the Aquarium, one of very few located in a town centre, which attracts over 70,000 local visitors annually with minimal publicity, is buried in Le Mans Crescent, and it seems to be a local secret, with the bulk of the visitors coming from Bolton.

However, the Museum, Art Gallery, Aquarium, Archives, and Libraries public services have suffered from severe long-term underinvestment. This seems to echo the Sheffield Art Gallery and Museum Service history, although less extreme. However, these services hold significant regional and national collections of outstanding quality which are currently unavailable to local people and in their present state attract over 200,000 visiting the Museum and Art Gallery and a further 70,000 local people visiting the aquarium. On the other hand, the Central Library, another cultural asset, receives 600,000 visitors annually.

It is notable that The Wolverhampton and Vienna Cultural Quarter examples include as cornerstones council services such as the Museum, Art Gallery or Theatre.

8.4 The Existence of a Cultural Infrastructure and the Cultural Tourism Influence

There is an extensive cultural infrastructure, although this is rarely quantified, including amateur theatre, art clubs and societies in the Bolton Borough, which is recognised and connected to the larger cultural organisations. This is based on extensive community arts work over the last ten years, and has resulted in substantially improved participation in the arts. The issue for the Bolton Cultural Quarter model is how these activities are connected and networked into the quarter and its activities to mutually support each other. This is an issue for all planned quarters.

Cultural tourism, another economic driver associated with places such as Bolton, has yet to realise its potential. The town is unexplored including its cultural infrastructure, particularly as Bolton was a major centre for the beginnings of the industrial revolution. The Borough has set a target of a 10 per cent visitor increase in its community plan by 2007. This will require a major tourist attraction in addition to the existing provision, which would sustain a family visit for at least the morning or afternoon. At present, the town does not have such a tourism asset. The total annual tourism visitors in Bolton (2003) were 8.4 million, an 8 per cent increase on the previous year, and visitor expenditure was in the region of £165 million, representing a 5 per cent increase on 2002, according to the tourism department at Bolton Metropolitan Borough Council. The question here is how a 10 per cent increase can be achieved without developing the cultural infrastructure, and more to the point a major destination attraction such as the MuseumsQuartier, Vienna, and Temple Bar, Dublin, although as has been noted earlier the tourists attracted to Dublin are not necessarily the "right" ones.

8.5 Graduate Retention and Added Value Jobs

There is a need to retain the best emerging talent, particularly cultural industry graduates from the University of Bolton and surrounding universities, who can contribute to the economic growth, social and cultural life of the town. Currently the University produces over 150 creative industries graduates a year, in disciplines such as Art & Design, Computer Games, Film and Broadcast Media. These graduates are most likely to set up creative businesses and live and work in the area, thus making a contribution to the local economy, but also stimulating the cultural life of the town through their activities and lifestyle.

Both Wolverhampton and Sheffield have based their developments on the incorporation of the University as a key stakeholder, investing in the Quarter, providing students and graduates and supporting existing businesses. The issue is how do we do this?

8.6 The Information Technology Phenomenon

Access to information technology is vital to any contemporary economic, social or cultural development strategy, and, consequently, the Department of Culture, Media and Sport (DCMS 2003) published a new strategic framework for the public library service: Framework for the Future. The policy document outlines the government's long-term strategic vision for the role of public libraries as cultural assets that have the capacity to make information widely available through technology. Its purpose is to help local and library authorities agree on the key objectives for the public library service with central government and local communities.

The new strategy is intended to enable libraries to build on existing strengths and ensure they position themselves at the heart of the communities they serve. Public libraries are a valuable infrastructure, which have the potential to help local councils deliver their corporate agenda. The best libraries are doing so already through a range of innovative programmes. By clarifying key priorities Framework for Future provides a focus for the future work across the sector. It provides a basis for authorities to prioritise and plan services to meet the needs of citizens, adapted to best suit local circumstance.

How, then, does Bolton keep pace with the digital revolution which is integral to the creative industries and supports the people in keeping themselves informed, skilled and employable?

The Bolton Library Service as a cultural asset is central to delivering this, but is restricted by the physical nature of the buildings and a lack of investment. There is a need to ensure that virtual networks with hubs are an integral part of the future of the town, not least because the cultural industries increasingly rely upon digitisation and the convergence of technology.

In the Framework for the Future strategy the Department of Culture, Media and Sport have identified the potential of Libraries to respond to changing circumstances:

Knowledge, skills and information are becoming more important to our lives economically, socially and as citizens. Libraries have a central role to play in ensuring everyone has access to the resources, information and knowledge they need – particularly those groups in society who will otherwise be disadvantaged, including people who are less affluent, and people with literacy problems.

The best libraries are showing the way forward. Libraries are developing new skills to help library users access ICT and use the Internet. There has been a big expansion in reader development work, eye-catching new library buildings have opened in a number of cities, and other places are seeking radically to redefine the ways in which the library services are developed.

The strategy states that:

We live in a society in which knowledge, skills and information are becoming more important to our lives, economically, socially and as citizens. Jobs in manufacturing and services increasingly demand higher skills, the ability to use computers and the capacity for continual on-the-job learning.

For example, the report cites Bournemouth's new Central Library, which is based in a bold, light, open and modern building, and it is already beginning to change the town.

There are 50 personal computers dotted around the building. In the foyer is a new cafe. An express area is designed for people to browse and choose from the most popular material, which includes videos, DVDs, CDs, as well as books. Teenagers gather in an area that they helped to design. The building is light, but quiet, and so an excellent place of the learning. A large proportion of the people coming into the library use it for study in the broadest sense of the word, rather than to take out books. Since the opening, visitor numbers have more than doubled. Book issues have risen by about 10%. The computers are used for about 2500 hours a week.

The Southeast England Regional Development Agency is studying plans to create a pedestrian piazza outside the library, which could be used for cultural events. That in turn is attracting local businesses. Investment in public space is creating the backdrop for economic growth. The new library building has been funded through a private finance initiative scheme.

Another idea which is described in the report concerns the London Borough of Tower Hamlets, where a new kind of library has been established, the Idea Store. The first Idea Store opened in 2002. It is open seven days a week for 71 hours. In the foyer people can study, read or have lunch in a large cafe. Across the hall a bank of Internet computers is in constant use. Staff at the library are drawn from adult education and libraries: they form a single integrated team. Idea Stores are a reinterpretation of what a library can be. Around the core stock of books and information the staff are helping people to learn, search for jobs, access public services, or simply to enjoy themselves. Visitor figures have trebled and issues are up by 65 per cent and rising. In the course of the next few years the Idea Store's brand will be rolled out across the whole authority in a network of purpose-built buildings, in time replacing the current library stock.

Despite the emerging importance of libraries in making information widely available and providing access to information technology they do not generally form part of a Cultural Quarter nor are they conceptually as important as other cultural assets, although they comfortably fall within the Williams cultural definition referred to in section 2.

8.7 The Importance of Cultural Diversity and the Bolton Profile

Recognition of cultural diversity and the consequent need to ensure that the Quarter is open to all Bolton residents is essential. This factor is universal and starts with a thorough understanding of the demographics of the area followed by a developed understanding of the cultural dynamics associated with this diversity – the richness in diversity principle. This has to be applied to all Cultural Quarters not least because the people already living and working in these areas are diverse.

The Bolton concern, as described in the community, economic and town centre strategies, would suggest that regional, national and international cultural exposure is poor, with some exceptions, and needs readdressing as a means of attracting inward investment and supporting the Council's aim of being a desirable place to live and work. Living in the Manchester shadow is unhelpful in this respect. The Vienna MuseumsQuartier has successfully raised the contemporary cultural profile of the city internationally.

8.8 The Manchester Shadow

The impact of the Manchester shadow effect, and the imperialistic ambitions to become a city region, has to be recognised and managed. There is a danger here that Bolton could become the Wakefield of the Leeds shadow or the Rotherham of the Sheffield city region. Bradford has been able to counter the shadow through the establishment of the National Museum of Photography Film and Television, and strengthening cultural business activity in Little Germany as well as promoting the strong cultural dynamics of the city.

Any development in Bolton has to take cognisance of the Manchester shadow and develop a unique and distinctive position to avoid city imperialism whilst at the same time taking advantage of the Manchester effect, particularly with regard to tourism. This is possible given the difference in geographical location, size, composition of the population, and social, economic and cultural infrastructure. It is worth noting that Bolton has been successful in gaining recognition for the Town Hall, and more recently the Reebok Stadium, as notable contributions to local and regional heritage and sports provision.

Chapter 9

The Nuts and Bolts: Outputs, Resources, Procurement Routes and Management

Essential to the successful delivery of a Cultural Quarter are resources, procurement routes and management. Inevitably, different models have emerged, particularly in management structures, resource and procurement patterns. The most popular mechanisms are described in this chapter.

The arguments for establishing a Cultural Quarter are concerned with the economic, cultural and social benefits to a geographical area. Outputs are important, and it is noticeable from the case studies that evidence can be found to support the economic and cultural impact of Cultural Quarters, but there is a paucity of social and marketing data and systematic analysis. This chapter provides summaries of the claimed outputs drawn from the case studies, followed by differing approaches to procurement and management. The inconsistencies in the evidence of success are due to the lack of evaluation – in some cases there is no published evaluation or associated data at all. This is surprising when the public sector is involved and their levels of accountability high.

9.1 Summaries of Outputs

Temple Bar, Dublin
- In 1992 there were twenty-seven restaurants, 100 shops, 6 arts buildings 16 public houses, 2 hotels, 200 residents, 70 cultural industry businesses and 80 other businesses in Temple Bar.

- By 1996, when most of the initial development schemes had been completed, there were 5 hotels, 200 shops, 40 restaurants, 12 cultural centres and a resident population of 2,000 people.

- During the construction phase some 5,000 yearly FTE equivalent jobs had been created in the building industry (most of them sub-contracted to Dublin companies).

- By the end of 1996 there were an estimated 2,000 people employed in Temple Bar, an increase of 300%. Monies generated from rental income are ploughed back into the property renewal programme and environmental action, and used to cross-subsidise cultural projects.

- Total public funding for Temple Bar was some IR£40.6 million, the bulk of which (£37 million) was spent on the Cultural Development Programme 1991–2001.

- A further £60 million has been borrowed and repaid through TBPL's commercial programme.

- From 1991 to 2001, the private sector is estimated to have invested over £100 million in the area.

Source: Montgomery 2003

In the case of the Sheffield Cultural Industries Quarter there is evidence generated more recently, with no published baseline of activity and, when the emphasis is on creative business generation and development, this seems a poor platform to assess the effectiveness of the quarter and its management. The following outputs are claimed:

Sheffield Cultural Industries Quarter
By 2004
In excess of 60,000sq m of CDI focused B1 broadband serviced move-on and incubation space available

Developing 6,000sq m of live/work accommodation

Sheffield Hallam University, Arts, Computer, Engineering and Science Faculty (8,000sq m) established

500 + student residences available

200 apartments for sale and let

2,500sq m of specialist sub sector move-on space (Dance/Theatre production Centre)

One new Hotel, (budget/mid price)

Public realm development, including street furniture and lighting

Approximately £100m + regeneration and investment activity

Source: Sheffield CIQ 2004

The MuseumsQuartier in Vienna established visitor numbers as a key measure for judging performance:

MuseumsQuarter, VIENNA

The MuseumsQuartier has attracted in its first year 1.6 million visitors, with the Leopold Museum as the star attraction with around 250,000 to 300,000 visitors, exceeding the original MQ target by 500,000.

Source: MuseumsQuartier Development Company

For other projects, as mentioned earlier, there is little published output evidence. Which, given the scale of resources involved and physical impact, is surprising, but is a general weakness of national and international Cultural Quarter development. Where systematic measurement has occurred, in cases such as Temple Bar, Dublin, the project has been successful by economic criteria; however, it is more difficult to judge the success of this project in social and cultural terms, although it has substantially raised the profile of a derelict area of the city and developed the cultural infrastructure. Again economic evidence can be found for Sheffield Cultural Industries Quarter, the numbers of businesses supported through the provision of dedicated space, for example, and the MuseumsQuartier, Vienna – success in attracting significant numbers of tourists. Audits of existing public and private sector provision in the designated area for Cultural Quarter development is essential, as described in chapter 5. This provides a baseline, which enables development to be measured accurately and consistently.

9.2 Procurement Routes

Procurement routes can be considered once a geographical area has been identified and should be incorporated at an early stage of planning because it will be necessary to acquire buildings and sites for redevelopment by public and private investors. Management and contractual vehicles need to be established to facilitate the procurement. After all, one of the primary aims is to regenerate a physical area, to sustain and attract creative businesses, jobs, and, increase income levels through the development of the existing cultural assets, a sustainable cultural economy based on creativity. As indicated earlier this approach requires an interaction between the local authority as planning authority, private developers and the people in the designated area, but perhaps above all else a visionary.

Common building types within a proposed Cultural Quarter, which can be found for example in Temple Bar, Dublin, and the MuseumsQuartier, Vienna, may include the following:

• Destination landmark scheme such as Tate Modern, London
• Cultural – Department of Culture Media and Sport/Local Authority

- Justice – Home Office;
- Education – Learning and Skills Council/Higher Education Funding Council for England and equivalents in Wales, Northern Ireland and Scotland;
- Leisure – Private Operators;
- Retail – Private Operators;
- Office – Private Operators;
- Housing – Private Developers.

The procurement routes for these building types may include the following forms of contract: traditional contracting, design and build contracting or design, build, fund and operate, which are known as Private Finance Initiative (PFI) or Public Private Partnership (PPP). The PFI and PPP contracting schemes were introduced to enable private investment in the public sector capital infrastructure, thus reducing the national government annual capital borrowing requirement. In the cultural field the first of these was the Royal Armouries in Leeds. The Royal Armouries, one of the oldest museums in the world, established in the fifteenth century, which has occupied buildings in the Tower of London since its construction, has developed and established an alternative approach to bringing together public and private sector interests. This model came about because the Royal Armouries, at one time a part of the Ministry of Defence, and latterly of the Environment Department, was determined as a result of the National Heritage Act 1983 when an independent board of trustees was established, to increase public access to its collections. In order to realise this fundamental strategic aim, the trustees initiated a development plan which included the establishment of two new museums, in Portsmouth and Leeds. Private sector funding was necessary to build and operate the £42.5m museum in Leeds, which was opened in 1996. (Roodhouse 1999)

Other examples of these approaches are:

Design, Build Fund and Operate Project
Treasury and Cabinet War Rooms
HOK Architects, worked with the HM Treasury and the Cabinet War Rooms to write the brief for the following projects:

- Occupier Brief for the Office and Museum;
- Output Specification for the Office and Museum.

The PFI project was then advertised and tendered by the OJEC process. HOK worked with Phil Reid, the Director of the Cabinet War Rooms and Sir Terence Burns, the Parliamentary under Secretary for HM Treasury.

The preferred PFI bid for the project included the following:

- Offices for the Treasury;
- Hotel facilities overlooking Whitehall;
- Residential Facilities overlooking St James Park;
- An extension to the Cabinet War Rooms/Churchill Museum.

The facilities included cultural leisure, hospitality and residential and business facilities.

Funding for the Museum Project included PFI and HLF funding. This required extensive negotiation between the Imperial War Museum and the PFI consortium.

The Cabinet War Rooms committed to financing the scheme by virtue of an annual payment to the PFI consortium.

The £21m Darwin Centre Phase 1 project for the Zoology Spirit Building included the following funding.

- NHM Revenues from entrance receipts;
- Sponsorship;
- Grant in Aid Funding for the Capital project.

The Phase 2 project has successfully applied for Heritage Lottery Funding.

The NHM had to exercise financial prudence over a number of years to save the capital for the NHM Zoology Spirit Building. Sir Neil Chalmers, the Director of the NHM, was the Champion for the project.

Source: P. Richards, HOK 2004

Multiple Procurement Routes
Birmingham Eastside Cultural Quarter
The Cultural Quarter includes the following stakeholders:

- Birmingham City Council Urban Development Team, Director: Richard Green;
- British Waterways who owned the Digbeth Branch Canal and Grand Union Canal;
- Millennium Point, a £70m Lottery funded museum and education project for Central England University;
- Aston University (Bursar – David Packham), who are planning a £25m sports centre with a 50m Olympic standard pool;

- Matthew Boulton College, (Vice Principal – Ray Goy), have completed a £25m project with £8m from the Learning Skills Council;
- Alliance West Midlands;
- Birmingham Museum and Art Gallery, (Assistant Director – Graham Allen);
- Birmingham Library is applying for lottery funding for £150m library by Richard Rogers;
- Gostrabock, (Director – Peter Stratton);
- Land Securities and Hammerson;
- Royal Society of Organists;

The Cultural Quarter will include a new 9-acre city park, which will connect the City Centre to the Digbeth Branch Canal. Facilities will include museum, library, education, leisure, hospitality, business and residential space. HOK produced the Urban Plan for Birmingham Eastside.
   Funding consists of the following:

- Funding from land sales – Aston University, Matthew Boulton College;
- Learning Skills Council Funding – Matthew Boulton College;
- HLF funding – Millennium Point;
- Private Finance of Student Residential Schemes;
- Private Finance of Business Schemes;
- Private Finance of Leisure and Science Park Schemes.

Source: P. Richards, HOK 2004

A common principle underpinning the chosen form of procurement is the business need for mixed-use development. The preferred procurement route generally followed by national and local government is the design, build, fund and operate contract, PFI or PPP, which involves the public sector working in partnership with the private sector.

The involvement of a private developer with access to substantial funding is necessary for the development of all three procurement routes as each requires matched funding for public sector Lottery, Public/Private Credits and Foundations financial resources. Lessons have been learned from the British Museum, Sheffield Cultural Industries Quarter and Dublin's Temple Bar, who all engaged private developers at some stage in the development of their schemes. Therefore it is a priority for new quarters to identify a private developer with a track record in education and culture development at an early stage.

This type of public/private funding can deliver a complex mixed-use scheme for libraries, museum space, office accommodation and housing without the public sector borrowing substantially over the long term. Instead the authority, agency or government department enters into a long lease arrangement, which often includes facilities management or site operation. A vibrant mixed-use Cultural Quarter incorporating the core characteristics will require all of these functions. The private sector partners are generally focussed on developing schemes which maximise land values for private properties and generate a long-term income stream through lease and operate, whilst public sector partners are more often concerned with meeting the social cultural and economic needs of their communities.

The capital receipts from this have the potential to fund these types of schemes and make PPI projects viable as a commercial venture. This is again not dissimilar to the Temple Bar, Dublin, approach.

In the case of the Bolton scheme a complementary approach is possible. Le Mans Cultural Quarter Museum, Art Gallery and Aquarium as the cultural landmark building could also work in partnership with National Museums such as the British Museum, the Victoria & Albert Museum, London, the Science Museum, London, and the Imperial War Museum, London. In effect they could become regional outposts for the national museums, and access funding through the national museum. This would replicate the MuseumsQuartier, Vienna, and to a lesser extent the Grand Opera House, Belfast, models as a lead cultural landmark solution to a regeneration problem, declining town centre and nightlife.

Once a procurement route is chosen it will then be necessary to consider the following:

- Town Planning constraints;
- Conservation Area and listed building consent issues;
- Urban Design issues;
- Landscape Architecture issues.

It should be noted that many private sector development partners are generally insensitive to listed buildings, and it is essential to develop a good relationship with the local conservation officers and English Heritage (the government agency responsible for conservation) to produce at an early stage a Conservation Strategy for any Cultural Quarter area. This could form an integral component of the baseline analysis of the chosen designated geographical area. In addition the design of the public spaces needs to promote the new Cultural Quarter and reflect the history and character of the place.

The next steps normally expected prior to formalising a procurement route are as follows:

Step 1: To deliver a detailed master plan
Step 2: To prepare a detailed conservation strategy
Step 3: To complete a detailed business plan for a mixed-use development

9.3 Management Structures to Deliver the Development

In the case of the Sheffield Cultural Industries Quarter, much of the early stages of the development were undertaken directly by the City Council. However, over the last two years an agency has been established to take the Quarter into the next stages of realisation. The Agency role as regeneration delivery vehicle for the part of the city centre is to steer and work alongside partners to realise the Cultural Industries Quarter as the foremost area to grow production capacity and opportunities for cultural producers.

The CIQ Agency is a not-for-profit company limited by guarantee. It has an executive team and board made up of key stakeholders of the area (at CEO or equivalent levels) as follows:

Sheffield City Council – Executive Director (Deputy Chief Executive); Sheffield First Partnership – Director Local Strategic Partnership; Sheffield Hallam University – Director, School of Culture; Sheffield Technology Parks – Director; Sheffield Media Exhibition Centre (the Showroom/Workstation) Group – Chief Executive Officer (CEO); Yorkshire

---

The Agency Approach
Sheffield Cultural Industries Quarter Agency

- The Agency is a not-for-profit company limited by guarantee.
- The Agency is expected to develop digital and creative industry businesses in the Sheffield CIQ, but also in the sub-region, South Yorkshire.
- The Agency acts as a statutory consultee on all planning applications within the CIQ. It has Finance and HR subcommittee and Advisory group reviewing Development and Investment in the Quarter. The DiG group is made up of officers from:

1. SCC planning
2. SCC highways
3. SCC property services
4. Sheffield One – (Urban Regeneration Company)
5. Sheffield First for Investment (inward investment)
6. Townscape Heritage Initiative THI (Lottery funded capital repair programme)

- The Agency is funded by a combination of European, SRB, single pot, lottery – some as core and others as project-based activity. Increasingly they are gaining contract and consultancy income streams.
- The private sector investment has been mainly in-kind and individual sponsorship in the core activity of the Agency.

Artspace Society – Director; Site Gallery – Director; Inspiral – Chief Executive Officer; (CEO); Community Media Association; Studio of the North – CEO; and BD Properties – representative.

Temple Bar, Dublin, on the other hand set out with a clearly defined strategy from the outset based on the urban principles referred to earlier:

The Publicly Owned Property, Facilities And Marketing Management Company Temple Bar, Dublin

- Temple Bar Properties Limited, a state-owned development company established in 1991. TBPL is a small company with a limited shelf life;
- Temple Bar Properties engaged in acquiring properties, renewing them and negotiating rents with occupiers and by undertaking development schemes on its own volition or as joint ventures with private owners and developers;
- It relied on EU grants and a State guarantee;
- Cultural projects to act as urban "chess pieces": localised strategic interventions to create activity and interest – these include a Film House, sculpture gallery, photography gallery, music venues and the old Olympia Theatre;
- Provision of business grants and loans to help young cultural and other entrepreneurs set up in business;
- Responsible for training in business skills and the various cultural industries, but also in catering and venue operation to develop businesses;
- An overall policy approach to property management and upgrading based on balancing the need to improve the area's environment with the need to retain existing activity;
- The introduction of vertical zoning linked to the provision of grants and tax relief status;
- Promoting design of new buildings by young Irish architects, with the accent on modern design within the context of the historic street pattern as policy;
- Responsible for marketing using good modern design.

Temple Bar Properties Limited was established to ensure that the future development of Temple Bar corresponded to the set of cultural planning, urban stewardship, mixed-use planning and urban design principles discussed earlier, and as a mechanism for attracting and channelling public funds to the development.

After Temple Bar Properties had completed its work the area was intended to have its own life. However, a little like the MuseumsQuartier Development Company, Temple Bar Properties has continued to manage certain key property holdings as well as putting on various events, thus operating as a facilities and marketing company. It is not yet clear how TBPL will disengage from its responsibilities as a landlord.

The Vienna MuseumsQuartier, employed an equivalent model, a publicly owned facilities and marketing company, is also a "brand name" for a particular physical single cluster site, which at present comprises about 40 diverse cultural organisations and culturally related activities occupying 53,000 square metres of useable space. This includes two new museum buildings, and two discrete theatres with seating capacity of 1,200. Additional exhibition space is available for hire along with offices, workshops and ateliers. This short-term space has been grouped together under the brand name Quarter 21. Many of the smaller cultural organisations are included, the Quarter 21 described as a structure of self-responsible, constructively competing content-entrepreneurs, a modular-action platform for independent small institutions, culture offices and temporary initiatives.

This model was employed by Sheffield City Council in transferring the Art Gallery and Museum Service to an independent Trust, the Sheffield Art Gallery and Museum Trust. A charitable Trust was the preferred option, although consideration was given to management buyouts and worker controlled industrial provident societies. The independent charitable Trust as a legal vehicle was acceptable to the Council and also other key stakeholders such as the Arts Council and the Museums, Libraries and Archives Council.

It provides safeguards for Council assets, as councillors are trustees, and enables new management to work independently of Council constraints. The Trust model is used extensively in the delivery of leisure services, and increasingly nationally applied to museums, galleries and related services; for example, York City Council Museum and Gallery Service has been recently established as a Trust, and the Ironbridge Gorge world heritage site is a well-established independent Trust.

The Council's view of the benefits was explained by Keith Crawshaw, the Director of Leisure Services, as

- The Trust can produce a more focused approach to service delivery, and business development opportunities may be more available utilising other experiences and resources;
- Opportunities may arise to involve a wider group of stakeholders, for example local community interests, in managing the business by involvement on the management board;
- The Trust may have access to external resources, both revenue and capital which are not available to the local authority;
- It has potential to develop new ways of working in an external environment;
- Cash savings can be made where the Trust can benefit from charitable NNDR relief provisions and VAT relief.

However, there are negative aspects to this, which are:

- The need to sustain ongoing management input and capacity to maintain relationships;
- The problems of making Trusts properly accountable for the spending of public monies or the use of public resources, because under Trust arrangements direct control by the City Council cannot be exercised;

- Cost savings are not always evident, and additional costs are often incurred in the short term as a result of legal and accountancy requirements;
- Legislation may preclude the City Council from having direct control; relationships will need to be built using influence rather than control;
- Charitable NNDR relief depends upon fairly strict statutory tests, and it is not achievable for every aspect of leisure provision. It will depend upon whether the charity is in rateable occupation and the use to which the premises are put. To qualify may require that the whole model of occupation of a particular facility may need alteration, thereby affecting income potential.

The Management Trust
Sheffield Art Gallery and Museum Trust
Independent legal entity with its own governance

Responsible for its own affairs and accountable to the Trustees

Independent management responsible to the Trustees for delivering the purpose of the Trust

Has the ability to directly raise and attract public and private funds to achieve the Trust purpose

Operates through contractual relationships normally with the local authority by providing an independent management service

It receives a guaranteed income over a specified period of time for these services which provides stability

---

Individual council officers responsible for the cultural services in a quarter would have full control, with the approval and guidance of the council and committee members. For example, Wolverhampton, where the Cultural Services Chief Officer has been instrumental in identifying the need to invest in the public cultural services by attracting external funding such as EU and National Lottery funding which requires matched funding from the Council. This mechanism enables the Council to direct resources it receives and can access for economic, social and cultural regeneration. This often requires the support of the senior Council executive and the controlling political party. However, it is in unpopular model for attracting private sector investment.

An example of cultural public/private partnership is the British Museum Study Centre, which housed collections for Egyptology, Conservation, Ethnographic Studies and visitor facilities was a £33m PFI Procurement – a design build fund and operate scheme. The British Museum Study Centre was designed from the outset as part of a PFI Procurement process. The funding elements of the project were:

- HLF Finance £8m;
- Private Finance Initiative Funding £25m;
- The PFI Consortium consisted of a developer, Parkes; a Contractor and facilities management company, Bovis; and a hotel group, Granada.

The distinguishing features of this project included; a roof-level hotel by the hotel partner; museum storage facilities for the British Museum with high-level specification for organic and non-organic collections; and a ground floor retail outlet by the retail partner.

The British Museum intended to enter into the PFI arrangement on the basis of an annual charge for capital replacement and facilities management Services. The PFI consortium and the Museum worked closely with the Heritage Lottery Fund to secure the offer of £8m worth of funding for a 'World of Textiles' exhibition. In effect the private investor receives an annual income from both the public and private occupants of the centre as a means of recouping the initial capital investment.

9.4 The Availability of Public Resources to Support a Cultural Quarter Development

Funding is complex and derived from many sources, including the private sector, and the majority of resources available provide capital, not revenue, as was the case in the Grand Opera House, Belfast, where the capital funds were available but not the additional revenue requirements to run the new theatre. A distillation of the recent public funding sources for cultural industry quarters in England are:

- Local Authority Council;
- European Union funds;
- Regional Development Agency;
- Single Regeneration Funds;
- DCMS/MLA (Re:source);
- Heritage Lottery Funds;
- New Opportunities Fund;
- Arts Council Lottery Fund;
- Learning and Skills Council;
- Private Sector;
- Regional Development Agencies;
- Private Sector Developers;
- Large Construction Contractors.

However, all these schemes are restricted in one way or another, and often require matched funding. For example, the Arts Council England North West: Grants for the

Arts: Capital Funding 06/07 bidding round for this funding takes place approximately every two years and is a two-stage process where projects can request up to £500,000.

The Heritage Lottery Fund on the other hand has two funding streams, 'Your Heritage', a fund that provides grants of £5000 to £50,000 and 'Heritage Grant', which funds capital projects over £50,000 to support the cultural heritage including buildings.

EU schemes are a significant source of funding and provide key finance for the Temple Bar, Dublin, scheme and Wolverhampton, for example. They are, however, complex to access, and the regulatory framework is demanding, including as it does accountability and outputs, which are almost always associated with job and business generation. EU schemes always require matched funding, normally of 50 per cent, often less, dependent on the EU designated status of the region or area.

What becomes obvious in any consideration of funding resources is the complex mix of sources and conditions required to be packaged together. Whatever the public sector package amounts to, Cultural Quarters require private sector finance to deliver the totality of mixed use. It is possible, however, to take the key components of a Quarter and match the resources against each element, as illustrated in the Bolton project. This would be a typical mix of funding streams necessary to realise a Cultural Quarter.

An Example of Potential Funding Sources for the Key Components of the Bolton Cultural Quarter

Museums, Gallery and Aquarium
- Bolton Borough Council;
- Heritage Lottery Fund;
- Department for Culture Media and Sport/Museum, Library and Archives Council;
- Learning and Skills Council;
- New Opportunities Fund;
- European Union Funds;
- Wolfson Foundation;
- Esmee Fairburn Trust;
- Sponsorship;
- Private Sector.

Octagon Theatre
- Arts Council Lottery Funds.

Theatre Incubator
- Jerwood Foundation;
- New Opportunities Fund;
- NESTA.

Managed Creative Industries, Workspace
- European Union Funds;
- Arts Council Lottery;
- Regional Development Agency;
- Private Sector.

Ateliers, Live/work space
- Housing associations;
- European Union funds;
- Private Sector.

Knowledge Civic Centre
- Bolton Borough Council;
- European Union funds;
- National Lottery/Communities;
- Private Sector, hotel/conference facilities;
- Department for Culture Media and Sport/Museums Libraries and Archives Council;
- NESTA;
- New Opportunities Fund.

The Market extension
- European Union funds;
- Regional Development Agency;
- Bolton Borough Council.

The Boulevard
- Bolton Borough Council;
- Regional Development Agency;
- Planning Gain.

Whatever public resources are available there remains a need for matched private sector funding as described in the procurement example of the British Museum Study Centre, and regular revenue streams, which are likely to come from private sector activity such as retail, housing and office and workspaces – a partnership of mutual interests working with the community through its agents. This and the engagement of private sector funders emerge as principles in the majority of Cultural Quarter cases.

Chapter 10

Public Sector Decision-Making: Two Crescents: One Place?

The case studies highlight the key role local authorities play as the focal point for Cultural Quarter development. They are the local democratically elected public bodies responsible for representing the interests of their communities and providing statutory and non-statutory services for their benefit. This includes social services from housing and care to education, refuse collection and disposal, road and street maintenance, economic development, libraries, museums, archives, cemeteries, lighting and planning.

Elected councillors representing wards in a defined electoral boundary form a council that meets regularly, which is divided into political parties mirroring the national system, and which is responsible for managing the affairs of the authority. The Council is accountable to the local electorate. The mechanism for managing the council business is often through a cabinet of councillors drawn from the largest political party, with executive powers and accountable to audit committees comprising a political cross section of councillors. Professional officers report to the cabinet councillor with responsibility for their area of work, and are led by a chief executive who reports to the leader of the council. This explains the plethora of local policies referred to in chapter 4. Local authorities have the power to raise income through a local tax, the council tax, to provide the services required by that community. However the national government provides the bulk of income and as a result determines to a large extent local priorities. In this case Cultural Quarters do not constitute government cultural policy, however, zoning is recognised as a formal component of national planning regulations. This does not, however, prevent a local authority from incorporating the quarter concept into local cultural policy. It is generally the case that local authority cultural services will loosely mirror national policy not least in order to access funds. What follows is an illustration of a typical local authority approach to decision-making.

The development of a Cultural Quarter has to conform to the approved economic, planning, social and cultural policy frameworks established by the council, such as the town centre development plan or cultural strategy. It is also helpful to coordinate the proposal with regional and national strategic ambitions, not least because this may enable the authority to access additional sources of funds. It also gives the regional and national authorities influence on policy at a local level. Structure is fundamental to authority decision-making, and this chapter includes a generic approach, but perhaps above all else there needs to be a clearly defined and shared purpose.

Assuming the initial analysis of locality, appreciation of the spatial context and consultation with stakeholders provide sufficient empirical evidence to justify the establishment of a cultural or cultural industries quarter in a town such as Bolton, the local authority, often the lead player because of their statutory planning role and community service responsibilities, is faced with options to address as the process unfolds. Generally the options available, given the cultural economic and spatial context, are:

- Take no action;
- Adopt a single-cluster site model;
- Adopt a designated, cultural industries quarter.

How these options materialise in practice will vary given the context specificities; the Bolton experience, however, provides a typical picture.

10.1 No Action

The Council could stand still and watch the world go by, in other words choose not to proceed with the Cultural Quarter, and develop the town centre through, for example, a retail driven model, like many other places. This may lead to a possible decline in investment for Council-owned cultural assets for the common good. The Council would as a result ignore its strategies, which repeatedly stress the necessity to regenerate the town centre and the importance of digitisation, and access to information and knowledge.

Little would be made of the best of its impressive industrial revolution past, and an opportunity may be lost to create an imaginative, dynamic national and international future, in the spirit of the industrial revolution and its history, through culturally led regeneration as many other towns and cities have already done. In addition there may be a failure to support young graduates wanting to live and work in the town, the next generation of knowledge workers who are most likely to stimulate the local economy by setting up their own businesses.

Such a failure to act would have the effect of limiting access to regional and national public project funding and matching private sector investment in the town centre through a Council-led cultural initiative, thus denying tangible benefits to the community.

10.2 Adopt a Single-Cluster Site

Alternatively, the Council could consider specifically developing Le Mans Crescent site, a cultural model, which is the present location for the library, museum, gallery and aquarium, as a single building with the existing cultural services occupants. It would provide a lower cost solution, improve the cultural services provision in the town and potentially attract more tourists. However, this is unlikely to be satisfactory due to the long-standing practical issues of exhibition space and storage required by the Museum, Art Gallery and Aquarium, as well as the Central Library. Furthermore, it would not act as a catalyst for the development of the surrounding area. It is clear from earlier analyses of Le Mans Crescent (Bradshaw Gass And Hope Construction Design Consultants 2003), without even the remainder of the building coming into use, it would not be possible to house both the Central Library and the Museum, Art Gallery, Aquarium, and records in the refurbished building.

The difficulty with this approach, therefore, is re-locating the Central Library and meeting storage requirements, and whilst this may enable the public cultural services to marginally develop it is unlikely to act as a catalyst for regeneration as the Grand Opera House in Belfast or the Newcastle Studios have, without a planned development of the immediate surrounding area.

The Vienna MuseumsQuartier is a single-cluster site model, which has a correlation with the Le Mans Crescent. However, the Vienna MuseumsQuartier is a substantially larger, rectangular building incorporating two open squares, and consequently has been able to house 34 cultural organisations, two new-build museums, and provide incubator and studio space for creative businesses along with bookshops, cafes and restaurants.

10.3 Adopt a Designated Cultural Quarter, Two Crescents – One Place

A third option for the Council could be to proceed with a designated Cultural Quarter, an economic model, as a regenerative tool, by building and adding to the cultural industry strengths in the town centre such as:

• The Museum, Art Gallery and Aquarium;
• The Archives;
• The Central Library;
• The original Civic Centre and the Town Hall as major architectural features and focal points for services to the public;
• The Market, a thriving hub of activity in the town centre;
• Existing cultural businesses and networks;
• Young creative industries graduates;
• Existing historic and contemporary places and spaces;
• Transport links;
• Cafes, bars and pubs;
• The Octagon Theatre, an important regional theatre;
• Public and private performance spaces.

This approach has been adopted by Wolverhampton and Dublin, in particular, with Sheffield placing a greater emphasis on cultural industry development. In addition, the Cultural Quarter option has been successfully used to regenerate rundown buildings incorporating new build, providing living and working space as well as improving the nightlife of the town and city. In the case of the Dublin Temple Bar, it has become a significant centre for parties from the UK and a cultural attraction during the day time. It has also attracted substantial private sector funding.

This option requires vision, leadership and long-term commitment, with a clearly defined purpose for the Quarter, reflecting to the town centre plan, zoning, regional and national priorities such as generation of jobs and businesses. This firmly positions public cultural service development within the economic development policy envelope.

This model requires a closer integration between Bolton Council cultural policy and economic and community plans if the Cultural Quarter is to be successful, and other cultural activities across the Borough are to be supported and linked to the Cultural Quarter focal point. The benefits are an improved cultural service, redevelopment of a significant spatial area of the town centre, attracting public and private financing that would not be available otherwise, and raising the profile of the town regionally, nationally and internationally, which is likely to result in attracting more creative business and tourists, thus increasing the number of jobs for local people.

A New Vision for Bolton

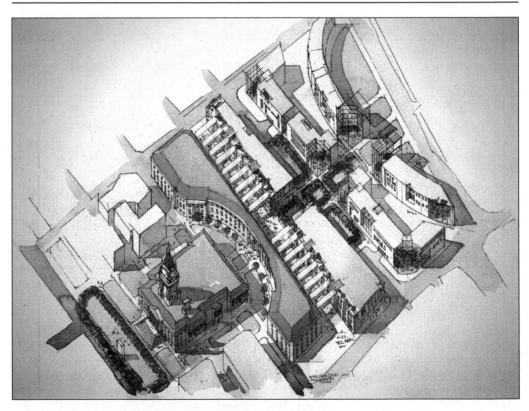

A phased approach to the development of the Quarter will be required, combined with a planned approach to funding, linked to the clearly defined marketing plan based on the Dublin Temple Bar model.

10.4 A Generic Structural Model

A suggested structural model which could be applied by a local authority to any situation is as follows:

- Agree a vision and purpose;
- Undertake a detailed feasibility study, which includes a detailed zone, spatial, transport, architectural, and cultural analysis;
- Develop a conservation plan;
- Develop a detailed, phased business case in partnership with the private sector;
- Establish a management vehicle to take the Cultural Quarter project forward;
- Identify key resources from the public sector, funding criteria, and phasing constraints;
- Continue consulting with local constituencies;
- Develop a marketing strategy, and implement at an early stage.

10.5 The Purpose of a Cultural Quarter

Earlier examples indicate the need to build on an existing asset base and exploit and develop the strengths of the local infrastructure. Based on this rationale it is suggested that the purpose of a Bolton Cultural Quarter would be:

- To contribute to the regeneration of the town centre;
- To profile Bolton regionally, nationally and internationally;
- To deliver the national cultural agenda and outstanding public cultural services locally;
- To act as a physical and virtual hub for cultural, social and economic development, innovation and learning networks;
- To attract tourists and retain graduates;
- To increase local participation in cultural and learning activity;
- To contribute to improving the quality of life for those living and working in Bolton;
- To create a sense of place;
- To attract private sector funding and major public sector project funding;
- To put Bolton's "family silver" to good use;
- To act as a catalyst for production and consumption of cultural products and services.

10.6 How Can This Be Achieved?

A means of achieving a Cultural Quarter which regenerates the town centre and provides high-quality public cultural services to support economic, social and cultural strategic objectives in the Borough, is as stated to build on existing assets, generate coherence and connectivity and recognise the rapidly changing world Bolton people have to live and work in. There are critical conceptual factors which provide the basis for establishing a quarter and meet the needs of the local community. These could easily be applied to other community settings.

- The establishment of cultural industries and Cultural Quarters are public sector-led from the outset.
- The cultural industries and Cultural Quarter approach cannot be all things to all people; it has to focus on a clearly defined purpose. Consequently, expectations need to be managed from the beginning.
- A balance needs to be achieved between indigenous growth of cultural and related business activity with attracting significant cultural inward investment over time.
- A corporate policy objective to establish a regional and national profile needs to be explicitly articulated as a component of the cultural industry and Cultural Quarter purpose.
- A balance is needed between major iconic cultural infrastructure and networks.
- Cultural industries and Cultural Quarters are diverse, accessible and incorporate a wide range of cultural business activity without engaging in determining a public aesthetic, markets are important.
- A cultural industries and Cultural Quarter is a real and virtual matrix of network engagement and interaction, with hubs spreading beyond the immediate physical zone.
- A balance is needed between social, economic and cultural activities including consumption, production and living in the quarter.
- A lively and human place, which is attractive to those who live there and others, a great place to live, work and play.

The planning mechanism of identifying a physical area for cultural industry or cultural activity – that is zoning, provides an enabling tool to re-generate key services in the town centre, which in turn supports the business development networks of activity throughout the Borough and raises the profile of the town centre. This therefore progressively attracts inward investment by supporting indigenous growth of creative businesses. It is the "culturalnomic model" which has the greatest potential for local authorities as it cost effectively combines economic and cultural public services for the benefit of the local community by adding value. The following chapter describes the key components of a proposed Cultural Quarter.

Chapter 11

The Composition of the Cultural Quarter in Practice

ocal authorities are an important component. However, higher education institutions play a crucial role in Cultural Quarters and have been identified as key influencers in Wolverhampton, Sheffield and the emerging Bolton models because they provide cultural graduates, are employers of these people and provide facilities, business support and product development capacity. But, above all else, the key characteristic and success of the Cultural Quarter rely on the people involved, both public and private, who incorporate entrepreneurial instincts such as those which led the Newcastle studios, the Grand Opera House, Belfast development and the Custard Factory in Birmingham. This chapter profiles a typical composition of activity found in a Cultural Quarter, derived from the Bolton experience which includes cultural businesses, public cultural services education and training, information, living, working, eating and entertainment. These elements are of little value unless marketed, as evidenced in the MuseumsQuartier, Vienna, that is making the distinctiveness of the place known. In this case a marketing company owned by the key stakeholders would promote individual businesses, and public services locally, nationally and internationally, provide market intelligence, and gain publicity for individuals and organisations working and living in the area. Similarly Dublin Temple Bar carried out a sustained marketing campaign that successfully raised the profile of the quarter.

The composition of the quarter is based on the successful ingredients described in chapter 1.

11.1 Activity: Learning

A core characteristic and central to the emerging Bolton Cultural Quarter model is the University, not least because it is, like so many others, a generator of creative industries graduates as well as a repository of expertise with applied research capacity. The synergies that can be developed between a University and the Cultural Quarter are demonstrated in the Wolverhampton model as well as the Sheffield cultural industries quarter. Sheffield Hallam University has provided students and located activities in the Quarter, as catalysts to attract others. More recently it has relocated the students' union in the key iconographic building in the quarter. As a result it is important in any consideration of a quarter to create a genuine and dynamic relationship between the cultural zone and University. For planners this points to the importance of connecting and overlapping learning, innovation and cultural zones rather then delineating boundaries.

The utilisation of existing local authority cultural services and linking them to national cultural ambitions is well understood with the Sheffield Gallery and Museum Trust model involving the Victoria and Albert Museum and the Vienna MuseumQuartier. Similarly the Wolverhampton scheme incorporates local authority services.

Often the distinctiveness of a quarter is derived from the existing cultural infrastructure, and Bolton, an unremarkable northern town, is not dissimilar. The Crescent in Bolton, originally designed as a public cultural centre with the support of Lord Leverhulme at the turn of the twentieth century, could, for example, be reverted to its original purpose of a Museum, Art Gallery and Aquarium, with the addition of substantial temporary exhibition spaces to incorporate the potential needs of local artists and the exploitation of the existing British Museum partnership. In order to achieve this, it would be necessary to establish additional storage facilities, accessible to learners for the Museum, Art Gallery, Archives and Library services. In this context it is worth explaining the British Museum collaboration, not least because it would act as a quarter visitor catalyst, which is thought to take the form of providing material from the British Museum collection on long-term loan to supplement the existing collections in Bolton. More specifically these might fall under three headings:

- Material from parts of the world which are not well represented in the Bolton Museum collection;
- Material relevant to the main Bolton community groups;
- Material that takes into account Bolton's more recent role as a host to asylum seekers;
- Some Egyptian material to supplement recognised strengths in the collection.

This approach leads to further considerations, such as refurbishing the Le Mans Crescent lecture theatre and establishing a vocational learning centre in partnership with the further education colleges in the town. There would as a result be access to the Museum skills and knowledge resource base, with vocational courses provided by the colleges. This could, for example, enable the Museum, Art Gallery and Aquarium to develop Modern Apprenticeship Schemes, Part-time Foundation Degree Programmes, NVQs and Graduate Apprenticeships.

11.2 Activity: Information, Networks and Digitisation

Digitisation is as important to museums as to any other cultural industries sector, and any refurbished facilities in the Crescent, particularly the lecture theatre area, could include a digital cinema. In addition there is the potential to digitise the collections, which massively increases local and global accessbility and use. Virtual networks and galleries can be established and developed around the hub to support clusters of activity and connect the existing cultural and educational infrastructure.

The Central Library is another buried glory of this town, with notable historical collections, the second most important reference library in Greater Manchester, substantial holdings for children, and an excellent commercial reference library, but as yet has been unable to realise its full potential in the digitised new world. The Cultural Quarter model provides a mechanism for the town to establish a major twenty-first-century multimedia centre. The state-of-the-art facility would provide a physical and virtual nuclear hub for the development of a knowledge-based local economy by collecting data sets and building up a regional data spine. It is this ability to re-evaluate the existing provision within a Cultural Quarter conceptual framework, including financial arrangements, which provides the Council with an alternative analytical tool.

The creative and cultural industries are an accepted part of the knowledge economy concept (Cunningham et al. 2000) and this approach has been taken up and developed in Australia, for example, at Queensland University of Technology, (QUT) Brisbane, Australia, where the Creative Industry Faculty has been established in partnership with the state government to ensure that creative talent is fed into the knowledge economy in Brisbane. QUT has a long history of success in many of the disciplines that constitute the creative industries, which has uniquely positioned it to take advantage of the opportunities offered in this emerging area by connecting creativity and technology, and focusing on commercial or commercialisable applications of creativity.

In practice, teaching programmes, research and collaborations are focussed on the "content" or "copyright" industries, especially those involved in entertainment such as radio, television, interactive games and cultural services, where new intellectual property can be developed.

QUT's Creative Industries Faculty is the first of its kind in Australia and it is intended to contribute to the growth and diversification of the Queensland economy. The faculty is housed in a purpose-built creative industries precinct.

The creative industries precinct is the Brisbane home for innovation, networking, business and product research development, as well as the Creative Industries Faculty. The Precinct comprises:

- 24/7 all year around access;
- Fully "wired" and networked facilities;
- Flexible working environments;
- Exciting public spaces;
- A community of researchers, entrepreneurs and businesses, students, teachers, artists and designers.

The $60 million Precinct, opened in 2004, is the lead site in a $400 million urban development, the Kelvin Grove urban village that combines tertiary education, residential accommodation, leisure facilities and business opportunities. The village, which is a joint undertaking of the Queensland Government's Department of Housing and QUT, is Australia's first inner-city development of its kind. The facilities are located on the former Gona Barracks site at Kelvin Grove, as well as on adjoining land and on QUT's Kelvin Grove campus.

In Bolton by contrast, walking through the archway of the Le Mans Crescent into Cheadle Square towards the bus station is at present a depressing and dismal British experience. Cheadle Square is an unimpressive, rather shabby area surrounded by mediocre buildings and car parks, with little purpose or sense of life. The original intention when constructing the Crescent was to create a tree-lined boulevard as illustrated in chapter 4. The question is, however, where would a new boulevard take us? It could, for example, prove to be a connection between the old and a new civic centre with a state-of-the-art Library and Learning Centre, acting as a virtual network hub, open 24 hours a day, linked to the University, further education colleges and schools, as well as the existing library branches uniting the learning infrastructure through information.

Any multimedia knowledge centre has a responsibility to disseminate and, in this respect, the opportunity to establish a state-of-the-art building would of necessity include conference facilities with cafes, restaurants and other visitor facilities, including the provision of a showcase for the Council's range of community services. Bolton is desperately short of good quality conference facilities in the town centre and this could be developed in conjunction with the University to complement the Reebok Stadium sports and conference facilities to the west. It could link to the branch network and schools as it does already, as well as the library services in the Bolton Community College and the University of Bolton.

It is, perhaps, to all intents and purposes, a twenty-first-century digitised Mechanics Institute.

11.3 Activity: Performing Arts

The Octagon Theatre close to the Town Hall, part of the well-established and frequented local cultural infrastructure, could in these new arrangements be complemented by creating an equivalent to the Jerwood Space on Bankside, London. Funded by the Jerwood Foundation, a private arts foundation, Jerwood Space provides young dance and theatre companies with affordable spaces and facilities (25,000 ft.^{2}) to develop their work. Furthermore, it includes, for example, fully equipped rehearsal spaces for both established and emerging young drama and dance groups, a gallery, a meeting and an event space for the business sector, five studios, and design, photographic, music and dance agencies based there. A sliding scale set of charges according to the status and means of the users is employed. It is essentially a performing arts incubator, and as a result retains performing arts graduates. Established in a Bolton Cultural Quarter and managed by the Octagon Theatre it could provide the platform needed for graduates to smoothly transfer from study to professional practice. Such a practice-based facility has the potential to link into supporting the three specialist cultural secondary schools in the Borough. This would provide a useful connecting of the education and cultural zones.

11.4 Activity: Tourism and Hotels

The Bolton town centre like many others contains a number of hotels, including the Moat House on Higher Bridge Street and the Pack Horse Hotel in Nelson Square. Other hotels are at or beyond the ring road or are associated with the Middlebrook Reebok Stadium development. Visitors to a newly established Cultural Quarter from outside Bolton who stay overnight would find useful proximity between the town centre hotels and the Cultural Quarter, those staying elsewhere would probably need to rely on individual motor vehicle transport. As a consequence it would be sensible to include a new hotel, along with conference facilities, as the Dublin Temple Bar experience has demonstrated. This would in time contribute to the cultural tourism policy linked to conference facilities.

11.5 Activity and Meaning: Cultural Organisations, Voluntary Groups and Societies

By creating a Cultural Quarter with iconic hubs and established networks, both physically and virtually, over time existing and new cultural organisations will be attracted to associate themselves physically with the Quarter. This will be organic growth developed over time and determined by the needs and ambitions of the individual organisations in much the same way as the Sheffield Creative Industries Quarter developed.

Voluntary groups and societies are generally well networked into Museum and Library services. Developing a Cultural Quarter based on the existing Council cultural infrastructure would strengthen these networks and relationships by providing enhanced facilities and substantially improved access.

11.6 Activity and Meaning: Creative Businesses and Ateliers

It is critical to the success of any Quarter that there is a nucleus of people living and working there, with families who provide the inherent individual creativity and engage in cultural activity as businesses. This provides the key social interaction of work and living that will generate the dynamism necessary to attract other people to set up a business in the area.

Generally speaking cultural businesses are classified as micro, employing between one to five people on average, and have low average turnover of work – around £25,000 a year. (Roodhouse 2003) Consequently if indigenous businesses are to grow then the development of ateliers, that is, integrated live-work spaces, and low rental levels, are necessary. In a Quarter these can be incorporated as a new build proposition or an effective use of run-down buildings. This concept provides integrated work and office units for cultural businesses. This approach can be found in Huddersfield, for example, reflecting a long-standing civic approach established on the continent in cities such as Munich.

It also enables the bridge to be built between the University of Bolton and ateliers to ensure that there is interaction between a major learning institution, committed to the creative industries, and the Cultural Quarter, with a consequent retention of graduates.

11.7 Activity and Placemaking: Small Businesses and Shops

Diversity of primary and secondary uses, presence of an evening economy, including cafe culture and the strength of small firm economy, including creative businesses are central to a successful quarter. Existing small businesses and shops are attracted to remain in the Cultural Quarter regardless of their products and services because of the redevelopment, as long as rental levels remain within their reach. This makes for a lively and interesting mix of activity, although the overriding impression will remain one of the old and the new, best epitomised in the Vienna MuseumsQuartier.

11.8 A Sense of Place: The Marketplace

The multicultural Market in Bolton is popular and important to small traders. It breathes life into the town centre and deserves to be incorporated into any Cultural Quarter concept, as the Williams interpretation of culture suggests in chapter I. The Market currently focuses on multicultural food and clothes in mediocre accommodation. The Market could be expanded as an integral component of the quarter to include arts, crafts and design, with openings on Sundays as well as during the week. A similar model can be found in Greenwich Village, London, which has progressively over time become an established and popular part of the infrastructure. It has also built up a reputation beyond that of its immediate surroundings. In the case of Greenwich this approach has supported young makers with limited resources to sell their products, as a first step in establishing their businesses.

Bury, another cotton town in Greater Manchester, has often been highlighted as a local model of creative industry good practice. In particular, the Re: Work Studios in Bury have nine incubator spaces and readily available business support. They occasionally employ artists to perform at events in the market; however, they do not as yet have arts and crafts fairs.

11.9 A Sense of Place, Space and Fabric: The Town Hall and Public Events

Completion of projects such as the pedestrianisation around the Town Hall, an architecturally significant and nationally recognised Victorian building, and in front of Le Mans Crescent, are essential if the original concept of an integrated civic centre with a major public square is to be realised and a sense of special place generated. By completing such works the archways in the

Crescent would become a key feature and act as a gateway into the Civic Centre and square. Events, open-air temporary festivals and other public activities can then be incorporated into the expanded square, which includes the archway and the Boulevard. Leeds Civic Square provides just this facility. The quarter would become a unique place which is easy to walk around, sit in, eat, meet people and talk. Some areas may need to be covered in order to provide places for people to meet throughout the year regardless of the weather.

11.10 A Sense of Place, Space and Fabric: Street Furniture, Signage, Nature and the Environment

Street furniture and signage are the physical outward manifestation of places, often overlooked but a key Cultural Quarter characteristic. In order to create a distinct and easily identifiable district, one solution used in Dublin Temple Bar was to invite artists to work with planners to design and install unique street furniture and signage such as lamps and street names. This could in other settings such as Bolton include an inventive approach to pedestrianisation which respects the buildings such as the Town Hall by introducing creative solutions. This would inevitably give the Quarter a unique physical identity and as a consequence boundaries will be self evident. As Parkin suggests in his statement of urban principles; "*Spaces must be attractive, stimulating and delightful to the senses by use of colour, texture and surfaces, ornament, materials and decoration*".

Parks and green areas are important in urban settings. With mechanisms such as the boulevard it becomes possible to introduce trees into the built environment, complementing and contrasting with old and new architectural statements. Trees provide a habitat for birds and other animals as well as shade for people to sit, talk and eat during the summer months. In addition, trees assist in cleaning the atmosphere, given the levels of traffic in and around the town. It answers one of Montgomery's principles, "*form: the relationship between buildings and spaces*" and responds to Parkin's requirements," *Create microclimates, e.g. to trap the sun protect from the prevailing wind.*"

Creating a sense of place can also include planning guidelines specifically for the Cultural Quarter, and a role in planning as is the case for the Sheffield Creative Industries Quarter Agency, which ensures that any refurbishment, conversion and new build meet stringent environmental requirements. This opens the way to establishing an overarching architectural style required for all conversions and new buildings in the Quarter to create a coherent and distinct urban environment. This would include, for example, specifying appropriate materials, again suggested by Parkin.

11.11 Movement: Transport

Transport arrangements are fundamental to any development, and often involve multi-agency cooperation, complex and lengthy planning processes and significant resources.

The following paragraphs provide a pragmatic and specific example of this tortuous process, illustrating how one action relies on another.

There are far-reaching plans being promoted by the Greater Manchester Passenger Transport Executive and the Local Authority, to redevelop, as a transport interchange, the so-called "Railway Triangle" in Bolton, (a piece of land lying immediately to the north of the railway platforms and South of Great Moor Street and bounded to the East and West by the railway lines to Blackburn and Preston respectively). As well as the development of the "railway triangle" there are proposals for residential accommodation in the Shifnall Street area (presently the red-light district area to the south-east of the town centre) and the Churchwarf area (to the north-east of the town centre). Located close the Churchwarf development is Churchgate, leading from Deansgate to the Parish Church, and it is proposed to create a market area in this location that has echoes of former times. A further important development, principally retail in nature although it has important elements of residential development and accommodation for community activity, is in the Central Street area.

The programme for the development is in two phases, with the first phase being concerned with the provision of additional car parking at the railway station, the refurbishment of the booking office at the railway station, and a re-ordering of the layout of the Newport Street Bus Station, leading to greater operational efficiency. The second phase would involve the development of the Railway Triangle, with a mixed-use development including a bus station large enough to accommodate all existing terminating services to the town centre. This development is understood to be some way off, being, proposed as "development" led.

As a separate aspiration, but in practical terms entirely linked with the closure of the Moor Lane bus station, there is a proposal to create an inner "Town Centre Box", with buses moving anticlockwise around Great Moor Street, Bradshawgate, Bridge Street, St George's Road, Knowsley Street, Deansgate and Black Horse Street. General motor vehicle traffic would move in the opposite direction but generally be "access only traffic". These plans are at an early stage of development and would have an impact on the Bolton Cultural Quarter, as they would use Black Horse Street.

Other considerations then come into play, which are determined by the attitude of the public agencies and Councils to global warming and protection of the environment. So, for example, Bolton is a compact town with a substantial amount of housing very close to the town centre, and consequently there are a large proportion of people that walk into the town centre. Presently there is no specific high-quality provision for pedestrians entering the town centre, There are access points separate from highway routes into the town centre at the underpass to St Peter's Way adjacent to the Parish Church, across Topp Way at a pelican crossing, and via the underbridge to Marsden Road along St Helena Road. This latter route connects to Queen's Park. It is proposed that this latter link is upgraded and extended along the Middlebrook Valley to generate a green corridor to connect into the town centre.

Bolton was one of the earliest towns in the UK to pedestrianise its core, and this has been generally hailed as a continued success. Bolton, partly through the pedestrianisation, became a destination for shopping for residents of Greater Manchester and beyond, who valued the diversity of shops and also the market. The continued growth and development of this retail life has been affected, as have many other town centres, by the out-of-town shopping developments, including the Middlebrook Development. The inherent character of the town centre, coupled with its pedestrianisation, has helped it not lose out as much as it might otherwise have done to such developments.

The pedestrian heart of the town is attractive to shoppers during the core commercial hours of 9:00 am until 5:00 pm. Yet it is increasingly being recognised that evening economy activity, a key characteristic of Cultural Quarters, particularly in the case of Wolverhampton, is centred on locations other than the pedestrianised heart, because of the preponderance of shop frontages (and also civic frontages) that offer no activity during non-trading hours. Numerous efforts have been made by the local authority, through a tourism approach, to generate activity in Victoria Square to counter this sterility. Consequently, it will be important to strengthen, so far as possible, the pedestrian link from the Cultural Quarter to the proposed transport interchange on the south side of the town centre. While this link could be formed through the arch to Le Mans Crescent, it is worth re-confirming that pedestrians will always attempt to find the shortest route between nodes. From this point of view it becomes necessary to ensure that the link from the south-east corner of the area (that is, at the south-west Corner of the Le Mans Crescent Building) becomes a secondary "main entrance". Ashburner Street, with a pedestrianised Le Mans Crescent, would become pedestrianised as well, and there would be a ready link to the open area between St Peters House and the Apcoa Car Park immediately south of the Octagon Theatre. From here existing pedestrian routes are clear and relatively direct and assisted by a recently installed puffin crossing and quasi-boulevard leading towards the Morrisons Supermarket.

A further important secondary pedestrian link would need to be formed north from the site towards the proposed Central Street development, which is set to become a centre for community activity as well as having retail and residential elements. This route would also pass the main Post Office, and assist in revitalising this part of Deansgate. While original 1910 proposals for a boulevard from the Town Hall showed links across to Queen's Park to the west of the town centre, emanating from the Town Hall in a westerly direction, it is considered more appropriate to link to the park via the proposed "Green Finger", that will extend from the park through the present Chorley Street car Park, via St. Helena Road (and which continues along the banks of the River Croal into the Central Street development area). A link to Queen's Park is deemed necessary in order that the Cultural Quarter may fit into edge of town open space as well as the pedestrianised core of the town. Parkin advocates that it is best to try to concentrate pedestrian (and, indeed, cycle movements) onto one or two key routes that link to town centre gateways, and to link to other proposed infrastructure developments, rather than to attempt to create new and potentially rival alignments.

The pedestrianisation also creates a significant barrier for short-distance cross-town journeys by bicycle. This is unhelpful, as cycling is being encouraged by national government as a means of reducing congestion and reducing pollution below levels that might otherwise be achieved because of hilly topography and rainfall, two features of Bolton. Notwithstanding this, there is the potential to increase the catchment area for cycle access to the town centre by adopting appropriately attractive gateways into the town centre and linking these gateways back into the surrounding communities, with appropriate routes for cycle traffic. This could be adopted as a feature of the quarter and provide distinctiveness.

All this argues for using the Cultural Quarter zoning approach to provide economic, social and spatial coherence and the acceptance of environmental concerns as imbedded principles for communication planning in quarters.

The typical components described here can only function as a sustainable quarter if there is meaning derived from the history of the area, individual creativity and business supported by a positive local authority planning development regime. The key to this is:

The whole approach is to create a hub which provides the impetus for a new digitised creative industrial revolution in Bolton, based on understanding our past and gaining confidence from this to ensure that the town is the place to live, work and enjoy other people's company.

Chapter 12

Conclusion

Cultural or cultural industry quarters are emerging internationally as a democratic and effective sustainable model which is less dependent upon the conventional and traditional public cultural agency structure, and more on the local, social, economic and cultural community need. It is less about determining what is "good art" and more about creative business.

Florida, Bell and Jeyne have helpfully echoed the principles and realities of Cultural Quarters by suggesting;

> Designed to make the city more liveable, these encompass aesthetic improvements of soft infrastructure, ranging from the building of squares, the provision of benches and fountains to the greening of streets and improved public spaces, the establishment of late night shopping and 'happy hours', and cultural events and festivals. Augmenting this has been the support and promotion of creative and cultural industries such as advertising, architecture, visual and performing arts, crafts, design, film, music, performing arts, publishing, media and new media. With buildings and facilities such as museums, art galleries and arts centres, theatres convention and exhibition centres, as well as a supporting cast of restaurants, cafe bars, delicatessens, fashion boutiques, and other cultural facilities – the buzz of 'creativity, innovation and entrepreneurialism' brought about by the clustering of these activities in certain areas of the city centre is seen as crucial to contributing to the competitiveness of cities. (Florida 2002; Bell & Jayne 2004)

However, this approach to cultural regeneration and development tends to focus attention on one physical area at the expense of others, and ultimately drives rents up and creative businesses out. There is a continual danger of "gentrification" and a subsequent loss of the creative nucleus or life of the quarter. Sometimes the quarter development fails to act as hub for other cultural or related activities, as Sheffield illustrates, or attracts the "wrong culture", with stag and hen nights in Temple Bar, Dublin.

12.1 How Do The Cultural Quarters Compare?

The Vienna MuseumsQuartier approach compares favourably, in the sense that it incorporates the old and the new architecture, provides a focal point for cultural production, as in Quarter 21, and addresses cultural tourism by delivering a high-profile international centre. The weakness, however, of the Vienna MuseumsQuartier is the failure to link the development with existing networks in the city. This is overcome in Wolverhampton by building on existing public service infrastructures, and reinforcing well-established physical and virtual networks. The city has unashamedly taken a public sector finance-led approach to the Vienna MuseumQuartier development; however, it assumes that there is the political will and the public sector resources available to do this. One of the clear advantages of the Vienna MuseumsQuartier approach is the coordinated approach to marketing and promotion. Other quarters can learn from this, and it is suggested that wherever possible a marketing company is established to promote the individuals and organisations in the Quarter. Links with further and higher education are poor in the Vienna MuseumsQuartier, and although there are educational organisations incorporated in the physical parameters of the Quarter these tend to be individual education services.

Wolverhampton, on the other hand, needs to regenerate its historic centre, and continue to generate jobs, as does Bolton. Both Wolverhampton and Bolton suffer from city shadows and effects which have to be addressed in order to ensure the continued and successful national and international profile for the town, which in turn attracts public and private funding as well as businesses.

The revitalisation of the Bolton Art Gallery, by refurbishing the existing Victorian buildings and creating spaces for artists, resonate with the need in Bolton to invest in its cultural services and infrastructure to provide the basis for new generation production and consumption.

Wolverhampton local authority has committed to encouraging living and working in the town centre as a means of bringing a life back into the area.

The relationship with the University is clearly important, particularly in terms of encouraging graduates to stay, live and work in the town centre, and as a means of developing small businesses. Bolton on the other hand has a magnificent set of civic buildings which are far superior to those located in Wolverhampton and, in addition, can focus on a Museum and Art Gallery with more significant collections. In addition, Wolverhampton does not have an aquarium in the town centre. By building a new knowledge civic centre it is possible for Bolton to provide the digital focal point and network that Wolverhampton currently lacks. The focus in Bolton on creating a knowledge civic centre, and in that connection a twenty-first-century library, is distinct from the Wolverhampton Cultural Quarter and all the other examples included in this study. Wolverhampton has not put in place a marketing strategy for individual businesses as well as the Quarter as a whole.

Sheffield cultural industries quarter is distinctive in that it focuses primarily on supporting and developing creative businesses rather than an engagement with the wider cultural interests of the city. This is both the strength and weakness in that it highlights the lack of a coherent cultural interlocking strategy, which could provide significant benefits to the city. However, the focus on businesses enables the Quarter to attract and pursue an unambiguous mission. The involvement of the University is a strength as it provides a mutually beneficial relationship. This model does not necessarily translate comfortably into other settings, as in every case Cultural Quarters are creatures of their location.

Dublin Temple Bar, on the other hand, is unapologetically a physical regeneration project which has created a Cultural Quarter that can be recognised as inclusive and not necessarily dominated by education, or what can be described as the traditional arts interests, which are often substituted for culture. It has by its very nature generated a significant number of jobs and new buildings and raised rental levels. Creative businesses are located here, and people live, work and play in the quarter. In this sense it meets most of the characteristics for this type of development, and in addition has a physical presence that is unmistakable. This model is reliant, however, on substantial European Union funding, and would not have been possible to realise in the timescales and extent without access to this type of resource.

12.2 Critical Success Factors and Risks

The general critical success factors which are derived from the case studies and the principles to be applied to the design and delivery of these models can be found in the following box, and are based on the principles and policies described. They act as a general guidance for those planning to engage in establishing a quarter, and provide a useful set of initial performance criteria.

Success Criteria
Meeting Key Local, Regional and National Policy Priorities such as:
Town or city centre area physical redevelopment and regeneration

Regional, national and international profile raising through effective and targeted marketing

Significant generation of jobs, graduate retention, and business development, the benefit to individuals

Post 16 educational attainment and skills development, to be employable

Accessing national and regional public and private funds for local benefit

Providing and improving high-quality public cultural services to the community

Public and private partnerships and management structures to attract additional major private sector investment

Rental levels that are variable, to meet differing needs

Providing and Supporting Activity including:

The diversity of primary and secondary business uses

The extent and variety of cultural venues and events

The use of existing public and private cultural and business infrastructure

The presence of an evening economy, including cafe culture

The strengthening of the small firm economy, including creative businesses

Access to and engagement with learning providers

Working with creative people and organisations

The enabling of livework space facilities

Protecting and Developing the Built Environment by:
A distinctive physical reality

An environmentally responsive approach

An old and the contemporary architectural juxtaposition

Creative streetscape within style and material frameworks

Clearly defined useable public space, including squares and green areas

Encouraging active frontages which take advantage of pedestrianisation

A Meaning for the People Involved and the Place through:
Establishing important meeting and gathering spaces all year round

Genuinely recognising the area's history and progress

Creating an exciting place to live, work and play

Knowledgeability, a place to access learning and information

Networks, virtual and real

Stimulating richness in cultural diversity

Maintaining a healthy, safe and clean environment

As the Temple Bar and Bolton case studies demonstrate the key success factor is consultation with stakeholders, as this is essential when local authorities are involved and provides a means of encouraging genuine ownership of the project. The alternative is the cultural entrepreneur model when an individual provides vision, energy and drive to establish the project, as was the case in Newcastle. Inevitably, there are risks, and these need to be understood and addressed in any attempt at developing a quarter:

Risks in Establishing a Cultural or Cultural Industries Quarter
- Community expectations are raised and have to be managed;
- Development is focused on one geographical area at the expense of others;
- Funds are directed to the Cultural or cultural industries quarter, at the expense of other cultural projects;
- Building and transport realignments may not be delivered in time or at all;
- Public funds from agencies such as the Regional Development Agency, EU, or National Lottery cease to be available or are less than expected;
- Lack of private sector interest or investment;
- Conservation, land and building acquisition and planning objections;
- Other towns developing similar configurations nearby, resulting in competition and diminished profile;
- Lack of markets for creative industry business products and services;
- Lack of distinctiveness from other cultural quarter developments resulting in a failure to attract businesses and tourists;
- The overpowering influence of the city region shadow and cultural imperialism;
- Policy confusion between local need, regional requirements and national direction of travel;
- Lack of leadership and vision, with no champion.

Cultural Quarter principles have been practised and risks addressed through a spectrum of management vehicles, all of which require a differing public and private funding package mix, from the almost entirely MuseumsQuartier, Vienna State model to the private sector influenced Temple Bar, Dublin, project. The concept is now an integral component of regeneration strategies in the UK and internationally increasingly forms part of the emerging global knowledge economy developments, including the creative industries. However, in any venture focussed on culture, at the end of the day, success comes down to creative people being given a chance to make a sustained social and economic contribution to their communities.

Creative people, in turn, don't just cluster where the jobs are. They cluster in places that are centres of creativity and also where they like to live. (Florida 2002)

Bibliography

ALBERT DOCK COMPANY LTD (2004) 'The Albert Dock Company'. Albert Dock Company Ltd, Liverpool.

ALLEN, K. & SHAW, P. (2001) 'Continuing Professional Development for the Creative Industries: A Review of Provision in the Higher Education Sector'. Higher Education Funding Council for England.

ARTS COUNCIL ENGLAND (2002) 'Pride of Place: Urban Focus, Greater Manchester'. Arts Council England.

BAUMOL, W. & BAUMOL, H. (1994) 'On the Economics of Musical Composition in Mozart's Vienna'. In: Morris, J.E. (ed.) *On Mozart*. Cambridge University Press, New York and Cambridge.

BEGG, P. (1990) 'Geelong. The First 150 Years'. Globe Press, Geelong.

BELL, D & JAYNE, M. (2004) 'City of Quarters, Urban Villages in the Contemporary City'. Ashgate, Aldershot.

BLAIR, H. (2001) 'You're Only as Good as Your Last Job: The Labour Process and Labour Market in the British Film Industry'. *Work, Employment and Society* 15(1), pp. 149–169.

BODEN, M.A. (2003) 'The Creative Mind: Myths and Mechanisms'. Routledge, London.

BODDANOR, V. (2005) 'Joined up Government'. OUP.

BOLTON METROPOLITAN BOROUGH COUNCIL (2002) 'Bolton 2002–2007: A Cultural Strategy'. Bolton Metropolitan Borough Council.

BOLTON METROPOLITAN BOROUGH COUNCIL (2003) 'Bolton MBC Libraries Positioning Statement 2003'. Bolton Metropolitan Borough Council.

BOLTON METROPOLITAN BOROUGH COUNCIL (2003) 'Bolton Town Centre Strategy 2003–2012'. Bolton Metropolitan Borough Council.

BOLTON METROPOLITAN BOROUGH COUNCIL (2003) 'Vision for the Future Partnership: Bolton Borough's Community Strategy 2003–2012'. Bolton Metropolitan Borough Council.

BOLTON MUSEUM ART GALLERY & AQUARIUM (2004) 'Best Value Report'. Bolton Metropolitan Borough Council.

BOLTON STRATEGIC ECONOMIC PARTNERSHIP (2004) 'The Economic Strategy for Bolton 2004–2008: Summary February 2004'. Bolton Metropolitan Borough Council.

BOURDIEU, P. (1986) 'Distinction: A Social Critique of the Judgement of Taste'. Routledge, London.

BRADSHAW GASS AND HOPE CONSTRUCTION DESIGN CONSULTANTS (2003) 'Le Mans Crescent and Cheadle Square Scoping Exercise'. Bolton Metropolitan Borough Council.

BRITISH COUNCIL (1998) 'Britain's Design Industry: The Design Workshop of the World'. British Council.

BRENNAN, L. (2005) 'Integrating work based learning into higher education'. University Vocational Awards Council (UVAC), Bolton.

BRITISH COUNCIL CREATIVE INDUSTRIES UNIT (2004) 'Creative Industries'. British Council.

BROOKS, A.C. & KUSNER, R.J. (2001) 'Cultural Districts and Urban Developments'. *International Journal of Arts Management* 3(2), pp. 4–15.

BROWN, A., COHEN, S. & O'CONNOR, J. (2000) 'Local Music Policies within a Global Music Industry: Cultural Quarters in Manchester And Sheffield'. *Geoforum* 31, pp. 437–451.

CALHOUN, C., LUPUMA, E. & POSTONE, M. (1993) 'Bourdieu : Critical Perspectives'. Polity Press, Great Britain.

CANTER, D. (1997) 'The Psychology of Place'. Architectural Press, London.

CARR, M. (2002) 'Banking on the Gallery – Geelong's Bid for a Guggenheim: Proposing a Cultural Strategy for Economic Development'. In: *Proceedings of the New Wave: Entrepreneurship and the Arts*. p. 11. Deakin University, Melbourne.

CAUST, J. (2003) 'Putting the "arts" back into arts policy-making: How arts policy has been captured by the economists and the marketers'. *International Journal of Cultural Policy* Vol. 9, No.s 1/12, pp. 51–63.

CAVES, R. (2000) 'Creative Industries'. Harvard University Press, Cambridge, MA.

CHARLES, D.R. (2003) 'Universities and Territorial Development: Reshaping the Regional Role of English Universities'. *Local Economy* 18(1), pp. 7–20.

CITY OF GREATER GEELONG (2008) 'City of Geelong Plan, 2008–2012'. City of Greater Geelong, Geelong.

CLAES, T. (2002) '"It Was Not a Bad Idea ... ". Defining the University'. In: *Ivory Tower to Convienence Store*. Paper presented at The Idea of Education conference, Mansfield College, Oxford, 3rd–4th July 2002.

CORIO-NORLANE RESEARCH FORUM (2009) In: Meeting sponsored by Deakin University and the Corio-Norlane Neighbourhood Renewal Advisory Board, November.

COX, G. (2006) 'Creativity Something Something'. In: Paper presented at the Creative Industries conference, 5th December 2006.

CREATIVE AND CULTURAL SKILLS (2006) 'Footprints'. Creative and Cultural Skills, London.

CREATIVE INDUSTRIES DEVELOPMENT TEAM (1998) 'Work Spaces for the Creative Industries'. Bolton Metropolitan Borough Council.

CULTURAL INDUSTRIES QUARTER (2004) 'The CIQ Agency'. Cultural Industries Quarter Agency.

CULTURAL INDUSTRIES QUARTER (2003) 'CIQ Connected'. *The Quarterly*, Issue 3.

CULTURAL INDUSTRIES QUARTER (2003) 'Broadcast News'. *The Quarterly*, Issue 5.

CULTURAL INDUSTRIES QUARTER (2004) 'Sounds of the City'. *The Quarterly*, Issue 7.

CUNNINGHAM, S. (2002) 'From Cultural to Creative Industries: Theory, Industry and Policy Implications'. Creative Industries Research and Applications Centre, University of Technology, Brisbane, Australia.

CUNNINGHAM, S. (2004) 'The Creative Industries after Cultural Policy: A Genealogy and Some Possible Preferred Futures'. *International Journal of Cultural Studies* 7(1), pp. 105–115.

CUNNINGHAM, S., HEARN, G., COX, S., NINAN, A. & KEANE, M. (2003) 'Brisbane's Creative Industries 2003, Report delivered to Brisbane City Council, Community and Economic Development'. Creative Industries Applied Research Centre, Queensland University of Technology.

CURRAH, A. (2006) 'Hollywood versus the Internet: The Media and Entertainment Industries in a Digital and Networked Economy'. *Journal of Economic Geography* 6, pp. 439–468.

DCMS (1998a) 'Creative Industries Task Force Report'. Department for Culture, Media and Sport, London.

DCMS (1998b) 'DCMS Mapping Document 1998'. Department for Culture, Media and Sport, London.

DCMS (2001) 'Creative Industries Mapping Document' DCMS.

DCMS (2008) 'Creative Britain. New Talents for the New Economy'. Department for Culture, Media and Sport, London.

De PROPRIS, L. & LAZZERETTI, L. (2007) 'The Birmingham Jewellery Quarter: A Marshallian Industrial District'. *European Planning Studies* 15(10), pp. 1295–1325.

De PROPRIS, L. & LAZZERETTI, L. (2009) 'Measuring the Decline of a Marshallian Industrial District: The Birmingham Jewellery Quarter'. *Regional Studies* 43(9), pp. 1135–1154.

De PROPRIS, L. & WEI, P. (2007) 'Governance and Competitiveness in the Birmingham Jewellery District'. *Urban Studies* 44(12), pp. 1–21.

DEARING, R. (1997) 'Higher Education in the Learning Society: Report of the National Committee of Inquiry into Higher Education'. HMSO and NCIHE, London.

DEPARTMENT FOR CULTURE MEDIA AND SPORT (2003) 'Framework for the Future, Libraries and Learning and Information in the New Decade'. Online. Available: www.culture.gov.uk/global/publications/archive_2003/framework_future.htm [Accessed February 2004].

DEPARTMENT OF CULTURE MEDIA AND SPORT (2001) 'Creative Industries Mapping Document'. DCMS, London.

DEPARTMENT OF CULTURE MEDIA AND SPORT (2001) 'Green Paper: Culture and Creativity; the Next 10 Years'. Online. Available: http://www.culture.gov.uk/reference_library/publications/4634.aspx/ [Accessed 22nd March 2010].

DETR (1999) 'Towards an Urban Renaissance: Final Report of the Urban Task Force'. Department of Environment Transport and the Regions, London.

DETR & CABE (2000) 'By Design: Urban Design in the Planning System, towards Better Practice'. Department of Environment Transport and the Regions and Commission for Architecture and the Built Environment, London.

DIAMONSTEIN, B. (1978) 'Buildings Reborn: New Uses, Old Places'. New York.

ENVIRONMENT DEPARTMENT BOLTON MBC 'Town Hall Conservation Area'. Bolton Metropolitan Borough Council.

EPA (2009) 'About Brownfields'. Online. Available: www.epa.gov/brownfields/ [Accessed 24th June 2009].

ETZKOWITZ, A., WEBSTER, C. & GEBHARDT, R.C. (2000) 'The Future of the University and the University of the Future: Evolution of Ivory Tower to Entrepreneurial University'. *Research Policy* 29, pp. 313–330.

EXPERIAN (2004) 'Retail Ranking'. Experian, London.

EXPERIAN BUSINESS STRATEGIES AND BURNS OWENS PARTNERSHIP (2003) 'Benchmarking the Health of Cultural Businesses'. North West Regional Intelligence Unit. Online. Available: www.nwriu.co.uk.

FAGAN, R. & WEBBER, M. (1999) 'Global Restructuring. The Australian Experience'. Oxford University Press, Sydney.

FLEW, T. (2002) 'Beyond ad hocery: Defining creative industries'. Second International Conference on Cultural Policy Research, New Zealand.

FLORIDA, R. (2002) 'The Rise of the Creative Class and How It's Transforming Work, Leisure, Community and Everyday Life'. Basic Books, New York.

FLORIDA, R. (2003) 'Cities and the Creative Class'. *City and Community* 2(1) pp. 3–21.

FLORIDA, R. (2005) 'Cities and the Creative Class'. Routledge, New York.

FOUCAULT, M. (1971) 'Revolutionary Action: Until Now a Discussion with Michel Foucault'. *Actuel* 14, pp. 42–47.

FRONTIER ECONOMICS (2009) 'Creative industry performance. A statistical analysis for the DCMS.' DCMS, London

FROST-KUMPF, H.A. (1998) 'Cultural Districts: The Arts as a Strategy for Revitalizing Our Cities'. Americans for the Arts, Washington DC.

G21 (2007) 'The G21 Geelong Region Plan'. Geelong, G21.

G21 GEELONG REGION STRATEGIC PLAN (2003) 'G21 Regional Alliance'. Online. Available: www.G21.com.au

GALLIGAN, A. (2008) 'The Evolution of Arts and Cultural Districts'. In: Cherbo, Stewart & Wyszomirski (eds) *Understanding the Arts and Cultural Sector in the United States*, pp. 129–142. Rutgers University Press, Piscataway.

GARCIA, B. & REASON, M. (2004) 'The Cities and Culture Project. Phase One: The Long-term Legacies of Glasgow 1990 European City of Culture'. Online. Available: www.culturalpolicy.arts.gla.ac.uk [Accessed February 2004].

GARNHAM, N. (1987) 'Concepts of culture: public policy and the cultural industries'. *Cultural Studies* Vol.1, No.1, pp. 23–37.

GBN (2000) 'Guggenheim Dreaming'. *Geelong Business News* 75, October, pp. 10–13.

GCP GEELONG CULTURAL PRECINCT (2007) 'Masterplan Project Update Volume 3'. Major Projects Victoria and City of Greater Geelong.

GCP GEELONG CULTURAL PRECINCT (2008) 'Masterplan Project Update Volume 4'. Major Projects Victoria and City of Greater Geelong.

GDANIEC, C. (1999) 'Barcelona Case Study'. Online. Available: http://www.mipc.mmu.ac.uk/iciss/cas_barc.htm [Accessed February 2004].

GEUNA, A. & NESTA, L. (2003) 'University Patenting and Its Effects in Academic Research'. SPRU EWPS 99. University of Sussex, Brighton.

GLAESER, E.L. (2004) 'Review of Richard Florida's *The Rise of the Creative Class*'. Online. Available: www.creativeclass.org.

GODIN, B. & GINGRAS, Y. (2000) 'The Place of Universities in the System of Knowledge Production'. *Research Policy* 29, pp. 273–278.

GOULD, D.M. & GRUBEN, W.C. (1996) 'The Role of Intellectual Property Rights in Economic Growth'. *Journal of Development Economics* 48(2), pp. 323–350.

GRAVER, A. & HARRISON, J. (2002) 'Benchmarking Employment in the Cultural Industries'. North West Regional Intelligence Unit. Online. Available: www.nwriu.co.uk

GRAY, H.H. (2001) 'The University in History: 1088 and All That'. In: Paper presented at The Idea of the University conference, University of Chicago, Chicago, 17th January 2001.

GREATER LONDON COUNCIL, INDUSTRY AND EMPLOYMENT BRANCH (1985) 'London Industrial Strategy: The Cultural Industries'. Greater London Council.

GUMPORT, P.J. (2000) 'Academic Restructuring: Organizational Change and Institutional Imperatives'. *Higher Education* 39, pp. 67–91.

HADDLETON, M. (2005) 'How I survived the regeneration processes'. Online. Available: www. ihbc.org.uk/context archive/78/survive/haddleton.htm [Accessed May 2005].

HAMILTON, C. & SCULLION, A. (2002) 'The Effectiveness of the Scottish Arts Council's Links and Partnerships with Other Agencies: A Report to the Scottish Executive'. University of Glasgow.

HEALY, K. (2002) 'What's New for Culture in the New Economy?'. *Journal of Arts Management, Law, and Society* 32(2), pp. 86–103.

HEFCE (1999) 'Partners and Providers'. 99/25 HEFCE, Bristol.

HEFCE (2004) 'Strategic Plan 2003–08' (Revised April 2004). Higher Education Funding Council for England, Bristol, UK.

HEFCE (2006) 'Strategic Plan 2006–11'. 06/13 HEFCE, Bristol.

HEMELRYK, DONALD, KOFMAN & KEVIN (eds) 'Branding Cities: Cosmopolitanism, Parochialism, and Social Change' In Chapter: *Cultural Quarters in Branded Cities* pp. 75–88.

HENRY, N., MCEWAN, C. & POLLARD, J.S. (2002) 'Globalization from below: Birmingham – Postcolonial Workshop of the World'. *Area* 34.2, pp. 117–127.

HERD, N. (2004) 'Chasing the Runaways: Foreign Film Production and Film Studio Development in Australia 1988–2002'. Currency House Inc., Sydney.

HERITAGE LOTTERY FUND (2002) 'The Heritage Lottery Fund Strategic Plan 2002–2007: A Summary Document'. Heritage Lottery Fund, London.

HERITAGE LOTTERY FUND (2002) 'Your Heritage: Grants £5,000–£50,000'. Heritage Lottery Fund, London.

HERITAGE LOTTERY FUND (2003) 'Heritage Grants: Grants of £50,000 or more'. Heritage Lottery Fund, London.

HOLDEN, J. & LEADBEATER, C. (2003) 'Framework for the Future: Libraries, Learning and Information in the Next Decade'. Department of Culture, Media and Sport, London.

HOWKINS, J. (2001) 'The Creative Economy: How People Make Money from Ideas'. Penguin, London.

HUTCHISON, R. (1977) 'Three Arts Centres: A Study of South Hill Park, the Gardener Centre and Chapter'. Arts Council of Great Britain, London.

JEFCUTT, P. (2004) 'Knowledge Relationships and Transactions in a Cultural Economy: Analysing the Creative Industries Ecosystem'. *Culture and Policy* 112(1), pp. 67–82.

JOHNSON, L.C. (1990) 'New Patriarchal Economies in the Australian Textile Industry'. *Antipode* 22(1), pp. 1–32.

JOHNSON, L.C. (2006) 'Valuing the Arts: Theorising and Realising Cultural Capital in an Australian City'. *Geographical Research* 44(3), pp. 296–309.

JOHNSON, L.C. (2009a) 'Valuing the Arts and Culture in One Community: Geelong, Victoria'. *Asia Pacific Journal of Arts and Cultural Management* 6(1), pp. 471–487.

JOHNSON, L.C. (2009b) 'Cultural Capitals: Re-valuing the Arts and Re-making Urban Spaces'. Ashgate, London.

JOWELL, T. (2004) 'Government and the Value of Culture'. Department of Culture, Media and Sport, London.

KEA EUROPEAN AFFAIRS (2009) 'The Impact of Culture on Creativity'. The European Commission, Bruxelles.

KEA EUROPEAN AFFAIRS 'The Economy of Culture in Europe'. The European Commission, Bruxelles.

KERR, C. (1963) 'The Uses of the University'. Harvard University Press, Boston.

KERR, C. (1987) 'A Critical Age in the University World: Accumulated Heritage Versus Modern Imperatives'. *European Journal of Education* 22(2), pp. 183–193.

KINGDON, J. (1997) 'Agendas, Alternatives, and Public Policies'. Second edition. Longman, London.

LAMBERT, R. (2003) 'Lambert Review of Business – University Collaboration'. HM Treasury, London.

LANDRY, C. (2000) 'The Creative City: A Toolkit for Urban Innovators'. Earthscan Publications, London.

LATOUR, B. (2005) 'Reassembling the Social: An Introduction to Actor-Network-Theory'. Oxford University Press, Oxford.

LAW, J. (1994) 'Organized Mobility'. Blackwell, Oxford.

LAWRENCE T. & PHILLIPS, N. (2002) 'Understanding Cultural Industries'. *Journal of Management Inquiry* 11(4), pp. 430–441.

LEADBETTER, C. (2006) 'Britain's Creativity Challenge'. Creative and Cultural Skills, London.

LEADBETTER, C. & OAKLEY, K. (1999) 'The Independents – Britain's New Cultural Entrepreneurs'. Demos, London.

LEADBETTER, C. & OAKLEY, K. (2001) 'Surfing the Long Wave: Knowledge Entrepreneurship in Britain'. Demos, London.

LEE, N. & HASSARD, J. (1999) 'Organization Unbound: Actor-Network Theory, Research Strategy and Institutional Flexibility'. *Organization* 6(3), pp. 391–404.

LEGNÉR, M. (2007) 'The Cultural Significance of Industrial Heritage and Urban Development, Woodberry in Baltimore, Maryland.'. In: Nilsson, L. (ed.), *Stockholms Lilja.* Stadshistoriska studier tillägnade professorn i Stockholms historia Sven Lilja 23 juli 2007. Stads- och kommunhistoriska institutet, Stockholm, pp. 111–144.

LEGNÉR, M. (2008) 'Industriarv och kultumiljöpolicy i stadsförmyelseprocesser'. Norrköping, Baltimore och Milano, *Report* 2008:4, CKS: Norrköping.

LEGNÉR, M. (2009a) 'Historic Rehabilitation of Industrial Sites: Cases from North American and Swedish Cities'. *Report* 2008:1, Department of Culture Studies, Linköping University.

LEGNÉR, M. (2009b) 'Regeneration, Quarterization and Historic Preservation in Urban Sweden'. In: Legnér, M. & Ponzini, D. (eds) *Cultural Quarters and Urban Transformation.* Gotlandica förlag, Klintehamn.

LEGNÉR, M. (2009c) 'Historic Rehabilitation of Urban Spaces in Eastern Europe: Plans for the Reuse of a Public Building in Disna, Belarus'. In: Barelkowski, R. (ed.) *The Faces of Urbanized Space.* Ośrodek Wydawnictuw Naukowych, Polish Academy of Sciences, Poznan Bransch, forthcoming 2010.

LEGNÉR, M. & PONZINI, D. (2009) 'Introduction'. In: Legnér, M. and Ponzini, D. (eds) *Cultural Quarters and Urban Transformation: International Perspectives.* Gotlandica förlag, Klintehamn.

LONDON DEVELOPMENT AGENCY (2003) 'The Mayor's Commission on the Creative Industries: Improving Links in Creative Production Chains'. Online. Available: www.creativelondon.org. uk.

MALANGA, S. (2004) 'The Curse of the Creative Class'. *City Journal*, Winter, pp. 36–45.

MANCHESTER CITY COUNCIL (2004) 'Manchester's Cultural Strategy'. Online. Available: www.manchester.gov.uk/regen/culture/strategy [Accessed February 2004].

MANCHESTER CITY COUNCIL (2004) 'Northern Quarter Magnet!'. Online. Available: www. manchester.gov.uk/people/issues17/quarter.htm [Accessed February 2004].

MARCHART, O. (1999) 'Das Ende des Josephinismus. Zur Politisierung der österreichischen Kulturpolitik'. Edition selene, Wien.

MARGINSON, S. & CONSIDINE, M. (2000) 'The Enterprise University: Power, Governance and Reinvention in Australia'. Cambridge University Press, Cambridge.

MASKUS, K.E. (2000) 'Intellectual Property Rights and Economic Development'. *Case Western Reserve Journal of International Law*, Special Supplement 2000 32(2), pp. 471–500.

MASON, S. (1998) 'Jewellery-making in Birmingham 1770-1995'. Phillimore & Co. Ltd, Chichester.

MATO, D. (2009) 'All Industries Are Cultural'. *Cultural Studies* 23, pp. 70–87.

MCCLELLAN, A. (2008) 'The Art Museum from Boullée to Bilbao'. University of California Press, Berkeley.

MCMANUS, K. & MORIARTY, G. (2003) 'Releasing Potential: Creativity and Change. Arts Regeneration in England's North West'. Arts Council England, London.

MELIA, T. (2004) 'Review of 14–19 Education and Training in Bolton: Extended Executive Summary – Draft Report'. Learning & Skills Council, London.

MEYER, H.D. (2002) 'Universal, Entrepreneurial, and Soulless? The New University as a Contested Institution'. *Comparative Education Review* 46, pp. 339–347.

MILLENNIUM GALLERIES (2004) 'Sheffield Galleries & Museums Trust'. Online. Available: www. sheffieldgalleries.org.uk/coresite/html/millennium.asp

MILLER, T. (2009) 'From Creative to Cultural Industries: Not All Industries Are Cultural, and No Industries Are Creative'. *Cultural Studies* 23, pp. 88–99.

MONTGOMERY, J. (2003) 'Cultural Quarters as Mechanisms for Urban Regeneration'. Online. Available: www.planning.sa.gov.au/congress/pdf/Papers/Montgomery.pdf

MORAS-GALLART, J., SALTER, A., PATEL, P., SCOTT, A. & DUNCAN, X. (2002) 'Measuring Third Steam Activities. Final Report to the Russell Group of Universities'. Science Policy Research Unit, University of Sussex, Brighton.

MOULD, O., ROODHOUSE, S. & VORLEY, T. (2009) 'Realizing Capabilities – Academic Creativity and the Creative Industries'. *Creative Industries Journal* 1(2), pp. 137–150.

MUSEUMS, LIBRARIES AND ARCHIVES COUNCIL (2001) 'Developing the Twenty-first-Century Archive; and Action Plan for UK Archives, 2001–2002'. Museums, Libraries and Archives Council, Birmingham and London.

MUSEUMS, LIBRARIES AND ARCHIVES COUNCIL (2001) 'Renaissance in the Regions; the New Vision for England's Museums'. Museums, Libraries and Archives Council, Birmingham and London.

MUSEUMS ASSOCIATION BULLETIN (1996), p. 352.

MUSEUMSQUARTIER WIEN (2004) 'Museums Quartier Wien'. Online. Available: www.mqw.at [Accessed April 2004].

MYERSCOUGH, J. (1988) 'The Economic Importance of the Arts in Britain'. Policy Studies Institute, London.

NATIONAL MUSEUMS DIRECTORS' CONFERENCE (2004) 'A Manifesto for Museums: Building Outstanding Museums for the Twenty-first Century'. Online. Available: www.nationalmuseums. org.uk/images/publications/manifesto_for_museums.pdf [Accessed March 2004].

NEW ZEALAND MINISTRY OF FOREIGN AFFAIRS AND TRADE (2006) 'Glossary'. (Definition no longer available). Online. Available: www.mft.govt.nz/support/tplu/tradematters/glossary. html [Accessed 2006].

NORTH WEST CULTURAL CONSORTIUM (2001) 'The Cultural Strategy for England's North West'.

NORTH WEST DEVELOPMENT AGENCY (1999) 'England's North West: The Strategy Towards 2020'. North West Development Agency, Warrington.

NORTH WEST UNIVERSITIES ASSOCIATION CULTURE COMMITTEE (2004) 'The Contribution of Higher Education to Cultural Life in the North West'. North West Universities Association, Manchester.

NORTHERN QUARTER PROPERTY DATABASE (2004) 'Manchester's Northern Quarter'. Online. Available: www.nqpd.co.uk/nq.htm [Accessed February 2004].

NPS (2009a) 'Interpreting and Applying the Secretary of the Interior's Standards in the Historic Preservation Tax Incentives Program'. Online. Available: www.nps.gov./history/ [Accessed 24th June 2009].

NPS (2009b) 'Identifying Primary and Secondary Interior Spaces in Historic Buildings'. Online. Available: www.nps.gov/history/ [Accessed 24th June 2009].

O'CONNOR, J. & WYNNE, D. (1996) 'Introduction'. In: O'Connor, J. and Wynne, D. (eds) *From the Margins to the Centre*. Arena, Aldershot.

O'CONNOR, J. (1999) 'The Definition of the Cultural Industries'. Manchester Institute for Popular Culture. Online. Available: www.mmu.ac.uk/h-ss/mip/iciss/home2.htm.

O'CONNOR, J. (2004) 'A Special Kind of City Knowledge: Innovation Clusters, Tacit Knowledge and the Creative City'. *Media International Australia incorporating Culture and Policy*, 112(1), pp. 131–149.

ÖSTERREICHISCHES ZENTRUM FÜR KULTURDOKUMENTATION, -FORSCHUNG UND-VERMITTLUNG (1992) 'Darstellung und Analyse der österreichischen Kulturpolitik'. *Europaratstudie*. Österreichischer Nationalbericht, Wien.

PARNASS 'The Leopold Collection'. *Art Magazine,* 10th special edition.

PATON, K. (2009a) 'Interview with Louise Johnson 10th September 2009'. Manager, Arts and Culture, City of Greater Geelong.

PATON, K. (2009b) 'Interview with Louise Johnson 11th November 2009'. Manager, Arts and Culture, City of Greater Geelong.

PECK, J. (2005) 'Struggling with the Creative Class'. *International Journal of Urban and Regional Research* 29, pp. 740–770.

PICK, J. & ANDERTON, M. (1999) 'Building Jerusalem: Art, Industry and the British Millennium'. Harwood Academic Publishers, The Netherlands.

PLESCHBERGER, W. (1991) 'Staat und Kultur. Einige Überlegunegen zur Osterreichischen Kulturförderung in Rechtstheorctischer und Rechtspolltlscher Sicht'. In: Zukunfts- und Kulturwerkstätte (Hg.), *Kultur. Kunst. Staat. Aufschwünge und Abgesänge zur Zukunft der Kulturförderung'.* Wien. S., pp. 63–78.

POLLARD, J.S. (2004) 'From Industrial District to Urban Village? Manufacturing, Money and Consumption in Birmingham's Jewellery Quarter'. *Urban Studies* Vol. 41, No. 1, pp. 173–193.

POSITIVE SOLUTIONS (2009) 'A Cultural Precinct for Geelong: Geelong Performing Arts Centre'. Draft report prepared by Positive Solutions.

PRATT, A. (1997) 'The Cultural Industries Sector: Its definition and character from secondary sources in employment and trade, Britain 1984–1991'. *Research Papers in the Environment and Spatial Analysis* No. 41, London School of Economics, Dept. of Geography and the Environment, London.

PRATT, A. (2004) 'Creative Clusters: Towards the Governance of the Creative Industries Production System?'. *Media International Australia incorporating Culture and Policy* 112(1), pp. 50–66.

PRESERVATION TAX INCENTIVES PROGRAMME. Online. Available: www.nps.gov/history/ [Accessed 24th June 2009].

RE:SOURCE (2001) 'English Regional Museums Report'. Unpublished. Re:source, London.

RE:SOURCE (2001) 'Renaissance in the Regions Report'. Re:source, London.

RE:WORK STUDIOS (2004) 'Re:Work Creative Enterprises'. Bury Metropolitan Borough Council.

RICH, D. (1987) 'The Industrial Geography of Australia'. Croom Helm, London.

RODWELL, D. (2007) 'Conservation and Sustainability in Historic Cities'. Blackwell, Malden, MA.

ROODHOUSE, S. (1997) 'Interculturalism, in particular the relationship between artists and industrial imagery'. *Journal of Arts Policy and Management Law and Society* Vol 27, No.3.

ROODHOUSE, S. (1999) 'A Challenge to Cultural Sector Management Conventions – The Royal Armouries Museum'. *International Journal of Arts Management*, 1(2), pp. 82–90.

ROODHOUSE, S. (1999) 'Where Is Today's Arkwright?'. *Journal of Arts Management, Law and Society* 29(3), pp. 150–161.

ROODHOUSE, S. (2000) 'The Wheel of History – A Relinquishing of City Council Control and the Freedom to Manage: Sheffield Galleries and Museum Trust'. *International Journal of Arts Management.* volume 3, number 1, pp. 78–88.

ROODHOUSE, S. (2000a) 'What do we know about the creative industries in the UK?'. Conference proceedings, Australian Institute of Arts Management Conference, Brisbane, Australia.

ROODHOUSE, S. (2001a) 'Creating Sustainable Cultures'. *Art Reach,* pp. 9–12, New South Wales Museum and Galleries Foundation, Sydney, Australia.

ROODHOUSE, S. (2001b) 'Is there a place for the Heritage in the Creative Industries as an engine of economic growth in the UK?'. European Institute for the Advanced Studies in Management Workshop, Managing Cultural Organisations.

ROODHOUSE, S. (2002) 'Creating a Sustainable Culture for Everybody'. *The Reformer, Journal of the Centre for Reform* 9(2), pp. 22–23.

ROODHOUSE, S. (2003a) 'Have Cultural Industries a Role to Play in Regional Regeneration and a Nation's Wealth?'. *The International Journal of Applied Management.* Vol. 4, no. 1, pp. 180–217.

ROODHOUSE, S. (2003b) 'Essential Facts: The Nature of Designer Fashion and Its Markets, Report'. Bolton Institute.

ROODHOUSE, S. (2004) 'The MuseumsQuartier, Vienna, an Austrian Cultural Experiment'. *International Journal of Heritage Studies* Vol. 10, number 2, pp. 193-207

ROODHOUSE, S. (2006) *Cultural Quarters: Principles and Practices*. First edition. Intellect, Bristol.

ROODHOUSE, S. & ROODHOUSE, M. (1997) 'Cultural Intervention in British Urban Regeneration since 1945'. Conference proceedings, International Arts and Cultural Management Association Fourth Biennial Conference, San Francisco, USA, pp. 567–579.

ROODHOUSE, S & TAYLOR, C. (2000) 'Vital Statistics: The Cultural Industries in Yorkshire and the Humber'. Bretton Hall, University of Leeds.

ROTHERHAM METROPOLITAN BOROUGH COUNCIL (2000) 'Celebrating Our Past Together, Developing Our Distinctiveness Together, Creating Our Future Together: A Cultural Strategy For Rotherham Metropolitan Borough Council'. Rotherham Metropolitan Borough Council.

SALFORD CITY COUNCIL (2002) 'Salford Quays Milestones: The Story of the Salford Quays'. City of Salford.

SCHUMPETER, J.A. (1911) 'Theorie der wirtschaftlichen Entwicklung'. Duncker & Humblot, Leipzig (English translation (1934): 'The Theory of Economic Development'. Harvard University Press, Cambridge, MA).

SCOTT, A. (2000) 'The Cultural Economy of Cities'. Sage, London.

SCOTT, A. (2002) 'A New Map of Hollywood: The Production and Distribution of American Motion Pictures'. Regional Studies 36(9), pp. 957–975.

SCOTT, A. (2004a) 'The Other Hollywood: The Organizational and Geographic Bases of Television-program Production'. Media, Culture & Society 26(2), pp. 183–205.

SCOTT, A. (2004b) 'Cultural-products and Industries and Urban Economic Development'. Urban Affairs Review 39(4), pp. 461–490.

SELWOOD, S. (no date) 'Creative Industries'. ESRC seminar paper. LSE, London.

SHEFFIELD ART GALLERY AND MUSEUM TRUST (1999) 'Enriching the Future, Sheffield Art Gallery and Museum Trust Corporate Plan 1999–2002'. Sheffield Art Gallery and Museum Trust.

SHEFFIELD CIQ UNCOVERED: CULTURAL INDUSTRIES QUARTER (1982–2002) CD-ROM. Sheffield Cultural Industries Quarter Agency.

SMITH, B.M.D. (1989) 'The Birmingham Jewellery Quarter, a Civic Problem that has become an Opportunity in the 1980s'. In: Tilson, B. (ed.) Made in Birmingham:Design and Industry 1889–1989 pp. 96–112. Studley, Brewin Books.

SMITH, C., (1998) 'Creative Britain'. Faber and Faber Limited, London.

SLAUGHTER, S. & LESLIE, L. (1997) 'Academic Capitalism: Politics, Policies and the Entrepreneurial University'. Johns Hopkins University Press, London.

SOLESBURY, W. (2001) 'Evidence-based Policy – whence it came from, and where it's going'. ESRC Centre for Evidence-Based Policy and Practice Working Paper 1.

STÅHL, M. (1999) 'Pannhus 11: En utställning om industrisamhällets kulturarv. Arbetarhistoria'. Stockholm Papers in the History and Philosophy of Technology 4, pp. 42–43. KTH, Stockholm.

STORM, A. (2008) 'Hope and Rust: Reinterpreting the Industrial Place in the Late 20th Century'. Stockholm Papers in the History and Philosophy of Technology. KTH, Stockholm.

STRATTON, M. (1997) 'Structure and Style: Conserving Twentieth Century Buildings'. E. & F.N. Spon, London.

TEMPLE BAR PROPERTIES (2004) 'Temple Bar Dublin's Cultural Quarter'. Online. Available: www.templebar.ie [Accessed April 2004].

THROSBY, D. (2001) 'Economics and Culture'. Cambridge University Press, Cambridge.

TORONTO CULTURE (2001) 'The Creative City, a Workprint'. City of Toronto.

UNICO (2001) 'Annual Survey on University Technology Transfer Activities'. NUBS, Nottingham.

UNITED NATIONS CONFERENCE ON TRADE AND DEVELOPMENT (UNCTAD) (2008) 'Creative Economy Report 2008: The Challenge of Assessing the Creative Economy: Towards Informed Policy Making'. UNCTAD, Geneva.

WARBURTON, D. (2005) 'Raising the stakes in the jewellery quarter'. Online. Available: www.ihbc.org.uk/context archive/75/Jewelry.html [Accessed May 2005].

WARD, S. (2004) 'National Cinema or Creative Industries? Film Policy in Transition'. *Media International Australia incorporating Culture and Policy* 112(1), pp. 119–130.

WATERHOUSE, R. (2002) 'Widening Participation and the Distributed University'. In: Roodhouse, S. & Hemsworth, D. (eds) *Widening Participation in the Workplace: A New Agenda for Further and Higher Education* pp. 6–10. UVAC, London.

WILLIAM-JONES, B. (2005) 'Knowledge Commons or Economic Engine – What's a University For?'. *Journal of Medical Ethics* 31, pp. 249–250.

WILLIAMS, R. (1981) 'Culture'. Fontana Paperbacks, London.

WILSON, R. 2006. 'Vocational qualifications: Current issues, government responsibilities, and employer opportunities'. Institute of Directors, London.

WOLFSON FOUNDATION (2002) 'Annual Report 2002–2003'. Wolfson Foundation, London.

WOLVERHAMPTON CITY COUNCIL (2004) 'Cultural Strategy for Wolverhampton'. Wolverhampton City Council.

WOLVERHAMPTON CITY COUNCIL (2004) 'Wolverhampton Artists' Quarter'. Online. Available: www.wolverhampton.gov.uk/trenv/plans/artist.htm [Accessed February 2004].

WOLVERHAMPTON CITY COUNCIL (2004) 'Wolverhampton Evening Economy: Action Plan'. Wolverhampton City Council.

WORTHING, D. & BOND, S. (2008) 'Managing Built Heritage: The Role of Cultural Significance'. Blackwell, Oxford and Malden, MA. Online. Available: www.midlandsmedici.org [Accessed 3rd August 2008].

WYNNE, D. (2004) 'Creating Cultural Quarters'. Online. Available: www.unicatt.it/modacult/impreseculturali/Wynne.htm [Accessed February 2004]

ZUKIN, S. (1995) 'The Cultures of Cities'. Blackwell, Malden, MA.

Appendix 1

The Bolton Town Centre Action Plan

The Bolton town centre action plan, yet to be finally approved, is important as it provides an insight into the policy constructs being employed by a local authority. In addition it lays out a vision and detailed analysis.The complete report is not reproduced here,however relevant extracts have been included in this appendix.

Strategic and Local Issues

The development of tourism, leisure, and culture in Bolton town centre needs to be set in the context of local, regional/sub-regional, and, in some cases, national strategies.

The Greater Manchester Strategy contains specific objectives for the development of tourism, culture, and sport at a sub-regional level. These will in turn relate to the North West Cultural Strategy adopted by the NorthWest Regional Assembly (NWRA) and the North West Tourism Strategy.

Locally, the published Bolton Cultural Strategy and Arts Action Plan identified key objectives and actions. Many of these are particularly relevant to the town centre, and all included within the emerging Town Centre Strategy Action Plan. Local priorities are suggested to be:

- Built Heritage and Townscape;
- Entertainment and Food;
- Visual Arts, Crafts, Fashion and Design;
- Events and Festivals;
- Cultural Diversity;
- Shopping;
- Business Tourism and Conferences.

The vision of the Strategy is to confirm Bolton town centre as:

A Leading Sub Regional Centre, A Place To Be Proud Of, Distinctive, Appealing & Popular With All.
The aspirations for the town centre are that it should build on its distinctiveness, strengths, and qualities to:

- Offer something for everyone in an exciting and ever changing environment;
- Provide quality spaces, quality shops, restaurants, and bar;
- Offer a welcoming and safe destination;
- Contain uses and activities that will attract existing and new visitors – not only local residents but also visitors from further afield to explore its history;
- Accommodate new distinctive mixed use town centre "neighbourhoods" – to allow for new activities in areas that are currently unused particularly during evening times;
- Enliven the town centre streets through the promotion of activity;
- Provide excellent access through new and improved transportation links.

To achieve this vision, the strategy should ensure that the town centre will be enhanced by:

- Creating a strong commercial, cultural, leisure, and civic centre which will continue to act as the economic driver of the Borough;
- Stimulating the physical renaissance of the town centre to make it an attractive place with many quality buildings and a public realm which will be safe, interesting, well managed, and accessible by all.

Benefits of Tourism, Leisure and Culture

Tourism, leisure, and the cultural product which supports these sectors is a fast growing, competitive market. The contribution it can make to the regeneration of cities and towns is well documented and it is recognised that any strategy relating to Bolton town centre needs to reflect the opportunities in respect of these sectors.

The key benefits of developing the tourism and leisure sector in Bolton are:

- Economic spend, new business development and creation of jobs;
- Developing a positive image of Bolton;
- Enhancing the quality of life for residents, underpinning leisure, culture, retail, and local services;
- Encouraging environmental improvements.

The Council considers them to be:

1. Investment in a Quality Tourism and Culture Product

- Build on key strengths – urban tourism, access to rural and city destinations;
- Improving the range and quality of accommodation;
- Invest in leisure/cultural attractions and events programme;
- Invest in people, tourism, and culture.

2. Focusing on the Customer

- Adopting a customer led approach to marketing – aimed at particular market segments to maximise economic return;
- Improving information services and developing electronic tourism services;
- Improving accessibility to the tourism and cultural product;

3. Towards a Sustainable Tourism and Culture Sector

- Developing local, regional, and national partnerships to maximise opportunities for the development of the sector;
- Encourage environmental, social and community responsibilities;
- Create and sustain a strong infrastructure of cultural organisations, spaces, activities, facilities, and services.

4. Developing a Cultural Quarter

- The majority of the town centre's cultural attractions are focused within the spaces provided by the finest quality buildings within the town centre around Le Mans Crescent. This concentration of heritage related buildings and spaces present an opportunity to develop a cohesive strategy linking the development of cultural and arts provision to the enhancement of the heritage of the town centre.